Visual Metaphors and Aesthetics

Also available from Bloomsbury

Advances in Experimental Philosophy of Aesthetics,
edited by Florian Cova and Sébastien Réhault
Names and Context, by Dolf Rami
The Aesthetic Illusion in Literature and the Arts, edited by Tomáš Koblíže
The Changing Boundaries and Nature of the Modern Art World,
by Richard Kalina

Visual Metaphors and Aesthetics

A Formalist Theory of Metaphor

Michalle Gal

BLOOMSBURY ACADEMIC
LONDON • NEW YORK • OXFORD • NEW DELHI • SYDNEY

BLOOMSBURY ACADEMIC
Bloomsbury Publishing Plc
50 Bedford Square, London, WC1B 3DP, UK
1385 Broadway, New York, NY 10018, USA
29 Earlsfort Terrace, Dublin 2, Ireland

BLOOMSBURY, BLOOMSBURY ACADEMIC and the Diana logo
are trademarks of Bloomsbury Publishing Plc

First published in Great Britain 2022
This paperback edition published 2023

Copyright © Michalle Gal, 2022

Michalle Gal has asserted her right under the Copyright, Designs and Patents Act, 1988, to be identified as Author of this work.

For legal purposes the Acknowledgments on p. xiii constitute an extension of this copyright page.

Cover image: Matteo Bianchi, Muffin Pouffe, 2011, Photo by: Rei Moon.

All rights reserved. No part of this publication may be reproduced or transmitted in any form or by any means, electronic or mechanical, including photocopying, recording, or any information storage or retrieval system, without prior permission in writing from the publishers.

Bloomsbury Publishing Plc does not have any control over, or responsibility for, any third-party websites referred to or in this book. All internet addresses given in this book were correct at the time of going to press. The author and publisher regret any inconvenience caused if addresses have changed or sites have ceased to exist, but can accept no responsibility for any such changes.

A catalogue record for this book is available from the British Library.

A catalog record for this book is available from the Library of Congress.

Names: Gal, Michalle, author.
Title: Visual metaphors and aesthetics: a formalist theory of metaphor / Michalle Gal.
Description: London; New York: Bloomsbury Academic, 2022. | Includes bibliographical references and index.
Identifiers: LCCN 2022004325 (print) | LCCN 2022004326 (ebook) |
ISBN 9781350127715 (hb) | ISBN 9781350326705 |
ISBN 9781350127722 (epdf) | ISBN 9781350127739 (ebook)
Subjects: LCSH: Metaphor. | Aesthetics.
Classification: LCC BH301.M4 G35 2022 (print) |
LCC BH301.M4 (ebook) | DDC 401/.43—dc23/eng/20220309
LC record available at https://lccn.loc.gov/2022004325
LC ebook record available at https://lccn.loc.gov/2022004326

ISBN: HB: 978-1-3501-2771-5
PB: 978-1-3503-2670-5
ePDF: 978-1-3501-2772-2
eBook: 978-1-3501-2773-9

Typeset by RefineCatch Limited, Bungay, Suffolk

To find out more about our authors and books visit www.bloomsbury.com and sign up for our newsletters.

For Shlomo Magril

Contents

List of Figures — viii
Preface — ix
Acknowledgments — xiii

1 The Visual Dimension of Metaphors: Framework and Main Argument — 1
2 Semantic Theories of Metaphor — 47
3 Cognitivist Theories of Metaphor: A Conceptual Turn — 61
4 The Advent of the Visual Perspective of Metaphors — 99
5 Metaphors and Ontology — 125
6 New Terminology for Metaphors: Visuality and Affordance — 157
Conclusion: A Definition of Metaphor — 173

Notes — 175
Bibliography — 191
Index — 199

Figures

1	Alex Padwa and Gilad Davidi, Padwa Design, *Powermat*, 2014	3
2	Job and Seletti, *Hot Dog Sofa*, Blow collection 2017	5
3	Jamie and Mark Antoniades, *Sharpener Desk Tidy*	6
4	Chocolate bar notepad	6
5	Matteo Bianchi, *Muffin Pouffe*, 2011	7
6	Nick Lerwill, *Cork Cactus*, 2021	7
7	Enrico Salis, *Caliteiro Toothpick Holder*, 2011	7
8	Shimon Levi, Arieh Cohen, *Ship Building*, Tel Aviv, 1935	8
9	Lemon purse, 2021	12
10	Alessandro Mendini, *Anna G, Alessandro M* corkscrew designs, 1993/2003	24
11	Ever Given cargo ship stuck in Suez Canal, Egypt March 2021	36
12	Jim Hannon-Tan, *Sweetheart Nutcracker*, 2020	68
13	Pablo Picasso, *The King* and *The Queen*, 1952, 1953	87
14	Nicolas Laisné and Manal Rachdi, *The White Tree*, Montpellier, 2019	107
15	Pablo Picasso, *La Venus du Gaz (The Venus of Gas)*, 1945	142
16	Neil Morris, *Cloud Table (Ameboid Table)*, 1947	147
17	Peter Behrens, *Turbine Factory*, Berlin, 1909	160

Preface

Visual metaphors are ubiquitous in our offices, streets, museums, and homes. One only has to visit a one-dollar store to see objects such as a piano-shaped sharpener, a cactus-shaped desk organizer, or a popsicle eraser. Our attachments to the iconic forms that accompany us through our lives ought not to be taken lightly by philosophy. The gravitas of the metaphor is a Rosetta Stone in the philosophy of human nature and ontology. Furnishing our surroundings, metaphors reach all the way from mundane objects to poetics from the utterly familiar to poiesis, art forms, and scientific breakthroughs. Metaphors can find their inspiration in the fleeting form of a passing cloud appearing as possessing a face or in the long gaze of a bedroom cabinet knobs. The phenomenon of metaphor progresses and solidifies into designs such as a lemon-shaped purse, or an alligator nutcracker entitled *Sweetheart*, as well as a reconstruction of life to be a journey, and a perspective-based Renaissance painting to be a window. Both Knowledge and the *White Tree* building in Montpellier (see Figure 14) complete the image of a tree with its roots, trunk, and branches, each in its own way.

Intellectual bewilderment at this immensely discussed phenomenon directs us to question what drives us to persistently reconstruct anew nature and artifacts, concepts, sounds, behaviors, cognitions, objects, and situations. My own answer is that it is an aesthetic motivation, fundamentally connected to the primary role that form plays in our lives, alongside our natural fascination with the power of composition. We are visual creatures: designing and perceiving reality through forms; reaching both banal and intellectual heights through the power of sensuous, external compositions.

Metaphors originate in the external sphere. We experience a physical depth and use it to reconstruct thought, because the composition of deep thought has beauty and richness. A sight of a solid or collapsing building can allude to reconstructing theories that solidify or collapse. Attached to the form of a face, we apply it to almost everything—everything may stare at us. The iconic form of a lemon wedge reconstructs a purse to be one. Metaphor is not a matter of a conceptual understanding or widening the semantic extension of predicates. It is an ontological composition. We are so metaphorical because metaphors, visual, linguistic, or conceptual, are essentially visual, and there is nothing more influential for us than the visual sphere.

I endorse the new voices that distinguish our era as going through a visual turn, and the admiration they hold for former canonical visual theories of the human being, thought, and cognition. Therefore, I make it a point in this book to offer a comprehensive reintroduction of magisterial visual theories, by Arnheim, Gombrich, Aldrich, and Housman, and then by Goodman and Beardsley. Their brilliant accounts of visual metaphor are rarely mentioned in the current literature, though they are prominent in visual theory. It is this framework, which points to the visual as the right sphere to focus a philosophical study on human nature and reality, that allows us to grasp the essence of metaphor. The ruling theory of metaphor from the 1980s onwards is a conceptualist one, which was favored by almost every single discipline, with open arms and little critique.

Contrary to the ruling conceptual theory of metaphor, externalism is the appropriate philosophical point of departure for the philosophy of metaphors. This closes the age of the linguistic and conceptual era of metaphors. Visual metaphors, rather than conceptual or linguistic, are paradigmatic. I denominate this the "visualist definition of metaphor."

A visualist ontological theory of metaphors is the primary objective of this book, insofar as I define metaphor as an aesthetic ontological construction, founded in visuality and the wonderfully rich possibilities that only the visual sphere can offer: the power of compositions. Metaphor, I claim, consists in *three parts*, rather than the two parts commonly propounded in literature—the source and target. These two elements are indeed two parts of metaphor, although they combine to constitute a third, significant, part: emergent properties. Emergent properties are those that are created by the fresh reconstruction of the target, drawing upon properties of the source and fusing them with those of the target. These lose their former identity—and are no longer distinguished separately—being possessed *only* by the metaphorical structure.

Metaphor is a form of composition that enables metaphorical properties to emerge. Compositions, established in antiquity, are powerful. They supply a context to the elements of metaphor that proffers significance thanks to their organization, mutual relations, and influences. A red stain in a green composition gains a specific unique composition-bound character. The same goes with depth, which is combined with thought in a composition. As we see the form of the 2019 *White Tree* building in Montpellier, or a tree shape combined with knowledge in the Cartesian metaphor, what emerges is an entirely different property. Disciplines as branches are different from balconies that branch off the trunk. These are the emerging third part of the metaphor: the essential constitutive parts, but they are also based on visual (or sensuous) abilities. I contend that visual metaphors are best placed to embody metaphoricity and are, to this end, paradigmatic. Conceptual or linguistic metaphors are founded on the visual construction.

This book is divided into six interrelated chapters and a Conclusion, arranged in deliberately didactic linearity. Chapter 1, "The Visual Dimension of Metaphors: Framework and Main Argument," presents the conceptual framework which is used in the book. I propose the argument that metaphor is an external, visual, ontological medium, that involves arranging categories and properties. I draw on the "attachment to forms" argument to explore the motivation of creating metaphors. This argument is aided by an analysis of the paradigmatic example of face metaphors and metaphors that are based on familiar forms: Gombrich's theory of Pygmalion Power and metaphor followed by Goodman constructivism are noted here. The framework of this argument is the current visual turn, which is introduced as supporting the need to redefine metaphors in visual terms. Finally, I argue that while metaphor is an imagistic-aesthetic phenomenon, the twentieth and twenty-first centuries' study of metaphors has been mainly led by a semantic-cognitivist model of metaphors followed by a conceptualist-cognitivist one. Therefore, I conclude the chapter by claiming that now is the time for philosophy to resolve the discrepancy in the field of metaphors.

Chapters 2 and 3 are respectively devoted to critical comprehensive surveys of the semantic and conceptual theories of metaphors that took over the stage in the 1980s. Conceptualism is presented as an internalist theory, which defines metaphor as an abstract cognition that is understood by referencing one to another. The external metaphors are but entailments of it. I track two main critical disadvantages of the conceptualist model, resulting from missing the power and significance of the visual sphere. The first is inconsistency, that is, it simultaneously points to mental content as the source of metaphor and external experiences as enabling this content. Second, it lacks the grasp of the emergent compositional and particular essence of each metaphor, which can neither be explained nor covered by a conceptual scheme. The survey on conceptualism in metaphor presents the main conceptualist theories of metaphors, such as the ones formulated by Lakoff and Johnson, Kovács, Gibbs, Fauconnier and Turner, Hampe, Steen, and Indurkhya. Additionally, I present critique from within the conceptualist school followed by new embodied-cognition theories, which manifest understanding that the conceptualist model is not enough to describe the human being.

This leads us to the fourth chapter: "The Advent of the Visual Perspective of Metaphors." Here I follow the line of thought that the visualists such as Gombrich, Arnheim, and Aldrich bravely developed amid a predominantly linguistic century. It is their early visualist theories that enabled the current visual turn to take place. They had acknowledged the status of the visual sphere in our ontology and lives and our visual nature, expanding theories of cognition and thinking to externalist approaches, and offering a constructivist theory of perception. Additionally, they were the first to detect visual metaphors and to address them theoretically. Their theories are very helpful for the next two chapters, which are devoted to the new visualist theory of metaphor, which presented both as an opposition to the conceptualist one and a positive autonomous one by itself.

Chapter 5, "Metaphors and Ontology," details the emerging third part of the metaphor, the ontological component, followed by an according theory of constructive metaphorical perception and an argument for the paradigmatic status of visual metaphors. I proffer an account of metaphor through the lens of material culture and everyday aesthetics. I do so to support the claim that metaphor is an ontological structure.

Chapter 6, "New Terminology for Metaphors: Visuality and Affordance," calls for a terminological shift from the conceptualist term of "understanding" to one of "affordance," which is the visualist consecutive term of "emergence." "Affordance," coined by Gibson, who was in discourse with the early visualists, is logically related, if not equivalent, to their notion of the power of the object and its dynamic character. However, it goes further by bringing us closer to the current visual metaphor theory and its corresponding theoretical visual turn. It is based on the *externalist* assertion that a theory may advance from the perception of visuality of surfaces, to the perception of what they afford owing to their ontological structure. Reintroducing ontology as the sphere of metaphors, adjoined with grasping metaphors' own materials, perceptual dynamics, and abilities to invite their own categorization, leads me to define metaphor in terms of its own space of possible relations with its audience. Characterizing metaphor in terms of visuality, emergence, and affordance leads directly to the Conclusion, which sums up by presenting a nine-part externalist and visualist definition of metaphor.

Acknowledgments

First and foremost, I thank my beloved, beautiful, and brilliant daughter Shira Gal, whose support, patience, and affording environment were crucial for the completion of the book. I thank my much-loved partner Shlomo Magril for being so noble and caring, allowing long hours of writing to be enjoyable. I benefited from our discussions of internalism vs. externalism and human nature.

I am most indebted to Garry Hagberg whose generous support of this project (and former ones) means the world to me. Thanks are sent to my close friend, Lyat Friedman: Our ongoing talks on philosophical externalism and metaphor were priceless; to Kristof Nyíri: His visualist theories are a significant source of inspiration, as well as his intellectual projects, in which he generously allows me to participate; to Yanai Toister for the departmental and institutional support and for being a friend; to Yeshayahu Shen, David Gill, and Eli Friedlander for supporting the outset of the project and to Menachem Mautner for an invaluable conversation about externalism and intentions from the vantage point of Law. My deep thanks are sent to the wonderful editor of Bloomsbury Publishing Philosophy, Colleen Coalter, and to Becky Holland and Suzie Nash for their superior editorial work throughout the process of preparing the manuscript.

1

The Visual Dimension of Metaphors: Framework and Main Argument

Metaphor is an aesthetic and creative medium, originating in the external visual-ontological sphere. In the visual-ontological sphere, metaphors operate by compositional means of cross-categorical allocations of properties, resulting in emergent properties of surfacing wholes. Metaphors thereby reconstruct groups, categories, and specific objects or phenomena as well as lay the foundation for all the various metaphorical practices, such as linguistic, conceptual, practical, material, or visual—along a line going from ordinary to artistic metaphors.

The creative process of metaphor is not a mere attribution, but a construction. It is said to progress from a source to a target—"source" and "target" being useful terms coined by the conceptualists to replace the linguistic ones, which will be used here as well—and then to an emergent structure and properties. However, contrary to the conceptualist definition—the most popular definition of metaphor in the twenty-first century—metaphors are not born in the mental sphere of thought or in understanding the target-concept through the source-concept, nor are they primarily formed as conceptual-mental content. Rather, creating a metaphor is an external ontological practice. It is from the visual-ontological sphere that properties, structures, forms, and relations are borrowed—actually, reproduced—to reconstruct the target and introduce it to a new ontological group. It is our perceptual experience and cognizance of the external things that we are exposed to which allows us to re-transfigure different phenomena—objects, practices, concepts, and mental contents, abstracts, and particulars. Therefore, visual metaphors are paradigmatic among the various kinds of metaphor, and the foundation of all of them.

According to conceptualism, following the linguistic theories of metaphors, metaphors are composed of merely two parts, which allegedly can be extracted post-production. Contrary to this, metaphors are composed of three elements, the third of which consists of an emergent metaphorical composition and properties that themselves emerge in the context of that composition. In summary, the use of the source to reconstruct the target creates a third element: an emergent, not predetermined composition, which is productive in itself and serves as a context for the newly modified emergent properties of the source and target. In addition to the reconstruction of the target, the metaphorical structure changes the source properties according to the context of the metaphorical composition, so they are new sub-properties. Addressing the emergent element of metaphor explains why, again contrary to the conceptualist theory of metaphor, the sphere of metaphor is not organized by internal, abstract, enduring type-metaphors, which the external metaphors are tokens of. Specific external metaphors gain their own emergent properties; those properties are not entailed by any alleged internal type-metaphor.

Not only is the external the source of the metaphorical composition, but visual metaphors are best in rendering and showing these emergences. Ernst Gombrich beautifully articulates Paul Cezanne's awareness of the potentiality of emergence made by visual composition. This awareness has been noted quite a few times in the literature. That Gombrich's formulation is especially instructive is just to be expected, taking into consideration that he was one of the first to theorize visual metaphors. Gombrich focused on their visuality rather than comparing them to verbal metaphors, and acknowledged their primary status. The following paragraph is from a subchapter of *Art and Illusion* entitled "Invention and Discovery," in which Gombrich asserts that comparing one of Cezanne's paintings to a photograph of Mont Ste. Victoire is unsuitable for aesthetic analysis because of the specific emergent properties of a composition:

> Cezanne's uncompromising honesty and his interest in clarity and structure made it manifest that if you were really faithful to your vision in every detail the equation would not work out: the elements will not fuse in the end into a convincing whole. This spelled the end of the mosaic theory of representation. New principles of organization had to be groped for. But Cezanne, if anyone, knew that you cannot plan these organizations because you cannot predict the mutual effect of all the elements of a picture.[1]

Thus, four interrelated propositions are presented here:

1. metaphors are essentially ontological;
2. metaphors originate in the visual sphere;
3. metaphors are structures that are composed from three elements, one of which is emergent and not predetermined;
4. visual metaphors are the paradigmatic and basic metaphors.

In addition, aesthetic externalist-formalist theory—visualist theory, as I would like to name it—is the right way to capture the essence of metaphors. These propositions will unfold throughout the book.

1.1 Ontology: categories and memberships

The pebble-shaped powermats (wireless chargers, Figure 1) designed by the industrial designer Alex Padwa constitute a beautiful example of metaphor. This functional and aesthetic object of design will be characterized later on as paradigmatic or representative of visual metaphor—being foundational to every kind of metaphor. Padwa's powermats are structured as members of the group of pebbles. This membership of the powermats in the group of pebbles, to be clear, is not exclusive, leaving intact their membership in the subgroup of powermats, the bigger group of chargers, as well as the even bigger group of gadgets. As metaphorical pebbles, there is no doubt they are not central members of the group of pebbles, dwelling in its periphery. But they are pebbles nonetheless!

Metaphor is a medium—one cannot stress this enough—a structure, a composition, an end product or artifact. A metaphor is actually the newly rearranged target that becomes a member, a real-albeit-peripheral member, of a group. It gains properties, real properties, from the source, and thereby gains emergent properties from the amalgamation of the source properties with their compositional context. The pebble shape, smoothness, appearance, and vibe, being possessed by the powermat, are clearly different from the counterpart properties being possessed by pebbles on the bank of a lake. The charger, along

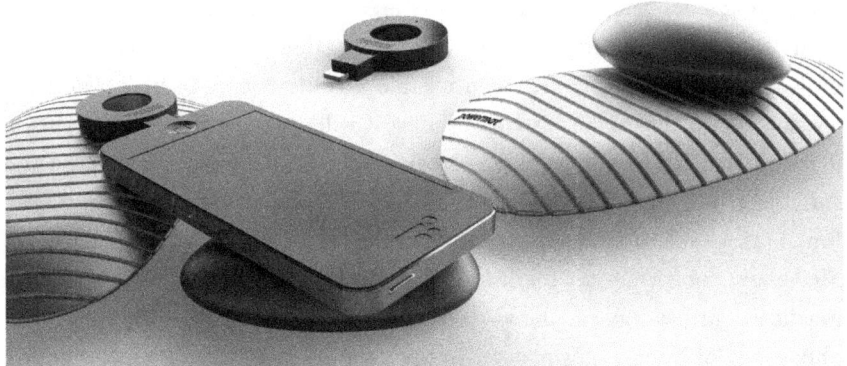

Figure 1 Alex Padwa and Gilad Davidi, Padwa Design, *Powermat*, 2014. Reproduced by permission of Alex Padwa, designer and photographer.

with the smaller pebble box containing parts of the charger, supplies a new context given their other properties and their relation to the new ones. Examples of the new context of properties and their relations include: the relation between the smoothness and its function as interface for the user; the horizontal roundness and its function as a platform of the cellphone or as a box for its plug; the very fact that the pebble properties are possessed by a charger rather than by a stone. All of these properties and relations are combined to render the visible metaphorical composition.

This metaphorical, emergent medium can neither be covered by a prior conceptual scheme, nor can it be preconceived. It is not an entailment of a primary, internal, abstract metaphor; if anything, it is the other way around. It is ontologically made, in the external sphere, and may subsequently result in entailing concepts.

Undeniably, metaphors have yet to be granted their own due ontological theory. Moreover, within ontology, the right sort of philosophical theory to capture the essence of metaphor is externalist-formalist—one that compels us to look at external ways of shaping metaphors, and tracks down the primary status of visual metaphors, which in turn may establish conceptual and linguistic metaphors. Accordingly, the terminology to be used in recharacterizing metaphors ought to shift from the ubiquitous mentalist-cognitivist, conceptualist, or linguistic one, to an externalist terminology including terms such as "form" or "composition," "property," "structure," "appearance," or "emergence," and "visuality," "medium," or "affordance." This is what I will try to do here.

Metaphors reconstruct thoughts to be deep and pictures to be expressive. They reconstruct emotions to be stormy, allow willows to weep and people to flourish. They rearrange theories to be buildings. They enable relationships to be at crossroads, and later at a dead-end. In the early Renaissance, the metaphorical model for painting was the mirror. Establishing further the practice of perspective projection, Alberti transfigured painting into a window, more accurately an open window, as he detailed in his *On Painting*: "I will say what I myself do when I paint. First, I trace as large a quadrangle as I wish, with right angles, on the surface to be painted; in this place, it [the rectangular quadrangle] certainly functions for me as an open window through which the historia is observed."[2] Metaphors sometimes set the infrastructure of philosophical movements and practices. For example, as the visualist Rudolf Arnheim notes, "the influential philosophy of Neoplatonism, based entirely on the metaphor of light, found its visual expression in the use of illumination by daylight and candles in the churches of the Middle Ages."[3] The metaphor of light appeared in modernist

Figure 2 Job and Seletti, *Hot Dog Sofa*, Blow collection, 2017. Reproduced by permission of Studio Seletti.

philosophy as well. Metaphors designated reason and rationalist maturity in Western ideology and culture as enlightened, and ignorance as dark. Metaphors create the Internet-based hypertext system as alternately a web that links countless sites in countless directions, a huge data storage facility, and an ocean that we surf. Not least, metaphors rearrange not only categories, but also particular objects—such as Alex Padwa's powermat as a pebble, Sia as titanium when singing David Guetta's "Titanium," and Job and Seletti's *Hot Dog Sofa* as a bun with a hotdog (Figure 2).

Particular metaphors are subsumed under the practice of categories and membership just like general metaphors. *Hot Dog Sofa*'s membership in the group of buns is unstable or ephemeral to be sure, but it is still a bun. Similarly, metaphors construct the Jamie and Mark Antoniades' pencils holder as some kind of a wooden sharpener and the sharpener as a pencil (Figure 3), or a chocolate bar–shaped notepad (Figure 4). Metaphors allow Matteo Bianchi's *Muffin Pouffe* (Figure 5) to belong to the group of muffins. They allow products designer Nick Lerwill's desk organizer and Enrico Salis's toothpick holder to be cactuses (Figures 6 and 7). A metaphor enables architect Cedric Price's *Fun Palace* (1961) to be "a people's workshop or university of the streets"—a modular, never-ending, flexible, process-oriented building—and to assume properties of a theatrical set, given that as Keller Easterling says, "Price designed architecture as

Figure 3 Jamie and Mark Antoniades, *Sharpener Desk Tidy*. Reproduced by permission of LOVEThEsign team; photograph by Michalle Gal.

Figure 4 Chocolate notepad. Photograph by Michalle Gal.

Figure 5 Matteo Bianchi, *Muffin Pouffe*, 2011. Reproduced by permission of Matteo Bianchi; photograph by Rei Moon.

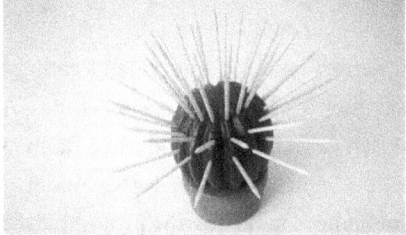

Figure 7 Enrico Salis, *Caliteiro Toothpick Holder*, 2011. Photograph by Michalle Gal.

Figure 6 Nick Lerwill, *Cork Cactus*, 2021. Photograph by Michalle Gal.

Figure 8 Shimon Levi, Arieh Cohen, *Ship Building*, Tel Aviv, 1935. Image produced by Wikimedia Commons: https://commons.wikimedia.org/wiki/Category:Shimon_Levi_house

a performance of components rather than a single object."[4] Furthermore, some say that his buildings are machines. A metaphor constructs Shimon Levi's and Arieh Cohen's 1935 modernist Bauhaus house as a ship, some would say a steam ship (Figure 8). Indeed, the modernist style of houses was deeply related to metaphors in borrowing prototypical forms of engineering and technology, such as the forms of airplanes, silos, ships, and industrial machines. This is noted in 1954, for example, by Gombrich in his "Visual Metaphors of Value in Art." There, he argues that metaphors originate in external artifacts, which serve as "areas of metaphors" used to form different styles of design:

> If the Victorians took their visual metaphors from the museum, we take ours from the operating theater and the factory... we are asked to see our house as "a

machine we live in." The machine itself, of course, or rather the world of engineering, has become an area of metaphor on which we draw. The "streamline" contour is employed metaphorically where no rapid airstream will ever cause friction, to suggest or "express" efficiency.[5]

This creative skill to re-transfigure something as an outcome of our labor is referred to by Gombrich as "Pygmalion power." Identifying different metaphors of various types beyond the linguistic ones involves this Pygmalion power. That is to say, this identification of metaphors involves the skill of adding a new member to a group by way of endowing the metamorphosed thing with a new ontological status due to its emergent properties. The ontological standpoint of Gombrich's account on metaphor is rarely mentioned in the literature, though time and again he explicitly points to "the difference between the narrower class of the real and the wider class of the metaphorical," namely, to the metaphorical segments of reality.[6] In coining the concept of "Pygmalion power," Gombrich alludes to Ovid's sculptor-hero in *Metamorphosis* who revealed the "awe-inspiring function of art when the artist did not aim at making a 'likeness' but at rivalling creation itself."[7] However, as is well known, Gombrich was a theoretician of visuality rather than a Latin literature scholar. Thus, his theory applies to *reality*, comprising everyday practice and everyday objects such as car lights staring back at us or a wooden stick transforming to a horse, "a ridable object," by a riding kid.[8]

What is more, looking at the example of what he dubs the "projecting" of ridability to a wooden stick and thereby transforming it into a toy horse, Gombrich rightly emphasizes that metaphorical practice is natural for us and common among children. This remains so even though metaphorical practice does not always result in self-standing or long-lasting metaphors. This insight is helpful in turning the focus of the study of metaphor from conceptual-cognitivism to ontology and world-reorganization. Gombrich subsumes the ontological practice of transfiguring things into new members of different groups under our primary creative practices. His main argument in "Psycho-Analysis and the History of Art" indicates both the naturalness of metaphorical practice and its ontological nature: "the child's baby doll is not an image of a baby so much as a member of the class 'babies'" given that it functions as a baby and the child takes care of it as it would a baby, by hugging it, bathing it, etc.[9] Another typical example of an exertion of this power that Gombrich presents, this time in his canonical *Art and Illusion*, is in making a snowman. That snowman's *ontological* status is characterized as follows:

> When we make a snowman we do not feel, I submit, that we are constructing a phantom of a man. We are simply making a man of snow ... It is only afterward that we may introduce the idea of reference, of the snowman's representing somebody ... But always, I contend, making will come before matching, creation before reference ... The pile of snow provides us with the first schema, which we correct until it satisfies our minimum definition. A symbolic man, to be sure, but still a member of the species man, subspecies snowman.[10]

We see, then, that an internal link between the practice of representation and ontology is delineated here, granting the ontological status of the artifact a primacy over its semantic load. What is more, according to Gombrich, not only is the snowman a thing rather than a symbol, being a member of the group of men, but the origin of the snowman is external rather than conceptual. Conceptually, "there was no such pre-existent snowman," he contends. The shape of the snow pile is corrected time and again until a man is recognized.

This Pygmalion practice, the ability to create a man out of snow, is named "metamorphosis" and "bodying forth" by Gombrich's contemporary visualist Virgil Aldrich in his 1968 essay "Visual Metaphor."[11] That essay was published more than a decade after Gombrich's "Visual Metaphors of Value in Art" and *Art and Illusion* first appeared, advancing toward a self-standing definition of the visual kind of metaphor. Like Gombrich, Aldrich was one of those whom it would be fitting to call the leading "visualist" theoreticians of the second half of the twentieth century, together with Rudolf Arnheim, whose work will be discussed at length later. They were the first to acknowledge the visual kind of metaphor and its significance in defining the essence of metaphor in general. Following this understanding, they were the first to relate metaphor to ontological practice.

A snowman is not clearly a metaphor, though in being a snowman, personhood has been attributed to a person-shaped pile of snow, and even though sometimes that snowman has a name and has been decorated with some human accessories. It is not clearly a metaphor because a metaphor must have a clear demarcated target, which is supposed to be reconstructed. In artistic terms, metaphor necessitates a ready-made target. However, the practice of personifying the snowman both enlarges the group of men and brings out new properties that emerge due to the special context of the new artifact—for example, the specific cold, white, crisp organs that can only be possessed by a snow-made person. Therefore, its formation could be subsumed under metaphorical practices. A snowman is still only ambiguously a metaphor, so let us turn to a surefire example from Gombrich: of artificial cowrie shell eyes affixed to a modeled skull from Jericho in about 6000 BCE. Analyzing it, Gombrich states that "to represent is to create." In other words, the essence of these shells is not that they symbolize or refer to eyes, but that they are created eyes that partially function as eyes:

> the difference between symbolization and representation is one of use, of context, of metaphor. In both cases, similarities present a starting point for what I have described somewhat pedantically as the "extension of a class". Here the class of eyelike objects can take the place of eyes because when they are put in position the skull will suddenly "look" at us.[12]

1.2 Attachment to forms

Just as much as the cowrie shells have the shape and properties of the eyes of the Jericho skull, and Selleti's sofa has the form of a hotdog, the pebble shape is not a natural property of power supply. The pebble shape was borrowed—actually, reproduced—from the source group in order to reconstruct the target object, the powermat, as some kind of pebble. *But its pebble form is not to be taken lightly.* For that matter, neither is the form of the sharpener (pencil holder), nor the forms of the piano or pencil (sharpener), nor the form of the ship (building), nor the form of the muffin (pouffe), nor the form of the cactus (desk cork or toothpick holder). And this is the important point, along the lines of the formulation of the ontological, externalist, formalist theory of metaphors here—forms are important to us! Canonical forms, whether whole or partial, such as the forms of building structure that reconstruct theories as solid, or of a ceiling that reconstructs the restrictions to career advancement of minorities and women. These forms are sensuously experienced by us, are significant for us, are carried by cultures through the generations, they come to be well recognized, they come to be culturally entrenched, and they are employed to reconstruct different kinds of phenomena in different media. As cute as the muffin pouffe, the hotdog sofa, and the sharpener-shaped pencil holder are—and as eye pleasing as the desk cactus, the pebble-powermat, and my daughter's lemon purse (Figure 9) are—these are not merely nice little things. These are serious things, which reflect our serious nature. Realizing this helps us to capture the essence of metaphors.

One should not take lightly the very common and ubiquitous use of canonical external-visual *forms* to continuously widen and rearrange our ontological sphere. Sometimes we do so using close-by and familiar forms, such as facial or

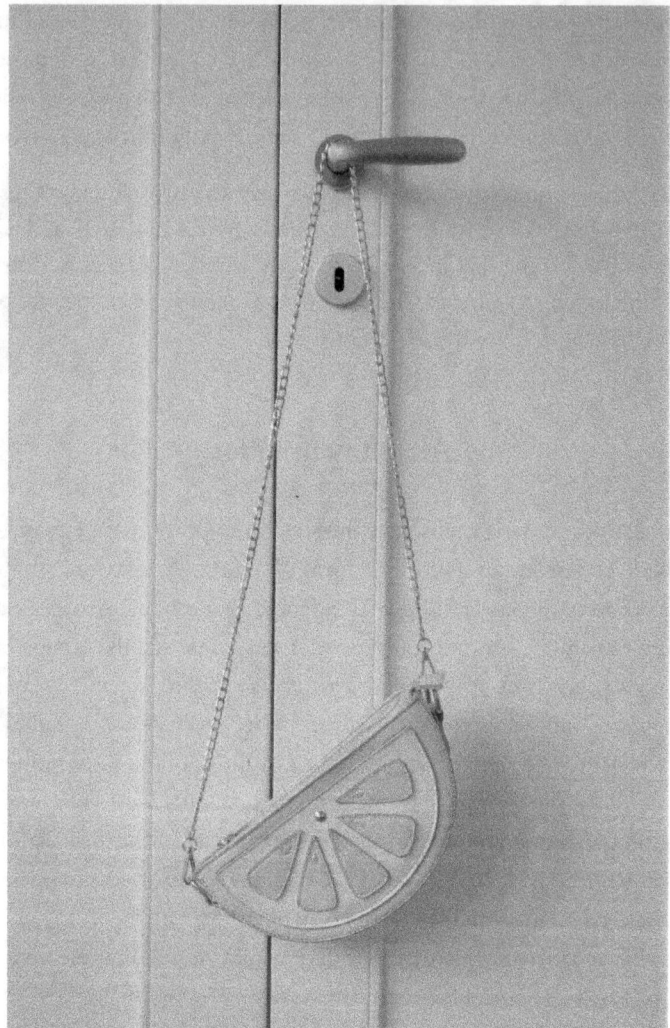

Figure 9 Lemon purse. Photograph by Matti Harel and Nira Pereg, 2021. Reproduced with permission.

bodily forms, projected onto almost everything possible: car fronts, buildings, electrical outlets, wine, clouds, organizations and states, or financial values. Sometimes this is casually done in everyday practice. Sometimes designers or artists, poets, writers or speakers create elegant metaphorical compositions reusing forms without their original functions. This could be a general form or a very specific one, such as the Bankside Power Station in London, originally designed by Giles Gilbert Scott and built between 1947 and 1963. This defunct power station faced demolition. However, a public campaign to preserve the very specific form of this landmark offered new possibilities for its use. Finally, in 1994 the Tate Gallery announced that Bankside would be the home of the new Tate Modern museum. Jacques Herzog and Pierre de Meuron won the subsequent international competition for the building's conversion, and 134 million euros were invested in the conversion of the power station to the museum that opened in 2000. This function-follows-form (inversion intended) instance is but one of many community-led campaigns motivated by the forms of buildings.

Since forms have their role in constituting identities, the sharpener-shaped pencil holder is no less a sharpener than it is a pencil holder. The pencil-shaped sharpener is no less a pencil than a sharpener. This is, at least, how my seventeen-year-old daughter labels them. True, the functions are significant properties of these objects. They were preconceived to function as they do and were made accordingly. However, one need not take the forms of these objects casually. They are more than merely decorative elements. They are leading elements in the constitution of the objects. They are related to what Gombrich names "sense of order" which is based on that perceptual "elementary expectation of regularity."[13] These are canonical or iconic forms that accompany us, are dear to us, and more besides, they accompany sharpenerhood or pencilhood. Therefore, the sharpener-shaped pencil holder is a member of the group of sharpeners. It dwells at the periphery of the group, no doubt, but it is still a member due to its iconic form. The same goes for the lemon-slice purse—everyone who is asked about it says that it is a lemon—as the lemon-slice has an iconic form. If I am right, this attendance of forms is what Arnheim means when he writes about *visual storage*, itself related to William James's idea of "preperception":

> William James uses the term preperception for such instances, in which stored visual concepts help to recognize insufficiently explicit perceptual patterns. However, James shows the traditional mistrust of unaided perception when he asserts that "the only things which we commonly see are those which we preperceive, and the only things which we preperceive are those which have been labeled for us, and the labels stamped into our mind. If we lost our stock of labels we should be intellectually lost in the midst of the world."

For Arnheim, preperception and stocked labels are visual, namely the organization of the world and its perception made by visual forms. He accordingly names them "visual knowledge" and "visual concepts," asserting that "visual knowledge and correct expectation will facilitate perception whereas inappropriate visual concepts will delay or impede it."[14]

Surely, these terms are closely related to the refutation of the innocent eye model, famously criticized by Karl Popper, Gombrich, and Nelson Goodman. Arnheim's take on this model is sheerly visualist. The structures that load the eye are derived from visual perception and the experience of pieces of ontology. These structures, it should be noted, are prototypical. Moreover, according to Arnheim—and this is a common assertion—the value and effect of the preperceived images depend not merely on the familiarity with prototype images, but also on "what the nature of the given context seems to call for," that is to say, "what one expects to see depends considerably on what 'belongs' in that particular place."[15] Perception or identification of kinds is innately connected to "norm images," as dubbed by Arnheim, which are stored in the visual storage of the observer.

The feelings of regret that caused by the evaporation of the iconic appearances of the pocket radio, the vintage television or the rotary-dial phone, and alternatively the feelings of pleasure evoked by their reuses and unexpected appearances in new things, are quite common. Parallel to it is the prevalent positive attitude toward new forms. Forms and styles of forms are quoted and requoted time and again in art, in all the disciplines of design, as well as in everyday aesthetics, all the way to the most ordinary visual things that furnish our everyday environments. Sometimes the forms are of the spatial kind, such as of objects, sometimes they are sequential or temporal, such as the form of a journey, of having a fight or of sleeping, of partying, of dining, of studying, of going to a funeral. Yes, these actions and situations possess visual forms and compositions, often iconic ones, as well as a very substantial visuality. We realize the iconic status of these temporal forms when watching, for example, a dance representing a couple fighting: fast and frequent hand movements where as one leaves, the other follows. We can see well-known repeating patterns of these kinds of situations. These visual forms are foundational to our being. These forms could be general; they could be derived from established categories such those of smiles, of houses, of trees, of frustration or anger, which emoji (both static and animated) manifest so well. They could be particular, the identity of which is not gained by a membership in a group, such as the forms of specific monuments, of a personal piece of jewelry or cloth or one's grandmother's tea set. Visual forms are carried through the generations, cherished, quoted, and alluded to. They are reused, they impart pleasure and comfort, they are borrowed or reproduced, they build cultures tier above tier, they arrange thoughts, ideas, and ideologies and they furnish our ontological sphere. *Visuality is in our nature. Visuality* is *our nature.*

Let us think again about the form of a pebble. I do not refer here merely to the fact that this form is the element that distinguishes Padwa's charger from other chargers. Nor do I-merely refer to Padwa's straight response to my queries about the creative process of this piece: "of course they were designed with the spirit of pebbles!" which I take to imply that the pebble shape was a central starting point in the creative process. What I would like to stress here is that the pebble form which is reproduced in Padwa's powermat is originally iconic, well established, easily recognized, as well as shown forth by the new object. Consequently, its metaphorical status notwithstanding, the pebble form is a strong property of the design object, the powermat, which is a metaphor by itself—a material-visual metaphor.

A possession of metaphorical property, such as that of "being a pebble," was brilliantly named "figurative possession" by Nelson Goodman in the framework of his theory of metaphors and expression. This kind of property possession is as actual as literal possession.[16] "Metaphorical possession is indeed not literal," Goodman explains in *Languages of Art*, "but possession is actual whether metaphorical or literal. The metaphorical and the literal have to be distinguished within the actual. Calling a picture sad and calling it gray are simply different ways of classifying it."[17] This realizes the significance of forms and thus explains why formal properties can prove to be salient even when they are metaphorical.

Goodman's pluralist ontology, explicitly influenced by Gombrich's, has an explanatory power with regard to metaphors' ability to use forms substantially in order to extend categories. Goodman is one of the few to capture the ontological character of metaphors, even if not in its entirety and not explicitly. Following Gombrich's blend of symbolic theory with constructivist ontology, and accordingly between representation and making, Goodman shows that metaphorical structure has to do with properties, their possessions and the subsequent classifications of the things that possess them. Accordingly, he claims that metaphorical truth and falsity are crucial in the fields of description of metaphorical properties. That is to say, like Gombrich and Aldrich, Goodman considers metaphor to be the properties-possessing thing—not the symbol, but the symbolized—the description of which has a truth value. He argues that both the metaphorical and literal properties that a thing may possess are exemplified by it, and they both in their turn label the thing as possessing them (thus belonging to a group). For example, being sad, just like being gray, equally labels Piet Mondrian's *Gray Tree* (1911) as belonging to the group of sad and gray things (and the subgroup of sad and gray pictures). Therefore, asserting that the picture is sad would be true and that the picture is happy would be false. If metaphorical attributions have truth values, then metaphors belong to the realm of facts rather than to that of understanding and mental contents. We see, then, that Gombrich and Goodman refer to ontological arrangements and rearrangements of external things as the core mechanism of metaphors.

Often, even a non-essential and external property of an object is one of the strongest in the hierarchy of properties, measured in terms of the durability of the property. For example, the short-lived desirability of each model of the iPhone is as strong a property as the iPhone's communicative function. By contrast, the pebble form is *not* a non-essential or temporary property of the powermat, but rather is a constitutive property. Using Arnheim's terminology which defines "type property" as structural, the pebble form is a type property as opposed to a mere attribution. Arnheim's distinction between type or structural property and attributions is drawn as follows: "a container concept is the set of attributes by which a kind of entity can be identified. A type is the structural essence of such a kind of entity. The abstraction characteristic of productive thinking are types rather than containers—in science as well as in art."[18] Accordingly, the following might explain the status of the pebble shape as a type property, its ontological work, and why visual metaphors are paradigmatic. The pebble shape takes hold of the charger and determines its structure, hence the charger's membership in the pebbles group as well (as mentioned earlier, this membership does not exclude any others). It assimilates the object's functions, and the means by which the functions are executed, i.e., the way the charger holds the cellphone and contains its connector, as well as how it feels when used, its appearance as an object that is used daily and present in our close environment. Moreover, one may claim that this form, similarly to other forms, is the very axis around which the identity of the object is determined. Indeed, the object lends itself to be perceived as such, shows forth its form, and viewers or users who are presented with it immediately declare, "It is a pebble!"

We see then that the pebble form, or "having a pebble shape," is neither a mere attribution of a foreign predicate, nor a mere source of understanding the charger. It is definitely neither a conceptual content nor a derivative of it. To be more precise, the pebble form, or shape, is accountable for constructing the charger and introducing it to a foreign group, of pebbles. It may not be very welcoming to chargers at first. But not being welcomed by the new group is what keeps the metaphor alive. From the opposite vantage point, the pebble form itself is amalgamated to the powermat properties, since it is a form of a charger now, not of a stone, and emerges as a modified property.

I claim that the emergence of these modified properties is the third part of metaphor, beyond the source and target, an integral part of any metaphor and the reconstruction of the target of it. Additionally, this is best shown by visual metaphors because the compositions of visual metaphors are more directly perceived than by those of the linguistic or conceptual ones. Moreover, the other kinds of metaphors borrow the emergence mechanism from visual metaphors, and the resources of metaphors are external-perceptual (this will be detailed and further explained later in this chapter and more thoroughly from Chapter 4 onward). These relations between metaphors, the significance of forms in our lives and the status of the visual sphere render the visual metaphors as the paradigmatic kind. The current visual turn in conjunction with the reintroduction of visualist, formalist, externalist theories to the field of metaphor studies provides an ideal opportunity to offer a new visualist theory of metaphor.

1.3 The visual turn

During the current age of interfaces, screens, and new media, accompanied by an increasing understanding that people are more visualists than conceptualists, the evolving visual turn of philosophy rightly presents the visual sphere as the right arena to analyze both the world and our ways of thinking about it—the medium of metaphor surely included. A clear exposition of the roots of the visual turn, and of the spread of visual media practices among the young, is given by András Benedek in his 2019 "A New Paradigm in Education: The Priority of the Image." It was published in the productive and revolutionary visualist project entitled *Visual Learning Lab*. Kristóf Nyíri and Benedek established *Visual Learning Lab* in 2009, and it has been one of the central voices of the theoretical visual turn ever since. In making a descriptive argument for the omnipresence of visual technology, Benedek reaches a visualist educational imperative:

> A truly significant turn has been brought about by the massive spread of touchscreen devices and the practice of personalized use commencing at a very young age among children ... Creating images, supplementing messages with diverse contents, applying specific genres (video, flash multimedia content and animation) have become an increasingly general practice in everyday communication. Storing, editing and sharing pictures, distributing them through networked communications systems became a basic social activity in the past decade, which has been modestly integrated into teaching and learning at schools. Modern curriculum theory highlighted the complex effect of cognitive and affective functions decades ago, which makes the pedagogical significance of utilizing pictures an issue of utmost importance.[19]

Benedek prescribes the use of pictures in education in order to make education suitable for the visual age, visual ontology, and visual practice. A recognition that the intensive visual turn is not random, but essential, stands behind this proposal. The various disciplines in philosophy should realize that as well, not least in the philosophy of metaphor—metaphor being a major aesthetic and creative medium.

Therefore, it is with this visualist awareness and spirit that an ontological, formalist, and externalist new definition of metaphor is presented here. Hopefully, this will capture metaphor's real visualist-ontological character, as opposed to the conceptual orthodoxy in the study of metaphor.

Two well-known philosophical turns preceded the current visual one. Curiously enough, the early twentieth century faced the linguistic campaign, not only characterizing the human being as a linguistic being first and foremost, but also setting language as the sphere of every single kind of philosophical analysis, and as the pick of humanity. The early parts of the linguistic turn promoted somewhat naïve, purely semantic, models of correspondence between language and reality. The later pragmatic models widened the extension of the definitions of meaning and language, coming from the realization that theorizing public, external, and particular structures of the use of language and of linguistic behavior is necessary in order to cover the linguistic sphere. But not much longer after this progress was made, an internalist (or at least mentalist), conceptualist, and cognitivist model of language took over the discussion, endowing a privileged status to mental content as *the* essence of the human being. The current conduct of the field of metaphor theory is a clear indication of this rule. Most of the theories of metaphor nowadays define metaphor as an internal scheme of thought and of understanding one concept through another, with the conceptual kind of metaphor enthroned as the paradigmatic kind of metaphor. From the mental-internal conceptual metaphor, they claim, one can derive not only the sub-conceptual metaphors as tokens of the main one, like the token "our relationship is at a crossroads" to the type "love is a journey," but one can also derive the different other kinds of metaphors: regular linguistic, poetic linguistic, material, or visual. Contrary to this view, I see visual metaphors as the paradigmatic and primary ones. I will go so far as to claim that even conceptual metaphors are derived from an external ontology, depending on an ontological reconstruction of one thing using properties of another, depending on the structures of perception in *seeing* or picturing one concept through a different one, which is enabled by the structural possibilities offered by visual media and originates there. I will argue, in Rudolf Arnheim's words from his *Visual Thinking*, for the primacy of the visual, "because it offers structural equivalents to all characteristics of objects, events, relations."[20]

Surely the philosophical study of metaphor is ready now to incorporate visualist studies, both of the visual and the cognitive, such as Arnheim's canonical and brilliant *Visual Thinking* from 1969. In it, Arnheim delineates an externalist theory of cognition, characterizing the human being as a perceiving visual being first and foremost, whose cognition dwells and develops in external, perceptual compositions and activities. He asserts that: "the cognitive operations called thinking are not the privilege of mental processes above and beyond perception but the essential ingredients of perception itself." By "cognitive operations" Arnheim refers to: "exploration, selection, grasping of essentials, simplification, abstraction, analysis and synthesis, completion, correction, comparison, problem solving, as well as combining, separating, putting in context."[21] For Arnheim, these operations are not the birthright of any mental function. Consequently, his systematic, visualist, ontological approach dissolves the distinction between thinking and seeing; or better yet, he presents thinking as depending on the visual external sphere coupled with its sensuous perception and as residing in that sphere. According to Arnheim's visualist characterization of us, "human thinking cannot go beyond the patterns suppliable by the human senses. Language then argues loudly in favor of the contention that thinking takes place in the realm of the senses."[22]

Arnheim offered his visualist theory of thinking in the midst of the linguistic age of philosophy, which then was assimilated into the cognitivist turn. In 2016, Nyíri, an ardent reader of Arnheim and a prominent figure in the twenty-first-century visual turn, who holds that "the human mind is a visual one," expresses his concern "that the visual approach is still entirely foreign to main-stream philosophy."[23] Nyíri goes against what he calls the "linguistic bias in philosophy." Hence in 2019, seventy years after Arnheim published his *Visual Thinking*, Nyíri finds it necessary to remind us that there is "such a thing as visual thinking" in the context of a return to John Dewey's philosophy of knowledge and education. In collaboration with Benedek, in a volume entitled *The Victory of the Pictorial Turn*, Nyíri progresses toward a visualist prescriptive account of education, submitting that: "no sound education is feasible without a recognition of the significance of the visual: mental images, physical pictures, moving images, the logic of the pictorial."[24] In that sense Arnheim's voice, as well as other visualist voices such as Gombrich's and Aldrich's, has fortunately been expressed parallel to linguistic and conceptualist voices. This expression has continued in the study of the visual to this day, waiting for philosophy to conclude its linguistic and then conceptualist turns in order to initiate its visual turn. The visual turn ought to include a visualist general philosophy, along with a visualist approach to metaphor, the vantage point of which is the visual sphere.

The study of metaphors within figurative language shows that the origins of most conceptual or verbal units are in the physical world, as Arnheim argues. Accordingly, these origins are given in perceptual and physical experience. Let us look at Arnheim's characterization of the very existence, not to mention the conceivability and conceptualization, of the typical metaphor of a "depth of thought" as being dependent on the experience of an external, physical depth:

> "Naive physics" is found in the figurative speech of the most divergent languages. The universal verbal habit reflects, of course, the psychological process by which the concepts describing "non-perceptual" facts derive from perceptual ones. The notion of the depth of thought is derived from physical depth; what is more, depth is not merely a convenient metaphor to describe the mental phenomenon but the only possible way of even conceiving of that notion. Mental depth is not thinkable without an awareness of physical depth.[25]

Voices that acknowledge the role and priority of the visual sphere in constructing our world can also be found in the fairly new disciplines of everyday aesthetics and material culture. These voices are significant for the visual turn, though that fact has not yet been sufficiently acknowledged in the literature. In particular Yuriko Saito, a prominent scholar of everyday aesthetics, has recently proposed that "western aesthetics today should be considered as restoring aesthetics to its original task: investigating the nature of experiences gained through sensory perception and sensibility."[26] Their brave study of the daily environment and practice of human lives, looking straight at the particularity of the disarranged parts of the world, teaches us a great deal about the role of ontology: the role of the external; the role of the visual; the role of "the practice of conceptualizing and constructing modernity [not modernism] in material form" in our being.[27] This focus leads us to the real essence of metaphors.

Conceptualist theories of metaphor insist on presenting a mind-ontology order: an internal base of conceptual scheme of meta-metaphors or primary abstract metaphors, whose structure is quite universal and whose token-metaphors, the metaphorical entailments, arrange big parts of our lives. They see this order as an arrangement of conceptual center, one which projects its branches all the way outside. Contrary to this picture, theories of externalist and ontology-oriented material culture, and of everyday aesthetics, are cognizant of the various directions of associations between types of thought and the external—with its particularities and its concrete and idiosyncratic phenomena. The historian and theoretician of material culture and design Judith Attfield, in her *Wild Things: The Material Culture of Everyday Life*, claims that materiality of the everyday should be explored in "terms of space, time and the body," a context which she classifies as a "physical entity." She therefore argues that "containment is the figure that provides a means of understanding this complexity reflected in the hybrid nature of contemporary material culture which cleaves to open-ended juxtaposition and metaphor rather than resolution."[28]

Similarly, and even more sharply, in her recent book *Aesthetics of the Familiar* Yuriko Saito calls for widening the scope of philosophy and especially aesthetics, both to all the particularities and practices and to the not-well-arranged space in which they exist. Abstraction with regard to life and ontology will not do, given its multiplicity and peculiarities, she contends, as opposed to conceptualism:

> Our lives consist of diverse experiences, some more aesthetically oriented than others, some more contemplative while others more physical in nature, some experienced literally daily while others only occasionally. I think it is a mistake to limit what counts as the legitimate ingredients of everyday life for everyday aesthetics discourse: life does not come in neat packages of different experiences and everyday aesthetics should embrace its complexities with all the messiness created by them.[29]

However, this diversity, complexity, and messiness should not be presented as a list of all of life's elements. Rather, Saito calls for defining the concept of the everyday: "by reference to the typical, usually practical, attitude that people take toward what they are experiencing."[30] This includes routine, monotony, and positive, as well as negative, aesthetic textures. Thus, Saito does not go along with the line of thought that classifies the aesthetic under the unfamiliar, and rightly so. One of Saito's most significant propositions is that the everyday aesthetic sphere does not need what she calls the "artification strategy" to be aesthetic, namely, the "defamiliarization of the familiar to render the ordinary in our life extraordinary." The key to aesthetic experience is reflection and attentiveness, which dwells in well-designed things as well as in the most ongoing or fragmentary practices:

> We can capture the aesthetic texture of ordinariness experienced as such, as long as we pay attention to what we are experiencing rather than acting on autopilot. Being attentive is a prerequisite for any kind of aesthetic experience and it does not necessarily compromise the ordinariness of ordinary life. Such experience of the ordinary is also captured by attending to the aesthetic experience of doing things, such as cooking and laundering.[31]

Here, Saito's theory of everyday aesthetics opens a vent to our not-always-organized existence, an existence which is full of non-abstract specificities. As opposed to the conceptualist definition of the human being as one operating from an organized *a priori* abstract scheme to its entailments, everyday aesthetics, by emphasizing that the aesthetic could be non-honorific, shows that we usually start our day by our externally oriented practices and objects within the visual sphere. Establishing that the subject of aesthetics also appears in the realm of the everyday has two relevant implications for the visual turn. First, that the visual sphere must be widened to include both everyday aesthetics and how everyday aesthetics can demonstrate the significance of visuality in our lives. Second, to understand that the motivation of metaphors, among which there are as many that are ordinary and ubiquitous as there are poetic and artistic, is aesthetic or at least visual.

A previous emphasis on the particularities of life and culture is found in Richard Rorty's theory of metaphor. Though he famously introduced the expression "the linguistic turn" to philosophy, Rorty himself went on to become one of the leading critics of this movement and an avowed anti-cognitivist. Endorsing an aestheticist and externalist approach, he views Western intellectual history through a filter of metaphor in order to renounce its teleological viewpoint. He argues that:

> to see the history of language, and thus of the arts, the sciences, and the moral sense, as the history of metaphor is to drop the picture of the human mind, or human languages, becoming better and better suited to the purposes for which God or Nature designed them, for example, able to express more and more meanings or to represent more and more facts.[32]

Indeed, metaphor is a matter of ontological strata rather than of concepts and thoughts. These strata are enabled by the external visual-material sphere, which is certainly sometimes, but only sometimes, followed by conceptual schemes. How can anyone deny the primacy and substantiality of physicality over conceptuality? The concept of depth, if it is conceivable at all, is barren without any real deep oceans, holes, or even bakeware. We are sensuous creatures; we primarily live in a material world. The fact that one says "I see" when one understands something is not casual but serious, crucial, and informative. We use the depth of these external physically deep things, as well as the physical walls of the holes or the floor of the ocean, to construct thoughts of depth in a manner that contains all of these and many other parts which each emanate from a serious, literal, preceding thought. But thoughts of depth contain more than just parts: they are compositions. Being visualist in our nature, we actually recompose thoughts of figurative depth to be more akin to the physical, introducing them to groups of preceding thoughts with which we are physically familiar. The metaphorical practice of familiarizing things is the topic of the next subchapter.

1.4 Face metaphors: familiarity-based metaphors and passing metaphors

The portrayal of metaphor as partially motivated by the wish or tendency to bring things closer to us through applying familiar labels to them is presented in the framework of "physiognomic perception" theory by Gombrich, Arnheim's contemporary visualist. "Physiognomic perception" is the title Gombrich gives to the universal, and immediate, ability and tendency to recognize facial and bodily expressions—both human expressions and other kinds, in other fields. That is to say, physiognomic perception is a categorizing perception of expressivity. The point of focusing on physiognomic perception is in its explanatory power regarding the composition of metaphors and metaphorical practice, including the everyday examples that one could call "passing metaphors" such as a frowning cloud, staring car lights, a dancing corkscrew or even a gloomy country. It is no wonder that Alessandro Mendini's Anna G, Alessandro M. corkscrew designs (Figure 10, 1993/2003) are so very popular.

Passing metaphors that are based on physiognomic perception are common among metaphors of the familiarizing kind; they are often found among the primary and ubiquitous kind of metaphor that reconstructs things from close visual categories so they are more familiar. This tendency, Gombrich asserts, "testifies to the constant scrutiny with which we scan our environment with the one vital question: are you friendly or hostile, a 'good thing' or a 'bad thing.'"[33] This might sound too simplistic, but Gombrich is definitely right in pointing to the formalist tendency to apply familiar forms on our surroundings, and in saying that ordinary compositions, as well as artistic and poetic ones, rely on the physiognomic response. That is to say, visuality and sensuous properties serve as an infrastructure for these compositions. I see Gombrich's analysis as supportive of the claim that we are attached to forms, and that this attachment is part of our metaphorical tendencies. Forms of all kinds used by all disciplines, he claims, have the power to be expressive and invite us to recognize their expressivity:

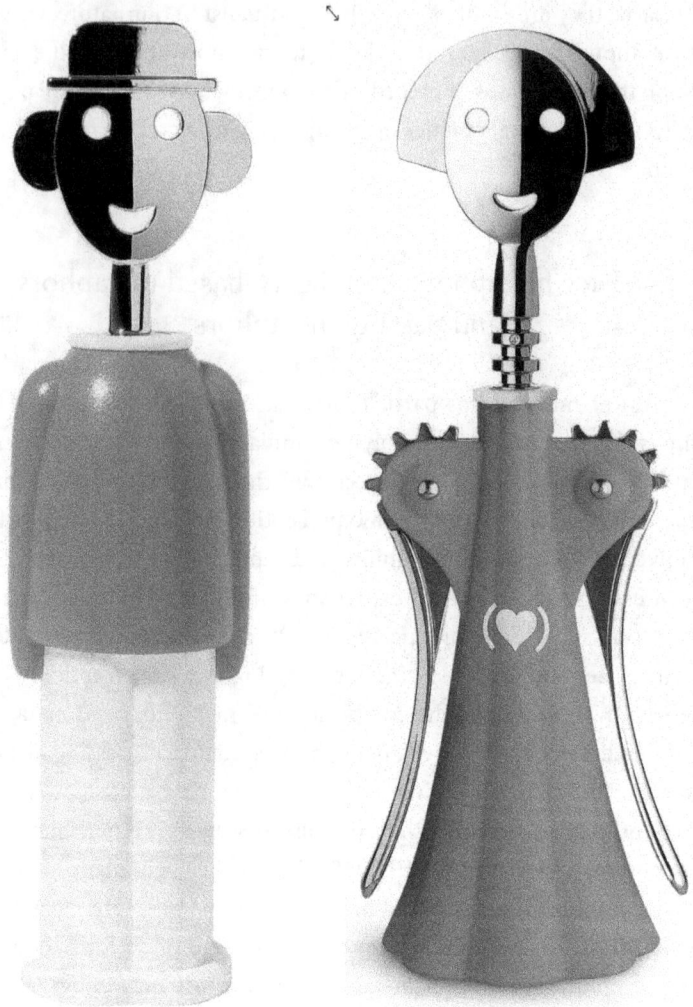

Figure 10 Alessandro Mendini, Anna G, Alessandro M. corkscrew designs, 1993/2003. Photograph by Michalle Gal.

What we call the "expressive" character of sounds, colors or shapes, is after all nothing else but this capacity to evoke "physiognomic" reactions. There is no theory of art, old or new, which ignores this element altogether. The ancient theory of music, for instance, elaborated the "expressive" character of modes and keys, orators discussed the physiognomy of words, rhythms, and sounds, and architects had something to say about the physiognomy of the various "orders" in architecture. Even in the visual arts, the expressive possibilities of shapes and forms as such were by no means neglected by the writers of the academic tradition.[34]

Gombrich's theory of expression in art defines it as a property of composition. The elaboration of this definition by his follower Goodman sheds light on Gombrich's philosophical approach here. For Goodman, expression is a metaphorical exemplification of properties possessed by the expressive thing: "works are said to express only such properties as they metaphorically exemplify when interpreted as aesthetics symbols."[35] Like Gombrich, Goodman links between expression, viz. metaphorical exemplification, and categorization. A thing exemplifies a few of its properties, those that categorize it in specific groups. Thereby that thing takes part in ontological practice, as said in "Fact from Fiction" in his canonical *Ways of World Making*: "serving as sample of, and thereby focusing attention upon certain shared or shareable forms, colors, feelings, such works induce reorganization of our accustomed world in accordance with these features, thus dividing and combining erstwhile relevant kinds, adding and subtracting, effecting new discriminations and integrations, reordering priorities."[36] Thus expression, or metaphorical exemplification, sets standards of rightness of classification of the exemplifying thing as a member of a group—this is what Goodman means by "interpretation."

Both of the expression and metaphor theories of Gombrich and Goodman are anti-mentalist, in the respect that they do not trace the source of expressivity of a piece in the mental content of its creator, but rather in that piece's own properties and their status in the composition. Additionally, parallel to the immediacy of physiognomic perception, the expressed properties are described by Goodman as ones that the work "makes manifest, selects, focuses upon, exhibits, heightens in our consciousness—those that it shows forth."[37] Goodman points to Gombrich's renunciation of the innocent eye model as his constructivist vantage point both in a review of *Art and Illusion* and in his own *Languages of Art* and *Ways of World Making*. Reflecting on Gombrich's theory of expression through Goodman's theory, we see that Gombrich takes the key externalist-visualist step of attributing primacy to physicality—both in constructing metaphors and in conceiving their conjoint relations with metaphorical perception.

Though not formulating a comprehensive self-standing definition of metaphor, Gombrich was one of the first to point to metaphor's visual source and ontological import. He was also one of the first to address the visual kind of metaphor as the right point of departure for a general theory of metaphor. He accordingly opposes the semantic theories of metaphor, which characterize the import of metaphors in extensions of meanings. "Metaphors are not necessarily 'transferred' meanings, linkages established, as the classical theory of metaphorical expression has it," he claims, and later suggests that metaphors have a visual foundation:

They are rather indicators of linkages not yet broken, of pigeonholes sufficiently wide to encompass both the blueness of a spring sky and a mother's smile. It adds to the interest of these categories that they are so often intrasensory: the smile belongs to the category of warm, bright, sweet experiences; the frown is cold, dark, and bitter in this primeval world where all things hostile or unpleasant strike us as similar or at least equivalent.[38]

We may now move one step forward in our account of the familiarizing kind of metaphors, and its contribution to the visualist theory of metaphors. Accumulating the main concepts of Gombrich's texts or paragraphs on metaphors, I see that beside "physiognomic perception" the main concepts, which together may amount to a complete visualist theory of metaphor, are "the area of metaphor," "projection," and "active perception." Gombrich's reasoning combines ontology with perception, as with Arnheim and Goodman after him. Gombrich accordingly conditions metaphor upon ways of seeing, which is a constructive notion that he calls "active perception." He also refers to this as "perception as a process of categorizing," which has an ontological bearing.[39] While psychological and biological expectations, needs, and tendencies are acknowledged to be crucial in his account, he maintains that metaphors and metaphorical practices are nonetheless *external* constructions. Critically, the fact that the tendencies of the perceiver are involved in making metaphors does not mean that the metaphor itself, as medium, is internal or contains internal mental contents by itself. Similarly, when Goodman speaks about conceptual schemes he refers to convention-dependent schemes, the sources of which are external and public.

Active perception involves the tendency of isomorphic personification: viz. of applying familiar anatomic forms and categories to targets, in order to reconstruct them as somewhat closer to us. This is part of the general formalist tendency to apply forms from one field to another in general, as betrayed by visual metaphors. Surely, the isomorphic tendency is well related to the fact (already mentioned in Chapter 1.2) that we are attached to forms, especially to familiar ones. An interesting dialectic element in Gombrich's theory is the revelation that there is a part of active, constructivist, perception that is not necessarily motivated by innovative or adventurous tendencies. Rather, our perception is sometimes motivated by conservative propensities, whose roots are our attachment to familiar forms and the wish to reconstruct relatively unfamiliar things in a manner which brings them closer to us. Of course, this practice may result in innovative constructions. For Gombrich, metaphor is a *dialectic* artifact;

sometimes metaphor consists of contradictory elements or forces, which mutually enable and enrich each other to a dialectic whole. What characterizes metaphor is not solely our creative faculty of innovation. Our inventive faculty is not that which allows us to present or to label something as something else, thus reorganizing our categories. Scrutinizing Gombrich's theory, we see that the psychological-epistemological roots of metaphor, and of Pygmalion practice, are not always our cravings for the new, but for making things and categories familiar to us and thus treatable by us. What stimulates Pygmalion practice is our perceptual fixations on familiar forms and conservative tendencies to personify what is different than us, making it more familiar. A main very commonly used form is that of a face: " a window can be an eye and a jug can have a mouth."

In January 2021, the United States House of Representatives assembled to consider the impeachment of Donald Trump, for his alleged role in the assault on American democracy by his supporters who stormed the US Capitol. One of the pro-Trump mob, Richard Barnett, broke into House Speaker Nancy Pelosi's office. A photograph of Barnett casually sitting in her office, with one of his feet on her desk, became one of the central images of the storming of the Capitol. Appealing to Republican colleagues to vote in favor of impeachment, Pelosi cited lines from Israeli poet Ehud Manor's *I Have No Other Country* (1982): "I can't keep silent in light of how my country has changed her face / I won't quit trying to remind her / In her ears, I'll sing my cries until she opens her eyes."[40] And again, Pelosi repeated, "I can't keep silent in light of how my country has changed her face."[41] This strong plea, coming from Pelosi, acquired almost immediate canonical status thanks to Manor's imagistic reconstruction: of a country having a face with shut eyes and closed ears, which one hopes will open again, to listen and to see—such a familiar form! Manor wrote this poem after the very controversial Lebanon War, which drove bitter divisions and much defiance among the Israeli public. How confident was Pelosi that this metaphor, in which a country gains a face, would be absorbed and endorsed by the American public? Given that she knew many people would be tuned in to the broadcast, Pelosi must have been certain that the *face metaphor*—so imagistic, so visual, and not least possessing *facial expressivity*, a familiar visual expressivity, of human aloofness, detachment, and alienation—would deeply impact her audience.

Gombrich writes a lot on face metaphors and facial expressivity in relation to metaphors. He shows us that the building on the right of Pieter Brueghel the Elder's *Dulle Griet* (*Mad Meg*, 1563) "becomes a devouring face, aided by the juxtaposition with a more realistic image of the mouth of hell." He adds that it is metaphor that shows us that the class of things called an eye, a mouth, or a face is much wider than the anatomist's concepts may provide. A progress from what Gombrich calls "the narrower classes of the real" to the classes of the metaphorical that inwardly absorbs familiar forms is famously exemplified by Pablo Picasso's *Baboon and Young* (1951): a sculpture of a baboon whose head is made of a car, that head thereby given the property of "being a car." At the same time, this metaphor is enabled given that many times the fronts of cars are transformed to look like, *to actually possess*, faces. Gombrich's analysis of Picasso's metaphor brings up all of these elements:

> The headlights of a car may look to us like a pair of glowing eyes, and we may call them so. The artist may use this similarity to work his magic of transformation. Picasso did precisely that when he created his wonderful bronze baboon with its young. He took a toy car, perhaps from the nursery of his children, and turned it into a baboon's face. He could see the hood and windshield of the car as a face, and this fresh act of classification inspired him to put his find to the test. Here, as so often, the artist's discovery of an unexpected use for the car has a twofold effect on us. We follow him not only in seeing a particular car as a baboon's head but learn in the process a new way of articulating the world, a new metaphor.[42]

1.4.1 Conservative visuality: making things look like us and look at us

Many theories of metaphors stress their defamiliarization, delineating their direction to be from the familiar to the new. It will be instructive to juxtapose our account with Rorty's account of metaphors, which he names "unfamiliar noises" or "unfamiliar uses of noises and marks."[43] Like Gombrich and the visualists, Rorty's point of view is externalist with regard to metaphor; he holds that metaphor is a creation, an "event in the world," and in that sense not merely a symbol but a thing in itself. For Rorty, metaphors shape consciousness, ideas, and thoughts, rather than the other way around. He therefore follows Donald Davidson's assertion in his "What Metaphors Mean" (nothing metaphorical, according to Davidson) that given "the distinction between what words mean and what they are used to do ... metaphor belongs exclusively to the domain of use."[44] The prevalent contemporary theoretical stance, which Rorty and Davidson opposed, was that of the semantic-cognitivist theories of metaphors: one that regarded the metaphorical mechanism as a linguistic meaning-producing mechanism. That stance was followed by the still-current conceptual-cognitivist theories, which regard the metaphorical mechanism as a mental mechanism of conceptual content. Davidson and Rorty relocate metaphors outside the semantic realm and inside the pragmatic realm. The difference between the literal and the metaphorical, in the way Davidson presents it, is not their corresponding links to literal and metaphorical meanings but between "familiar and unfamiliar uses of noises and marks."[45] While old theories enable us to get by with familiar noises, new noises push us to develop new and passing theories. In that respect, and given that they are self-declared anti-cognitivists, Davidson and Rorty are to be classified as pre-externalist or pro-externalist. In other words, they both submit that metaphors dwell in practice. Metaphor is in the business of making, not of symbolizing or conceptualizing.

However, for Rorty the impetus for metaphorical practice, ahead of culture, is the ever-refreshing practice of newness generated by the unfamiliar. He therefore endorses the high esteem the Romantics had for the role of imagination over that of rational analysis. This rationale leads him to broadly support Davidson's theory of metaphors: a theory that directs us to realize the pragmatic (as opposed to semantic) role of metaphors in both collective and personal dynamics and transformations. Davidson, Rorty argues,

> lets us see metaphors on the model of unfamiliar events in the natural world—*causes* of changing beliefs and ... He lets us see the metaphors which make possible novel scientific theories as causes of our ability to know more about the world, rather than expressions of such knowledge. He thereby makes it possible to see other metaphors as causes of our ability to do lots of other things—*e.g.,* be more sophisticated and interesting people, emancipate ourselves from tradition, transvalue our values, gain or lose religious faith.[46]

Rorty presents Davidson beautifully, and definitely holds an eye-opening theory of metaphor himself—characterizing it as an external cultural engine. He claims to endorse Davidson's opposition to the correspondence picture of language; specifically, they both oppose "the notion of language as something which can be adequate or inadequate to the world or to the self," and claim to realize the contingency of language in ways that the correspondence theory does not. According to Rorty, "recognition of that contingency leads to a recognition of the contingency of conscience, and how both recognitions lead to a picture of intellectual and moral progress as a history of increasingly useful metaphors rather than of increasing understanding of how things really are."[47] This is another wedge between Rorty and the cognitivist-conceptualist, as they would define metaphor as conceptual understanding. He also attributes a significance to visual and material kinds of metaphors, especially of artistic kinds. Then again, Rorty's interpretation of Davidson's theory goes too far in assuming that

Davidson stresses newness more than he really does. In actuality, Davidson does understand that what seems new in metaphor results from the success of composition rather than that of revolutionary elements, contending that "what we call the element of novelty or surprise in metaphor is a *built-in aesthetic feature we can experience again and again*, like the surprise in Haydn's Symphony No. 94, or a familiar deceptive cadence" (my emphasis).[48] It is noteworthy that this point was made by Davidson, given that he was a philosopher of language and mind, not an aesthetician. But then again, not once do philosophers of language and mind turn to art and aesthetics for their explanatory capacities. Davidson's point about the novelty in metaphor actually being based on repetitive experience sheds light on Gombrich's stress on familiarity in metaphors. That consequently brings us closer to a formalist-externalist definition of metaphor, taking into account our attachment to forms and its role in metaphorical practice, perception, and creation. Let me explain it further.

Like Davidson and unlike Rorty (in this respect—of his emphasis on newness) Gombrich shows that more often than not, the motivation of metaphors dwells in our attachment to familiar categories and forms or even our fixation on them. We tend to project these canonical forms on distant and new things alike to make them familiar to us and fit our experience. The direction of this kind of metaphor is, then, from the new to the familiar. When we transform something into something else, it is very often not by using a familiar thing in a new way; instead, we use a new thing in a familiar way. The aim is to visually familiarize the new and to draw it toward us. In this manner, we introduce it to a nearby category. We thus project familiarity onto mountains, furniture, clouds, and stars. Simply put, we want everything—still life, animals, plants, nature—to be like us, or even to see us in them. So we simply endow them with faces. "We know that there are certain privileged motifs in our world to which we respond almost too easily. The human face may be an outstanding example among them," says Gombrich, adding that the tendency to reconstruct things using faces involves the wish to set some order. "Whether by instinct or by very early training, we certainly ever disposed to single out the expressive features of a face from the chaos of sensations that surrounds it and to respond to its slightest variations with fear or joy."[49] In addition to our sensitivity to the expressive character of things, we reconstruct them to interact with us, even for a short while. This may apply to a plate of fruit, a building we walk by or a couple of side-by-side door handles. Gombrich, who very accurately presents our visual relationships with our environments, describes it in this manner: "our whole perceptual apparatus is somehow hypersensitized in this direction of physiognomic vision and the merest hint suffices for us to create an expressive physiognomy that 'looks' at us with surprising intensity. We may see faces in the pattern of a wallpaper, and tree apples arranged on a plate may stare at us like two eyes and clownish nose."[50] Interestingly, notwithstanding the conservative motivation, the corollary reorganization of categories is creative. Cars now do not only drive, plants do not only grow, but they acquire their own expressive properties not rooted in their origins: like the ability to smile, to gloomily bend or to stare.

It does not end here, though. The familiarity of anatomic categories results in the direct recognition of their types of expressivity. This direct recognition is what Gombrich classifies as "physiognomic perception." Gombrich describes the ease of physiognomic perception as follows: "we all experience this immediacy when we look into a human face. We see its cheerfulness or gloom, its kindliness or harshness, without being aware of reading signs."[51] The significant proposition for my argument is that physiognomic perception, combined with our attachment to forms, promotes the frequent creation of familiarity-based metaphors and *discloses their visual foundation*. Indeed, Gombrich proceeds by asserting that the metaphorical visual practice of exercising physiognomic perception is prompted by various kinds of things creating passing or stable metaphors, ordinary or artistic:

> This type of "global" and immediate reaction to expression is not confined to the reading of human faces or gestures. We all know how easily a similar response is evoked by other creatures, how the penguin will strike us as grave, the camel as supercilious and the marabou as wise. Moreover, the metaphors of our speech testify to the ease with which we carry this physiognomic perception into fields even further removed from rational inference; we speak of cheerful colors or melancholy sounds. Any poem, good or bad, will furnish examples of this extension of physiognomic perception, also known as the pathetic fallacy, telling of smiling skies and menacing clouds the caress of the wind and the soothing murmur of the brook.[52]

The "pathetic fallacy" was coined by John Ruskin in *Modern Painters III* to denote and criticize the sentimental tendency of eighteenth- and nineteenth-century poets to ascribe feelings and emotions to natural things and phenomena, which results in "falseness in all our impressions of external things."[53] Ruskin ridicules the tendency to familiarize things by making them closer to us. A sheer realist, anti-constructivist, externalist who holds the imperative "truth to nature" as Ruskin is, he classifies the "greatest poets" as sticking to pure facts, contrary to the "second order of poets." This imperative was formulated against aestheticist constructivism, which was proposed by his Oxford colleague Walter Pater, and later on by their disciple Oscar Wilde. Indeed, Wilde claimed in "The Decay of Lying" that nature is created by us and furthermore: "as for the infinite variety of Nature, that is a pure myth. It is not to be found in Nature herself. It resides in the imagination, or fancy, or cultivated blindness of a man who looks at her."[54] Ruskin denotes, "the difference between the ordinary, proper and true appearances of things to us; and the extraordinary, or false appearances, when we are under the influence of emotion, or contemplative fancy." Ruskin strongly asserts, "the foam is not cruel, neither does it crawl." These are, for Ruskin, false appearances which are "entirely unconnected with any real power or character in the object, and only imputed by us," while the first order poet refrains from these types of projection and expressivity, rooting for a rationalist conduct of truth to facts.[55]

Gombrich, Arnheim, Aldrich, and Hausman hold a more moderate externalist view, and would not endorse a description of such a sharp wedge between external things and perceptions. Their ontology is more intricate than Ruskin's, allowing for the percepts to possess expressivity by themselves. Things can be constructed and utterly external at the same time. Consequently, the poet does not subjugate her poetry to facts, but to a modification of reality.

> Even the poet's metaphor of the smiling sky suggests, as do all metaphors, a looser network of categories than do the tighter meshes of literal and rational language: the poet lives in a world where all things can still be divided into those that smile and those that frown, he has preserved the child's capacity to probe and question anything in nature and anything in nature will answer him clearly enough to allow him to 'sort' the world into these "physiognomic" categories.[56]

Arnheim too tries to decipher the immediacy of physiognomic perception, both of animate and inanimate things, and links it to metaphorical perception and creation. Like Gombrich, his visualist aim is to characterize: "how the perception of shape, movement, etc. may convey to an observer the direct experience of an expression that is structurally similar to the organization of the observed stimulus pattern."[57] He accordingly stresses in his *Towards a Psychology of Art* that "expression is an integral part of the elementary processes of perception. *Expression, then, could be defined as the 'psychological counterpart of the dynamic processes that result in the organization of perceptual stimuli'*" (emphasis in original).[58]

To delineate an isomorphism of the physical and psychological as the foundation of expression and metaphor, Arnheim uses the Gestalt theory while developing Theodor Lipps's then-innovative definition of perception as projecting oneself onto the object—meaning that perception is active and constructive. Lipps's proposal sheds a light on visual storage and attachment to forms, which I referred to earlier as being the basis of metaphors. According to Arnheim, Lipps offered a structural similarity between the perceptual appearance of an object and the psychological dynamics for the observer of physical and mechanical forces, "whose existence in an inanimate object is inferred by the observer through past experience."[59] Lipps applies this similarity, for example, to the relationship between the rhythm of musical tones and the rhythm of psychical processes that occur in the perceiver or listener. He calls this isomorphism between the object and the observer an "association of similarity of character," thus realizes a "possible inner similarity of perceptual patterns and the expressive meaning they convey to the observer."[60] Arnheim supports this theory, claiming that it preceded the Gestalt principle of isomorphism (which in turn served as a foundation of its theory of expression). He shows that correspondences between physical and psychical behavior, which is the basis of expression, has an explanatory power with regard to the directness of detecting expressivity, which Gombrich calls "physiognomic perception." This led Gestalt psychologists to maintain that:

> expressive behavior reveals its meaning directly in perception. The approach is based on the principle of isomorphism, according to which processes that take place in different media may be nevertheless similar in their structural organization. Applied to body and mind, this means that if the forces that determine bodily behavior are structurally similar to those that characterize the corresponding mental states, it may become understandable why psychical meaning can be read off directly from a person's appearance and conduct.[61]

What is crucial here for the visuality of us, and of metaphors, is that all the kinds of metaphors are based on our ability to grasp their compositions—and this ability is based on structures we have experienced beforehand. Look at how well Arnheim links external physicality, perception, and philosophy of metaphor. It is clear why he and Gombrich were the ones to endow philosophy with the foundation of the visual turn and recapture our visual nature. "To perceive any object or event," Arnheim clarifies,

> means to see it as a configuration of forces, and an awareness of the universality of such configurations is an integral part of all perceptual experience. Metaphors could not be so elementary and widespread a property of languages as they are if, for example, looking into a gorge did not inevitably involve the universal qualities of depth, darkness, and penetration-qualities that permit us to discuss abstractions in words.[62]

What the visualist grasped and the conceptualist missed is the ongoing and long-term influence of visuality over us. This influence is the source of metaphors and their omnipresence. The experience of physical depth, for example, accompanies us in the construction of many of our metaphors. Of course, this is also the case with the iconic forms to which we are attached; they accompany us in reconstructing various things.

Ian Verstegen, one of the most interesting recent interpreters of Arnheim's visualism, argues that for Arnheim the expressive force of external things is not based solely on the emotions and feelings we apply to them, but on "metaphor-like processes that recognize the isomorphic structural qualities of diverse sensory situations." However, he interprets Arnheim's theory as attributing a privileged status to metaphor over perception; he claims, "Arnheim does not derive metaphor from physiognomic perception but rather vice versa, physiognomic perception from metaphor."[63] This is an interesting reading of Arnheim. I tend to think that the metaphorical act is the very response to the physiognomic properties of things and events, rather than the other way around. But I will leave this controversy moot for the time being, because the significant point that underlies both readings is that metaphor and physiognomic perception are internally linked—thereby they support visualism with regard to metaphors.

A clear significant point regarding Arnheim's visualism is that he definitely prioritizes expression and its perception over mere properties. This is coherent with his holistic Gestalt theory. After all, his Gestalt theory points to emergent compositional relations between elements, revealing themselves within the whole as the base of ontology. "In the Gestalt Theory of Arnheim, the cultural object is emergent from the physical substrate," as Verstegen puts it.[64] This view goes well, of course, with Arnheim's characterization of visual metaphors as natural to us. It also explains the paradigmatic status of visual metaphors, since their holistic, dense, and continuous character is the foundation of what makes linguistic or conceptual metaphors compositional as well.

Arnheim's priority of expression over pure forms is expressed in his *Art and Visual Perception* in the following manner. First, he describes the common somewhat mistaken or not fully perceptive idea that forms are clean:

> we have come to think of perception as the recording of shapes, distances, hues, motions. The awareness of these measurable characteristics is actually a fairly late accomplishment of the human mind. Even in the twentieth-century Western man, it presupposes special conditions. It is the attitude of the scientist and the engineer, or of the salesman who estimates the size of a customer's waist, the shade of a lipstick, the weight of a suitcase.[65]

Second, Arnheim describes the depth of the forms we encounter, the expressivity of our environment, and our active perception. The visualist theories of physiognomic perception which were formulated by Arnheim and Gombrich underlie not only the general visual turn in philosophy, but they specifically underlie everyday aesthetics as well. Arnheim exemplifies the ordinary occurrence of physiognomic perception in the following, which opposes the approach to forms as being simple:

> But when I sit in front of a fireplace and watch the flames, I do not normally register certain shades of red, various degrees of brightness, geometrically defined shapes moving at such and such a speed. I see the graceful play of aggressive tongues, flexible striving, lively color. The face of a person is more readily perceived and remembered as being alert, tense, and concentrated than it is as being triangularly shaped, having slanted eyebrows, straight lips, and so on. This priority of expression, although somewhat modified in adults by a scientifically oriented education, is striking in children and primitives, as has been shown by Werner and Kohler. The profile of a mountain is soft or threateningly harsh; a blanket thrown over a chair is twisted, sad, tired. The priority of physiognomic properties should not come as a surprise. Our senses are not self-contained recording devices operating for their own sake.[66]

Active perception is explained by social constructivism, specifically by the viewer's tendency to apply preexisting conventional forms to both natural things and artifacts, as opposed to passive seeing. A recent example is in the immediate transnational conveyance of metaphorical attachments, applications, and projections made in light of the photos of *Ever Given*—the giant container ship, 400 meters long, loaded by 200,000 tons, wedged in the Suez Canal in March 2021 (Figure 11). This obstruction of one of the world's busiest trade routes created a queue of hundreds of ships. A whole week passed with many failed attempts to dislodge it. Subsequently the photo of a power shovel, standing next to the huge ship in order to dredge sand from beneath while "touching" it, brought about a great many reactions from all over the world (Figure 11). These reactions manifested its expressivity in its meeting a physiognomic perception: the shovel looked sad, even pathetic, as it pitifully tried to help and console the huge, miserable, stuck creature. Suitably, when *Ever Given* refloated, tugboats honked their horns in salute and the whole world treated the vessel as a giant creature being set free.

Accordingly, Arnheim's and Gombrich's theories of expression—along with their follower Goodman's—are externalist. They dissuade us from accepting the romanticist or mentalist view of expression as stemming from the speakers or creators of mental content. Instead, expression stems from known cultural forms.

Figure 11 *Ever Given* cargo ship stuck in Suez Canal, Egypt, March 2021. Alamy Stock Photo.

As quite a few Gombrich scholars know, by using physiognomic perception to explain the expressive effects of works of art, "he offers a more plausible explanation for the potency of these works, because he locates their effectiveness within a social and cultural matrix rather than seeing them as the product of the artist's unconscious."[67] Naturally, Arnheim holds a parallel constructivist version of realism, characterizing perception as active. In a chapter titled "The Intelligence of Perception," he claims that the difference between passive reception and active perception shows even in ordinary and primary visual experience: "as I open my eyes, I find myself surrounded by a given world: the sky with its clouds…the window, my study, my desk, my body—… it is given. It exists by itself without my having done anything noticeable to produce it."[68] This nonetheless does not cover the essence of perception, according to Arnheim.

> That given world is only the scene on which the most characteristic aspect of perception takes place. Through that world roams the glance, directed by attention, focusing the narrow range of sharpest vision … following the flight of a distant sea gull, scanning a tree to explore its shape. This eminently active performance is what is truly meant by visual perception … The world emerging from this perceptual exploration is not immediately given. Some of its aspects build up fast, some slowly, and all of them are subject to continued confirmation, reappraisal, change, completion, correction, deepening of understanding.[69]

Arnheim is aware of the fact that many would agree with the "active perception" proposition. However, he adds, they miss the fact that these perceptual actions are where intellectuality takes place. He refutes what may be named "the conceptualist etiological stance" which presents the material as becoming non-perceptual from the moment thinking is involved, abstracting concepts in order to "disrobe them completely, to free them from their visual character, and thereby make them suitable for intellectual operations."[70] The mind, Arnheim claims, is absolutely dependent on visuality for its function.

Some recent cognitivist theories of metaphors, those which realize the principal status of visuality in the operations of the mind, still cannot let go of the idea of abstraction that governs metaphors. A cognitivist metaphor theory that considers visuality and relates metaphor to active perception and ontological import is offered by the cognitivist Bipin Indurkhya. As we will see in Chapter 2, he developed the (formerly semantic) interaction theory of metaphors of the mid-twentieth century. Contrary to former semantic definitions of metaphors, he claims that metaphorical interaction takes place between the world and the perceiver, more so than between the metaphorical elements. Indurkhya is an explicit follower of Goodman and his assertions are analogous to the active perception theories of Gombrich, Arnheim, and Goodman. In a 2012 interview about his ideas and the intellectual road he took, he claims, "our perceptual system is not a passive receptor of sense data, but actively constructs the perceptual experience. Our perception of color, motion, and depth does not just depend on the stimulus, but reflects our past experiences of integrating similar stimuli into our actions, which is sometimes referred to as sensorimotor contingencies."[71] Like the visualists, Indurkhya links metaphorical practice to active perception while stressing its ontological boundaries and the context of the structure of metaphor, but combines this with the cognitivist (anti-visualist) assumption that metaphors are arranged by scheme: "in the framework of active perception metaphors play an irreducible epistemological role for they correspond to the gestalt or top-level template or schema that filters and organizes the sensory impressions. This, in my view, is the central tenet of the interaction theory."[72] Indurkhya offers to see metaphors in terms of pre-theoretical model formations, some of which are designed by accommodation (environment-driven) and some of which are designed by projection (subject-driven). We then see that, even though Indurkhya's account of metaphor is progressive in its grasp of the status of ontology in the field of metaphors, his perspective ultimately fits the cognitivist-conceptualist approach—an approach that attributes to metaphor a well-ordered mechanism of scheme and embodiments, or an abstract internal type and tokens.

Therefore, for too long the visuality-dependent mind has not been addressed in the field of metaphor. This results in an interesting discrepancy between the ruling conceptualist-cognitivist discipline of metaphor and the essence of such an imagistic, visual, aesthetic phenomenon as metaphor. In what remains of this chapter I shall elaborate on this incongruence.

1.5 A discrepancy in the metaphorical study

In the rich and ever-growing literature on metaphors, only a few ontological theories of metaphors are to be found. The lack of ontological analysis of metaphors in the literature does not represent the essence of the medium of metaphor, which no doubt has had an impact on both ontological categories and the properties of specific objects or phenomena. Nevertheless, the twentieth- to twenty-first-century study of metaphors has been mainly led by a semantic-cognitivist model of metaphors, followed by a conceptualist-cognitivist one. In the current visual turn, a crucial question to address and readdress in metaphor studies is how such an ontologically ubiquitous aesthetic, imagistic, visual, compositional, and creative phenomenon as metaphor, which furnishes a large portion of our environment and the conduct of our lives, has been taken over by a conceptualist-cognitivist approach whose links to aesthetics are very thin.

In his important essay "Criteria of Creativity," the visualist Carl Hausman emphasizes the aesthetic and philosophical significance of metaphor. He rightly argues that not only are metaphors autonomous, but that studying their formation informs us of the general nature of creative things. While metaphors are often used in language to analyze new creations and intelligibilities, Hausman writes, "more important, metaphors are themselves creations. Consequently, examination of their structure is suggestive of the general character of the structures exhibited in all creations. And if this is so, then metaphors will conform to the criteria of the phenomena for which they are intended to account."[73] Playing a crucial role in shaping the world, these reconstructions—instances of the *medium* of metaphor—are ontological in essence. Metaphors are primarily *aesthetic* pieces of ontology in the simplest sense of that term. In particular they are creative compositions, motivated more than anything else by visual tendencies. Accordingly, they are recognized by metaphorical seeing, which in turn reveals our visual nature.

One of the most important paragraphs in twentieth-century ontology and aesthetics is the following one by Arnheim. In it, he challenges the linguistic-followed-by-conceptualist turn and its admiration of language and abstract content. Arnheim indicates the visual sphere as instead having the upper hand in understanding our ontology and being. This paragraph comprises the essence of the controversy between conceptualism and visualism:

> The visual medium is so enormously superior because it offers structural equivalents to all characteristics of objects, events, relations. The variety of available visual shapes is as great as that of possible speech sounds, but what matters is that they can be organized according to readily definable patterns, of which the geometrical shapes are the most tangible illustration. The principal virtue of the visual medium is that of representing shapes in two-dimensional and three-dimensional space, as compared with the one dimensional sequence of verbal language. This polydimensional space not only yields good thought models of physical objects or events. it also represents isomorphically the dimensions needed for theoretical reasoning.[74]

Nonetheless, the ruling conceptualist theory of metaphor ignores the visual sphere and relies on an internalist philosophy of our nature. It mistakenly defines metaphor as an abstract, well-ordered, mental content. According to the conceptualist definition, the external metaphors are merely lesser and subservient tokens of the abstract internal one. Therefore, the discipline of the history of ideas ought to track the source of the discrepancy between the aesthetic-ontological essence of metaphor and the ruling conceptualist theory of metaphor. This discrepancy is rooted in the Western attribution of a privileged status to conceptuality over visuality when it comes to understanding the world, its perception and portrayal, and accordingly to analysis over seeing and to meaning over composition. A few reasons for this, from a philosophical point of view, will be presented here. I of course pick the reasons that best shed light on the essence of metaphor, but they also enlighten us on the big subject of ontology and our perception of it.

The discrepancy between the visual-ontological sphere of metaphorical structures and the conceptualist dominance of the field of metaphor stems first from a systematic ignorance of the fact that metaphor is an autonomous medium. What is more, despite the fact that metaphor is essentially rich in formats and kinds of media, as well as ontologically and intellectually productive, the ruling conceptual approach incongruously is internalist and reductionist—though a few very recent conceptualist appeals to widen its scope are heard, as will be presented in Chapter 3.3. Gombrich, Goodman, Arnheim, Rorty, and others present a much wider definition of cognition than the conceptualists do, seeing cognition as dwelling in physical spheres. Metaphors are central in the practice of what Arnheim names "visual intelligence" and accordingly "visual concepts," given that they renovate groups while using the familiar characters of the members of the group in a new way, leaving their former boundaries unstable. They challenge thereby our recognition of objects, phenomena, and categories. Arnheim notes that the recognition of visual things comprises the most common interaction between visual perception and visual memory. He argues that:

> visual knowledge acquired in the past helps not only in detecting the nature of an object or action appearing in the visual field: it also assigns the present object a place in the system of things constituting our total view of the world. Thus, almost every act of perception involves subsuming a given particular phenomenon under some visual concept—an operation most typical of thinking.[75]

Goodman's ontology, according to which perception involves labeling the percept, is surely equivalent to these claims—metaphor is dominant among the objects which invite us to relabel groups and remake the world.

If we are to capture the real nature of the medium of metaphor, as well as to understand why it is often unobserved by current theoretical propensities, understanding the source of this reductionist internalist approach is a significant aim for us. The most crucial factor in the scarcity of ontological theories of metaphors is the twentieth-century linguistic turn of philosophy, which endowed a theoretical authority to philosophy of language, linguistic studies, and cognitive science. The subsequent development of philosophy of mind had an impact as well. This paradigm begins from an internalist stance, characterizing humans as primarily linguistic-conceptual beings. Hence it was to be anticipated that, unfortunately, philosophy of language and cognitive studies would lead metaphor research. Under this influence, while proceeding to embrace an internalist view of metaphor, many theories failed to grasp the external origin of metaphor. They also failed to grasp the visual-material essence of the metaphorical medium—the fact that a metaphor is a structure or a composition—and that metaphors are motivated by *compositional* and formalist, if not aesthetic, creativity.

The conceptualist neglect of the medium of metaphor led a few critics of the conceptualist theory of metaphors to claim that such a theory gestures at schemes that are either too obvious or well established to be metaphorical, let alone used consciously. Riccardo Fusaroli and Simone Morgagni, two active theoreticians of metaphors, propose the conceptualist theory in their historical survey "Conceptual Metaphor Theory: 30 Years After"; they write,

> it is often suggested in the literature that conceptual metaphors are activated automatically during language use. Lakoff and Turner claim that when linguistic metaphors appear so hackneyed and conventional, they no longer pass for metaphors at all—as in everyday expressions such as *long* in *a long time*—this demonstrates that the conceptual metaphor (in this case duration is length) is alive and well. In the last decade, psycholinguistic and psychophysical behavioral evidence has begun to provide highly suggestive empirical support for this view.[76]

Raymond Gibbs has written a similar survey, claiming (as some psychologists and linguists argue) that many conventional expressions, such as "he attacked every weak point in my argument" or "your criticisms were right on target," are viewed by cognitive conceptualists as derivative of the abstract metaphor Argument Is War yet are not metaphorical but function as literal speech. They are neither motivated by conceptual abstract metaphors nor are they classified as metaphoric by ordinary speakers as well as scholars. Gibbs asserts, together with Steen, people may use metaphoric language as a matter of convention without necessarily having some underlying cognitive mapping occur between disparate source and target concepts. For instance, the simple phrase "John blew his stack" may be produced or understood to mean "John got very angry" without an individual having to access or compute some mapping between anger and heated fluid in the bodily container, as suggested by traditional cognitive linguistic analyses.[77]

I do not think that the subjects of conceptual metaphor theory analyses are not metaphorical. Rigidly conventional metaphors are still metaphors—though as I will explain in Chapter 3.3.1, using a distinction drawn by Gibbs and Steen, they are not always deliberate. However, I do think that conceptualism is essentially the *wrong* theory for metaphor and misses the point of metaphor from the start. Characterizing metaphors through the mentalist filter of a stable conceptual scheme is simply the wrong apparatus to grasp the phenomenon of metaphor and its visual power! I will elaborate on this point in detail in Chapter 3, but for now the following will suffice. The metaphor Argument Is War is commonly used as a clear example of a primary conceptual scheme, the entailments of which are common in our daily lives. But approaching the person whom we argue with as one would a rival in the battlefield is not founded on a conceptual scheme. This instead happens because of our aggressive urges, for example, or our innate wish to win, or because this person gets on our nerves, or because we are used to fighting. If we construct the argument to be some kind of war, it is only due to the external and visual composition of war which we have experienced and apply in this case. Then, further along in the process of metaphorical construction, we may conceptualize it. But the portrayal of the human being as a conceptual being whose particularities are universally and *a priori* guided is not compelling enough. Everyday conduct is more behavioral, particular, dependent on wishes and feelings or external habits. It sometimes happens because of aesthetic motivations or even random ones. It is all very external and visual.

Alongside the linguistic and then conceptualist occupation of philosophy, social sciences, cognitive studies and more, aesthetics took a linguistic turn of its own: neglecting the visual and addressing art as language. When it comes to aesthetics, its linguistic turn was logically linked to anti-formalism. Following philosophy in general, the aesthetics of the time defined artworks as symbolic and referential, in such a way that they essentially possess aboutness and meaning even more than syntax and composition. Endorsing the portrayal of humans as conceptual operators, aesthetics presented the ontology of artworks as based on conceptual order and comprehension, externally embodied only by derivation. While linguistic aesthetics gained impressive accomplishments, it also paid a high price of pushing away its own sphere of study: the visual, the sensuous, the composition and its power. Sometimes, it seems that while anti-linguistic formalism really appreciated visuality, the linguistic-turn aesthetics assumed an apologetic stance.

One of the leaders of this movement, a prominent aesthetician by any standard, is Arthur Danto, who famously formulated the brilliant paradigmatic definition of art as embodied meaning. Danto simultaneously made aesthetics a central philosophical discipline of the twentieth century, with its own history— again, brilliant and innovative philosophy—and pushed it to be superseded by theories of language and mental contents. Defining the artwork as an intellectual product results in the assertion that the idea of the work must first be captured by the beholders, who are only then able to figure out which visual properties of the object participate in the embodiment of this idea. An attack on the senses and a downgrade of the visual properties of artworks followed this approach, considering the senses as unsuitable to even recognize the ontological category of artworks and its relevant artistic properties.

In his account on metaphor, interestingly, Danto himself goes against what he calls "provincial conceptualism." He explains, "just because we find a good theory of linguistic metaphor may not mean that we have a good theory of *metaphor*." Nevertheless, Danto's view is internalist, characterizing metaphor as "having an *intensional* structure." That is to say, according to Danto, the medium of metaphor—linguistic and visual metaphors explicitly included—is conditional upon mental contents. This is confirmed by his assertion that "metaphors are minor works of art" with artworks characterized as mind-dependent things.[78]

Danto develops his internalist semantic theory of metaphor into a more reductionist cognitivist theory in a later article, "Metaphor and Cognition" from 1993. He argues for a link between metaphors and the prototypes through which our world is conceptualized. In particular he claims, "metaphor accordingly involves a distinction between essential and not essential (or accidental) attributes. Metaphors get to the heart of things." One of his examples of visual metaphors is that of Alice Boughton depicting herself as Queen Victoria. According to Danto, "she is telling us what she essentially is . . . This, I think, may be a cognitive dimension for metaphorical representation—for representation as—on the view that cognition traffics in essences and reductions. And I suppose to the degree that metaphoricity characterizes art, it accounts for the cognitive dimension of art as well."[79] Still one has to remember that Danto's theory, as internalist as it is, is an ontology of art—characterizing the ontological structure of artworks—the essential properties of which are the artist's intentions. Thus, contrary to the conceptualism, Danto's is an ontological theory. It is just of the kind which considers non-visual properties to be the constitutive ones.

Unfortunately, even the discussion of metaphor under analytic aesthetics gives way to the linguistic turn and its conceptualist successors. Thus, this discussion did not reach far enough to account for the omnipresence of everyday metaphors—indeed, it did not account for the material and visual metaphors that are experienced daily. The ruling conceptual discussion of metaphor neglects to apply, cannot apply, to the aesthetic, imagistic, and compositional foundation of this phenomenon. Fortunately, parallel to the development of linguistic-cognitivism, the visualists Gombrich, Aldrich, and Arnheim developed a counterpart understanding where metaphorical seeing and perception is an integral part of the creation of metaphors. Widening the scope to metaphorical perception allows a parallel expansion of the different kinds of metaphors that stem from everyday experience. This all ought to be subsumed under our visual creative nature, living in visual spheres. The modernist art historian T. J. Clark puts it nicely: "It is the form of our statements, and the structure of our visualizations, that truly are our ways of world-making—at any rate the ways that hold us deepest in thrall."[80] The expression "ways of worldmaking" was famously used by Goodman in a book titled with this name, in which he draws an innate link between perception, aesthetics, and ontology.[81]

In the case of metaphor, the link between perception and worldmaking is clear. As mentioned earlier, this link in a framework of constructivist theory of metaphor is surprisingly presented by the cognitivist Indurkhya. Indurkhya could indeed be classified as neo-Goodmanian, given that he draws both a distinction and internal relations between ontology and structure as a basis of metaphors. In his 1992 monograph *Metaphor and Cognition*, Indurkhya formulates what he dubs the "interaction view of cognition," laying out the relation between the perceiver and the external environment. He has developed his theory ever since, trying to support it with empirical evidence and to apply it to visual metaphors. According to Indurkhya, "ontology refers to the set of primitives in terms of which a structure can be specified; and structure refers to a particular configuration, or a particular description using those primitives. Thus, a structure always presupposes some ontology, but there can be multiple structures based on a given ontology." For him, this distinction is a presumption of the following contention: "a sensorimotor apparatus of a cognitive agent, and the cultural and social context in which it lives determines the ontology in terms of which it experiences the world. But then it is the autonomous world that structures this ontology." For Indurkhya, this is the essence of the interaction theory of metaphor: the world that a cognitive agent lives in is an interaction between the world and the agent. "But it is not completely arbitrary, for the world places objective constraints on structures that are possible within that ontology. For metaphor research, this has implications for the phenomenon of emergence of features and creation of similarity which were the key aspects of the interaction theory of metaphor."[82]

Given that even some cognitivists are aware of the role that ontology and sensory perception has in our nature and the nature of metaphors, one ought to revisit the big apparatus of Western aesthetics. Western aesthetics, given its prioritization of conceptuality and mental intentions over visuality, is partially accountable for the neglect of the ontological essence of metaphors. As Yuriko Saito descriptively and prescriptively claims, aesthetics traveled too far from the study of sensory perception. Saito, too, uses the concept of "making a world." In her 2017 monograph *Aesthetics of the Familiar: Everyday Life and World-Making*, she shows how broadening aesthetics to everyday particular experience will help aesthetics to return to its origins of addressing sensory sensibility and perception, which applies to sky or laundry—just like many visual metaphors, I will add.

Visual metaphors are discussed by a wide range of disciplines. However, it is high time that aesthetics widened its discussion of conceptual and linguistic metaphors to a comprehensive account of the visual ones, as well the general visual infrastructure of metaphors. Philosophy has been analyzing the essence of metaphors since antiquity. It is well known that in *Poetics* and *Rhetoric* Aristotle had already formulated the idea of transference of new terms to genus or species, which is usually termed "application" nowadays. Aristotle revealed the epistemological as well as rhetorical import of the transgressions of the natural kinds of predication, or rigid categories—by "making your hearers *see* things" (italics in original).[83] Metaphor, be it linguistic, visual, or any other kind, is an aesthetic phenomenon in its very nature. The necessary condition for this phenomenon is its visuality and materiality, it is understood by its structure and composition, and it is perceptual in essence. Following Richard Rorty (who opposed the semantic approach) in his discussion of metaphor, one may say that revealing the visuality of metaphor also has far-reaching implications for theories of intellectuality and cultural progress as being aesthetically, rather than cognitively, oriented.

However, since the linguistic turn, the majority of the philosophical discussion of metaphors has referred to the *conceptual* mechanism of transference, and later on to analogies and the interaction of concepts and predicates, as being the essence of metaphors. In the twentieth century, most of the aesthetics literature focused on the semantic mechanism, meaning and cognitive value of the different kinds of metaphors. Thus, even aesthetics employed the terminology of very influential work in philosophy of language for this purpose. Linguistic theories of metaphors, mainly the semantic ones, are the subject of the next chapter.

2

Semantic Theories of Metaphor

This chapter classifies as semantic the central paradigm of the study of metaphors, initiated in the mid-twentieth century and still ongoing, though its dominance has waned since the 1980s with the rise of the conceptual theory of metaphor. Many of the semantic theories were cognitively oriented, motivated by the idea that one of the main merits of metaphor is its cognitive value—viz. its ability to convey information and improve communication. The overarching aim of the semantic theories was to characterize the uniqueness of meaning of metaphor. In order to achieve this, a secondary goal was to establish the distinction between literal meaning and metaphorical meaning. "Literal" vs. "metaphorical" were the main terms, used by non-cognitivists such as Davidson and Rorty as well, though the extension of them was widened to include properties and ontology.

As is well known, the semantic discussion of metaphors in 1936 was (re)opened by I. A. Richards who characterized metaphor as an interaction between two co-present thoughts. He called the original idea or principal subject the "tenor," and the new idea the "vehicle," explaining that this interaction between the reference and the context results in a wide or multiple meaning: the metaphorical meaning. The interaction theory was elaborated by Max Black (from 1949 to 1977), by Monroe C. Beardsley (in 1958 and 1962), and later by John Searle (in 1979) to a definition of metaphor as a broad extension of a predicate. Black distinguishes between the focal word in the metaphor and the frame (the whole sentence), which imposes an extension of meaning on the focal word. In "man is a wolf," for example, "wolf" has its own system of associated commonplaces—i.e., things that are commonly held true about wolves—and the metaphor functions as a filter, transferring a few of these commonplaces to "man." Thus, both the extensions of "man" and the predicate "wolf" are broadened. A detailed and systematic semantic theory of metaphor was formulated by Goodman (1976, 1979). Even though Goodman was one of the first to formulate an ontological philosophy of metaphors, he characterized metaphor as a figurative application of a label—transferred from its home scheme of alternative labels to an alien realm and range of referents. Figurative application, for Goodman, is as actual as literal application, thus it has both meaning and a truth value. Given that he considered labeling to be a worldmaking act, his metaphor theory ultimately concerns itself with the ontological sphere.

While some subsequent linguistic theories emphasized the pragmatic constituents of metaphor, in 2000 Joseph Stern relocated the analytic characterization of metaphors to the semantic fields. He argues for the context-dependency of metaphors, in particular to attribute them with semantic qualities of indexicality. Stressing the non-literal contexts of metaphors, their cognitive and non-cognitive effects, and their expressive contribution to language, Stern nonetheless delineates the constraints of metaphorical interpretations. A recent anti-contextualist theory of metaphor is offered by Elisabeth Camp, within a unique account of figurative speech, poetic uses of language, and non-sentential representation. Camp redraws the semantic-pragmatic distinction; contrary to Searle, she claims that though metaphors do not do anything different in kind from literal speech, they are not dispensable because they, as she puts it, "enable speakers to communicate contents that cannot be stated in fully literal and explicit terms."[1]

These theories should be classified as *semantic-cognitive approaches to metaphor* since they all consider the cognitive merit of the metaphor to be its most significant element. In this cognitive approach, Mary Hesse's theory plays an important role. While all the aforementioned theorists kept the distinction between metaphors and literal units, in "The Cognitive Claims of Metaphor" from 1988, Hesse tries to dissolve it. Following Ludwig Wittgenstein's idea of family resemblance with respect to definitions, she formulates the network theory of meaning, according to which "all language is metaphorical."[2] For Hesse, though not all the literal is metaphorical at every given moment, they are on the same semantic-cognitive scale, differentiated by a matter of degree of shifts in meanings rather than differentiated in kind. Hesse's approach, one may assert, betrays the primacy of the literal which the semantic theories still hold. Nonetheless, we see that even an aesthetician such as Richard Wollheim, who developed magisterial theories about visual art as well as visual metaphors, in his "Metaphor and Painting" professes belief in "the paradigmatic character of literary metaphor."[3] Wollheim's aesthetics explicitly present the visual as being subjugated to the literal, and secondary to mental contents, which in that respect is typical of the condition of aesthetics in the linguistic and conceptualist twentieth century going on to the twenty-first. The problematic effect of the linguistic turn on the literature on metaphor, mainly that of visual metaphors, will be presented through contemporaneous developments in analytic aesthetics in the next subchapter.

2.1 The linguistic turn of aesthetics, metaphors, and anti-visualism

I would like to focus for a while in this subchapter on the impact of what can be titled "the linguistic turn of aesthetics" on the discussion of metaphors. By and large, the theoretical tendency in the discussion of metaphor in analytic aesthetics since the twentieth century is *to apply the traits of the verbal metaphor to metaphorical images and objects*, showing the symbolic function of images as parallel to linguistic units in ordinary language. This tendency was intensified in aesthetics by the prominence of the philosophy of language, from the linguistic turn at the very beginning of the twentieth century and on. Analytic aesthetics consequently redefined art as a symbolic-linguistic system. It reached its first peak in the 1960s and 1970s with the publication of Richard Wollheim's *Art and Its Objects: An Introduction to Aesthetics* and *On Art and the Mind*, Goodman's *Languages of Arts* and *Ways of Worldmaking*, and Danto's "The Artworld" and *The Transfiguration of the Commonplace*. In these works, they argued that artworks are necessarily semantic symbols, constituted by meaning, reference and aboutness, all rooted in thought. While Goodman held an externalist-nominalist view of metaphors in the frame of his ontology, Wollheim and Danto attributed a privileged status to thought and intentional mental content—as a condition to art, and accordingly to metaphors. Endorsing an anti-formalist view and denigrating the visual as being but an embodiment of mental content, they neglected the aesthetic and visual essence even of visual metaphors.

The elevated status that language and the conceptual mind are endowed with is deeply rooted in modernist philosophy. Interestingly, and less obviously than is often assumed, modernist philosophy has been commonly linked to flouting the visual sphere. For many years the cognitive mind has been considered the carrier of schemes of knowledge and its implementation, and accordingly language is deemed more capable of carrying information and delivering it than the visual.

Arnheim accurately describes and criticizes the intellectual tendency to elevate the status of language and thought in favor of the visual in this paragraph from his 1980 "A Plea for Visual Thinking," pointing to its roots: "Perception and thinking are treated by textbooks of psychology in separate chapters. The senses are said to gather information about the outer world; thinking is said to process that information. Thinking emerges from this approach as the 'higher,' more respectable function, to which consequently education assigns most of the school hours and most of the credit."[4] We see this the same year in which Lakoff and Johnson published their first internalist-conceptualist manifesto. Arnheim tried to dissolve the distinction between cognition and thought on the one side and visual reality and perception on the other. The first modernist to draw this distinction and claim for the cognitive hierarchy was Descartes, and accordingly Arnheim conveys,

> the passive ability to receive images of sensory things, said Descartes, would be useless if there did not exist in the mind a further and higher active faculty capable of shaping these images and of correcting the errors that derive from sensory experience. A century later Leibniz spoke of two levels of clear cognition. Reasoning was cognition of the higher degree: it was distinct, that is, it could analyze things into their components. Sensory experience, on the other hand, was cognition of the lower order.[5]

Arnheim's visualism challenges the contention of the linguistic movement that it is the semantic mechanism that allows the visual metaphor its acceptability as a "possible" image. Arnheim's wide philosophical visualist project shows that the visual metaphor is *not* constituted as an image by the semantic-cognitive result of the interaction of concepts, but rather by creative composition, and its classification by its perceiver. Though evocative and not obvious, the acceptance of metaphor is nonetheless possible thanks to the rightness of this composition. However, the linguistic framework coalesces with the anti-formalist attack, on both visuality and the senses, shared by the central streams in aesthetics.

To substantiate my judgment about the extreme linguistic tendency of analytic aesthetics, I would like to take a look at the account on visual metaphors formulated by Wollheim—one of the leaders of analytic aesthetics after the linguistic turn. Like Danto, Wollheim defines the visual as being subjugated to mental contents from which it gains its meaning. Wollheim understands that metaphors do more than convey a particular meaning, claiming even that metaphor is "ineffable": "The light is generated solely through conjoining the two terms, and just what we are enabled to see by the light of the metaphor, or how the metaphor asks us to conceive of the metaphorized term, is something that we can only very approximately express in words. Metaphor is fundamentally ineffable."[6] However, while Wollheim understands that metaphor cannot be paraphrased or reduced to literal expression, he surprisingly classifies the linguistic metaphor as paradigmatic. Moreover, "the paradigmatic character of literary metaphor" is the vantage point of his account of visual metaphors, one which borrows from linguistic metaphors the ways to identify a visual metaphor as such. Additionally, he presents an oversimplified definition of metaphor—which amounts to a conjunction of two things that consequently are "shedding light" on each other. The presented metaphorized element in a picture is argued by Wollheim to be a metaphorized term "under a special conception."[7]

Wollheim sets the following requirements for "an adequate account of pictorial metaphor": "it would have to be in the spirit of the best available account we have of metaphor in that area where we all can identify clear and undisputed examples of the phenomenon, i.e., language; it must ultimately fit into whatever general theory we believe to be correct of how painting acquires meaning."[8] These requirements clearly base the pictorial metaphor on language, disregarding the unique character emerging from composition that visuality imparts metaphor with. Metaphorical language merely borrows this character. What is more, Wollheim's linguistic anti-visualist stance leads him to argue that while linguistic metaphor belongs to the realm of pragmatics, pictorial metaphors are semantic, or better yet, "whereas linguistic metaphor is not a form of meaning, pictorial metaphor is." More accurately, according to Wollheim, while linguistic metaphors depend on the distinction between semantic and pragmatics, the distinction is not applicable to pictures. Rather than focusing on the visuality of pictorial metaphors, Wollheim characterizes them merely by attributing metaphorical meanings to them. What may come across as the most significant assumption in Wollheim's theory of pictorial metaphor is that its organizing factor is the concept that motivates the artist, and thus pictorial metaphor is what Wollheim dubs a "transference of conception." One of his main examples of this transference of conception is Titian's metaphorical manifestation of his "conception of the body" as what he calls, "the locus of vitality and emotion, intimately connected on the one hand with pleasure and on the other hand with the inevitability of death." According to Wollheim the pictorial metaphor consists of two stages, the first of which is conceptual. Initially, a representation of the body should be established in the spectator's mind. The second stage is a transference of the characteristics of the body to those of the picture as a whole: "between flesh and stone in the *Concert Champetre*, between young skin and sky in the *Three Ages of Man*."[9] That is to say, in 1993 Wollheim still theorizes in the manner of the linguistic turn; he still insists on founding, reducing is more like it, the visuality of the body—even as given in a complex visual composition—on a conceptual understanding of it. One might say that the price philosophy paid for the linguistic-conceptualist turn is too high to pay: the result is that we miss out on understanding the visual sphere we live in, which as Arnheim says is much richer than language given its multiple dimensions and compositions or configurations.

Wollheim implies that he sees metaphor as a symbol rather than a configuration. In that respect, his theoretical outline is parallel to Danto's and different to those of the visualists such as Gombrich and Arnheim. In his "Metaphor and Cognition," Danto applies his indiscernibility method of analysis to metaphors. He juxtaposes "Men are Animals" as a literal expression "taken as the assertion of biological fact" with a verbal or pictorial metaphorical counterpart such as a "famous caricature by Charles Philipon of Louis Philippe as a pear, printed in his magazine, *La caricature* in 1831."[10] Philipon made the king "reprobate and ludicrous at once, like a vicious clown, and took an artistic revenge for Daumier's imprisonment for having depicted the king as Gargantua, swallowing material goods."[11] This metaphor was so successful and so often employed, Danto reminds us, that Daumier reached a point where he "could simply have drawn a pear and everyone would have known who was meant."[12] That is to say, the metaphorical pear has meaning and aboutness which its counterpart, the mere drawing of a pear, does not. This analysis, ultimately, defines metaphors as revolving around their special meanings, with no underlying structure addressed. In this respect, the conclusion of Danto's theory of metaphors is that the metaphorical medium or composition is a communicative tool with no aesthetic qualities in and of itself. They "exist because of the truth that the mind is moved by representations," he claims.[13] As said in his *The Transfiguration of the Commonplace*, metaphors involve reference to a representation as part of their truth conditions, this reference pointing to the principal trait or essence that the creator of the metaphor wishes to manifest. Therefore, Danto deduces, metaphor reduces its referent to its metaphorical representation—e.g., Louis Philippe as a pear is reprobate and ludicrous—and gains its truth value therefrom. This leads Danto to the unfortunate, definitely inaccurate, and even surprising, conclusion: "while they serve in a powerful way to fix our images of things, powerful because of the essentializing and reductive character they have, I am uncertain they ever, as metaphors, tell us something we do not know."[14] If I am right, Danto's view of metaphors as nothing but symbols, and his use of a linguistic cognitive-value-filter to characterize visual metaphors especially, results in an overall misunderstanding of the structure of metaphor and its autonomous status, as well as its aesthetic motivations and productivity. Contrary to Wollheim and Danto's view of the visual metaphor, and metaphor in general as they limited it in light of the supposed primacy of language, a few semantic theories of metaphor did try to explain metaphorical productivity. In brief, these theories treated metaphorical productivity as deriving from the interactive nature of metaphors. These semantic interactive theories of metaphor are presented next.

2.2 Interaction and emergence

Initial formulations of a semantic-cognitive emergence within a metaphorical context of a linguistic expression were delivered by I. A. Richards, Max Black, and Monroe Beardsley. Their often-quoted theories referred to language as the sole and obvious medium of metaphor. Moreover, their cognitivist approach, moving back and forth from language to thought, was advanced by the prevalent conceptualist theory of metaphor. In particular, Black's "Metaphor" of battle thought through the vocabulary of chess ought to be explicitly credited as a source of the conceptualist theory. Given that my aim is to conjure up an ontological, visualist, formalist theory of metaphor, I will not present their work too deeply here. But a very focused recap is necessary to reveal two points, a positive and a negative one respectively:

1. The aestheticians who brought metaphor back into philosophy in the twentieth century were motivated, at least partially, by the cognizance that metaphor is a constructive medium. An essential part of this medium emerges from qualities that are unique to compositions and cannot be predetermined. It will be asserted later on that these compositional qualities are imagistic, aesthetic, and born in visuality. This motivation suits the essential structure of metaphor.
2. Despite this grasp of the emergent elements of metaphor, the semantic-linguistic theories could not apply to the pebble-powermat, nor to visual or material metaphors in general, unless they *impose* a linguistic frame on them. After all, as Richards asserts, "it is the word which brings in the meaning which the image and its original perception lack."[15] Along the lines of the linguistic turn of twentieth-century philosophy, to which aesthetics was committed as well, aestheticians of metaphors neglected ontological phenomena in favor of meaning. Thus external, imagistic, visually driven, compositional, aesthetic phenomena such as metaphors were mistakenly subsumed under the cognitivist study of language. This led directly to the study of mind as the framework of metaphor.

Following Richards, who in 1936 characterized the mind as a connecting organ and metaphor as "two thoughts active together and supported by a single word or phrase, whose meaning is a resultant of their interaction" together with what he names "interinanimation,"[16] Black developed from 1954 onward an interaction theory of metaphor. Its main elements are the focus of the metaphor (later named the "target" by Kövecses, Lakoff, and Johnson) and the frame—the latter being the whole metaphorical sentence, which has a "transforming function." Black asserts that within the metaphorical frame, the "focal word obtains a new meaning... which is not quite its meaning in literal uses, nor quite the meaning which any literal substitute would have. The new context (the "frame" of the metaphor ...) imposes extension of meaning upon the focal word."[17] In "man is a wolf," Black claims, the metaphor picks up relevant attributions of "wolf" to reorganize our view of man and the other way around—wolves, as a result of our use of the metaphor, may seem more human to us. In the frame of describing a battle in terms of chess, the battle is reconstructed with a system of implications by the following means:

> the enforced choice of the chess vocabulary will lead some aspects of the battle to be emphasized, others to be neglected, and all to be organized in a way that would cause much more strain in other modes of description. The chess vocabulary filters and transforms: it not only selects, it brings forward aspects of the battle that might not be seen at all through another medium.[18]

According to Black, this reorganization creates further "subordinate metaphors," thus the emergence could reach far afield.

Quite a few years after he published his "Metaphor" and "Metaphors and Models," in 1977 Black's "More About Metaphor" takes a "shift of formulation from conceptual analysis to a functional analysis" wishing in retrospect that his position would "help to understanding how strong metaphorical statements work," and therefore focuses on what he names "vital metaphors."[19] Seeking to stress the ability of metaphor to produce new attributions and consequently to reorganize the primary subject, in this essay Black replaces the term of "associated commonplaces" with "implicative complex." He explains the new term as follows:

> My notion was that the secondary subject, in a way partly depending upon the context of metaphorical use, determines a set of what Aristotle called endoxa, current opinions shared by members of a certain speech-community. But I also emphasized, as I should certainly wish to do now, that a metaphor-producer may introduce a novel and non-platitudinous "implicative-complex." The maker of a metaphorical statement selects, emphasizes, suppresses and organizes features of

the primary subject by applying to it statements isomorphic with the members of the secondary subject's implicative complex.[20]

However, this shift is too moderate in light of the ontological weight of metaphor, being pointed at by the progressive, visualist, and constructivist theories of metaphor being formulated at the time. Keeping his interaction theory as language-oriented as before, Black goes even further in aiming for an internalist stance, defining metaphor as "verbal action" whose interactive "outcome is of course produced in the minds of the speaker and hearer."[21] Even when imagery is involved in metaphor, such as in his example of Nixon as "an image surrounding a vacuum," Black categorizes it as subjugated to an alleged verbal origin of the image, or thought. The original verbal formulation, he claims, "still controls the sensory imagery and remains available for ready reaffirmation." So, like many others, Black does not capture the autonomous, substantial ontological status of metaphor as a creative medium. Then again, Black's theory is still one of the most significant in the field. After all, it presents not only the interactive structure of metaphors but also the ability of metaphors to be productive as a corollary of this interaction, as the interaction provides the emergent essence of metaphor. While reminding us of the opposition to his idea of metaphorical creativity, and unfortunately ignoring the contemporary visualist theories of metaphor that define metaphors in a manner which shows them to be cognitively and ontologically productive, Black rightly insists, "some metaphors enable us to see aspects of reality that the metaphor's production helps to constitute. But that is no longer surprising if one believes that the 'world' is necessarily a world under a certain description or a world seen from a certain perspective. Some metaphors can create such a perspective."[22]

Inspired by Black's interactive definition of metaphor, in 1958 and 1962 Beardsley developed his "controversion theory" of metaphor, which details the emergent modification of the migrated predicates under the foreign metaphorical context: "a metaphor is a significant attribution that is either indirectly self-contradictory or obviously false in its context, and in which the modifier connotes characteristics that can be attributed, truly or falsely, to the subject."[23] Black refuted Beardsley's classification of metaphors as "self-contradictory or obviously false," given that there are counterexamples to it. However, the important point is that Beardsley rightly named the source of the metaphor the "modifier" and the emergence element of metaphor the "metaphorical twist" of the modifier. He, too, realized that metaphor is endowed with the quality possessed by aesthetic compositions that enable them to transform their elements, naming it "logical form." Accordingly, Beardsley argues that "when a predicate is metaphorically adjoined to a subject, the predicate loses its ordinary extension, because it acquires a new intension—perhaps one that it has in no other context. And this twist of meaning is forced by inherent tensions, or oppositions, within the metaphor itself."[24]

Beardsley promises that his controversion theory explains metaphor's most important "capacity to create new contextual meaning" and to produce new ideas. "The reason is that the connotations of words are never fully known, or knowable, beforehand," Beardsley explains, "very often we discover new connotations of the words when we see how they behave as modifiers in metaphorical attributions. The metaphor does not create the connotations, but it brings them to life."[25] Still, along the lines of the treatment of metaphor that was typical during the linguistic turn, Beardsley endorses a relatively narrow view of metaphor, considering language as its obvious medium and the metaphorical interactions as interactions of meanings. Moreover, Beardsley submits that, their creativity notwithstanding, metaphors are paraphrasable. But his theory, and the idea of interactions being made by metaphors, planted a few seeds for future accomplishments, albeit accomplishments that a philosophy of metaphor should achieve nowadays by shifting to visualism.

An interpretive analysis of this line of argumentation of Richards, Black, and Beardsley is presented in Paul Ricoeur's well-known *The Rule of Metaphor* from 1975. He combines their theories under "the aegis of the semantics of the sentence" (because of the shift from the word to the sentence as the context and primary level of metaphor), offering a rich development of a linguistic interaction theory of metaphor which is based on semantics (as distinct from semiotics) and contextualism. Ricoeur names metaphor "a semantic event that takes place at the point where several semantic fields intersect," and like the interactivists, he promotes the idea that the essence of metaphor is its real-time productivity, rather than an internal abstract scheme: "the meaning-effect results from a certain interaction of the words within the sentence."[26] Contrary to the conceptualists, he emphasizes metaphor's significance in its open and active outcome of two words acquiring qualities they did not possess beforehand, at times even in contrast with their own prior qualities:

> metaphorical attribution is essentially the construction of the network of interactions that causes a certain context to be one that is real and unique. Accordingly, metaphor is a semantic event that takes place at the point where several semantic fields intersect. It is because of this construction that all the

words, taken together, make sense. Then, and only then, the metaphorical *twist* is at once an event *and* a meaning, an event that means or signifies, an emergent meaning created by language.[27]

Ricoeur details the productive structure as the resulting context of meaning.

Capturing the creativity of metaphor and its modifying ability—an accomplishment of Beardsley and Ricoeur—is much closer to capturing the essence of metaphor than Wollheim and Danto reached by their intensional-internalist theories of metaphors. Nevertheless, in considering "metaphor as the touchstone of the cognitive value of literary works,"[28] Ricoeur keeps his theorizing of metaphor within the narrow framework of cognition, semantics, and language, neglecting the wide and foundational field of visual metaphors and the visuality of metaphors. We should then move to a semantic visualist theory formulated by Carl Hausman to see how visualism, even in semantic theory, manages to come much closer to capturing the productive essence of metaphor. Hausman's theory comes closer to this essence than the four interactivist theories could because of the fixation of these interactivist theories on language.

2.3 Visual elements within the semantic theory of metaphor

In order to show the depth a comprehensive semantic theory of metaphor can reach, and move closer to an up-to-date interaction theory, it is instructive to read Carl Hausman's critique of Beardsley's account of metaphorical emergence. Hausman holds a semantic view of metaphor, but interestingly establishes it on ontology and visualism. The combination between semantics and ontology, one should note, characterizes Danto's philosophy of art as well, which contrary to his theory of metaphor is comprehensive and applies to the deep structure of artworks. This is not the case for Hausman who, like Goodman, offers an innovative theory of metaphors, which helps to explain the sources of the narrowness that typifies the linguistic and semantic view of metaphors (as well as the later conceptual views). Hausman's theory alternatively extends semantics to cover visual and other kinds of metaphors and their ontological import. As stated by Hausman, Beardsley did not aim far enough, given that even though he sees metaphor's productivity as essential, he does present the restriction that "the metaphor does not create the connotations, but it brings them to life"[29] nonetheless. Contrary to Beardsley, Hausman extends the definition of metaphor to apply to visual metaphors in his 1989 *Metaphor and Art: Interactionism and Reference in the Verbal and Nonverbal Arts*.

Not less significant for us, Hausman explicitly denotes what he names "extralinguistic" elements of both *verbal* and nonverbal metaphors by proposing an ontology of properties rather than predicates, as well as by noting the complex referents that emerge from metaphors. In doing so, Hausman is much closer than the linguistic semantic theoreticians to securing the role that metaphors play in an external ontological environment. For example, his analysis in his 1991 "Language and Metaphysics: The Ontology of Metaphor" of the modification of the property "being a sun" within the known Shakespearean metaphor "Juliet is the Sun" helps explain the individuation of metaphorical properties in the foreign context of the metaphorical object. He claims that "Juliet is the Sun" is a center of meanings that are relevant to Juliet the individual, such as her significance in Romeo's life, her innocence or tenderness—and also relevant to the actual sun, such as its warmth and radiance. These meanings combined together, says Hausman, "are productive of a unique individual that constrains and makes metaphor's meaning relevant to a condition of future referents of future metaphors that draw on the sun's qualities now qualified by Juliet's qualities."[30] Hausman is right to assert that in the frame of the metaphor, the sun is neither as harsh nor as much a source of discomfort as it was originally. That is to say, the property of being a sun, that is actually a cluster of properties, is modified so that it can be possessed by the new metaphorical thing—but no longer by its source. A woman-sun is not a celestial sun, though they both now belong to the same group. From this argument one may derive a groundbreaking ontological assertion, one which had been previously formulated by Gombrich, Arnheim, and Aldrich, but not under the relatively purist doctrine of analytic aesthetics—the metaphorical integration produces a new, unique, and individuated, not preconceived, ontological referent. This is how Hausman describes the consequence of the interaction of the warmth of the sun and the kindness of Juliet:

> as interacting with one another, they constitute an integration that is a whole structured by internal relations. The meaning of warmth here depends for its relevance in the metaphor on the character of Juliet's kindness, and vice versa. Each meaning depends on the other for its appropriate function ... The referent of such a meaning cluster is, of course, partially dependent on the unique organization and interactions of meanings. Thus it, too, is unique being an individual that approximates a determinateness that uniquely satisfies the integration of the metaphor. So the Juliet-sun referent constrains the unique integration of meanings drawn from Romeo, and the sun, the star of the solar system.[31]

Hausman's innovative ontology of the emergent referents of metaphors will be further addressed in Chapter 5, "Metaphors and Ontology." For now, I would say that Hausman still does not crack the wall of the linguistic turn and its conservative elevation of language. On the one hand, he proposes an informative and promising account of the ontological import of metaphor as creating new referents and things or objects. On the other hand, being influenced by the linguistic turn's apparatus and priorities, Hausman still considers (incorrectly in my opinion) the medium of metaphor to be merely *a symbol* of the emergent ontological new things with their new properties, rather than as that thing possessing the properties itself. But then again, metaphor is a thing-in-itself, dwelling in the ontological sphere—it is an autonomous piece of ontology. The common term "metaphor for" is misleading. Metaphor is not the symbol, nor does it symbolize things; it is the symbolized.

The recent interaction theory of metaphors and visuality which has been developed by Bipin Indurkhya is progressive and far-reaching. Not only does it hold a wide extension of "metaphor" to include visual metaphors, but it also sees visual perception as playing a crucial role in comprehension of all the kinds of metaphors and takes cognizance of the ontological status of metaphors themselves. In his (and co-authors') "Emergence of Features in Metaphor Comprehension" (2000), Indurkhya presents the main condition of interaction theory: "The interaction theory draws attention to the creative, 'online' strategic aspects of metaphor, although it allows some influences from a priori or more automatic or salient similarities."[32] Indurkhya's main methodical claim is that empirical studies of metaphors supply indispensable data for theoretical studies. Studying experiments which conclude that "metaphors are not built on old associations; on the contrary, they are used to create new associations and relations between,"[33] he conducts his own experiments, aiming to characterize what he names "metaphorical property (or feature)"—the newly combined property of the target and the source, and the "emergent feature," that was not possessed as such by either the source or the target before the creation of the metaphor. I will return to Indurkhya later, in Chapters 3 and 5. It is important to note here that while most of the interaction-emergence theories see metaphors themselves as symbols of things and situations rather than as real things, considering the emergence as happening "outside" of metaphors, Indurkhya offers an empirically well-supported theory that relocates the interaction between the perceiver, the thing, and the emergence as being integral to the metaphor. In that respect, among others, his approach is very related to the visualist ideas of active perception and visual construction. Reading the interaction and emergence theories renders the conceptualist philosophy of metaphor even more reductionist, entrenched in an internal stance far away from real metaphors. The conceptualist critique of the linguistic theories that "the locus of metaphor is not in language at all, but in the way we conceptualize one mental domain in terms of another. The general theory of metaphor is given by characterizing such cross-domain mappings,"[34] seems very far off. After all, rather than widening the scope from language to the omnipresent visual metaphors and metaphorical perception, the conceptualist-cognitivist theory of metaphor defines metaphor as abstract mental content. The next chapter is a critical discussion of the conceptualist-cognitivist theory of metaphor.

3

Cognitivist Theories of Metaphor: A Conceptual Turn

The conceptualist-cognitivist characterization of ordinary metaphorical reasoning is exemplified in the following description of an everyday practice, namely the commute: "For instance, the conclusion that you can 'save' time by taking the subway to work instead of walking derives from the 'time is money' metaphor that most of us take for granted."[1] This example from Indurkhya, a prominent current philosopher of metaphor, in his 2007 "Rationality and Reasoning with Metaphors" is inspired, so he notes, by the conceptualist-cognitivist theory which had become paradigmatic since it was formulated by Lakoff and Johnson. Indurkhya's rationale is more empirically and externally—or ontologically—oriented than Lakoff and Johnson's is. Nonetheless, quite often the conceptualist paradigm reveals itself in the infrastructure of his very profound research. The "time is money" example is more telling than it might seem. It betrays the cognitivist belief that we are conceptual beings; that we operate in a well-ordered manner, derived from conceptual schemes so internal and entrenched in the mind that often they do not even reach our awareness. I find the idea that taking the subway to work is motivated by an abstract internal metaphor to be hard to support. Actions taken at a different level of ordinariness, uniqueness, and ways of being are not as organized and mentally driven as the cognitivists would take them to be. Taking the subway is a practice that many undertake for any one of a number of reasons: because this is what people do; because they grew up seeing their parents doing it; because they went to sleep late or are in a hurry; because when they got their job, they were informed that the "D" line is the best way to get to the office; because they are too tired to walk. We are external, behavioral, and particular, much more than we are scheme-driven as conceptualist-cognitivists would have us be.

Indurkhya draws a distinction between two kinds of what the literature refers to as "metaphorical reasoning," in parallel with two corresponding kinds of metaphors: monotonous and non-monotonous. The former kind of metaphorical reasoning is "more commonly known as reasoning with similarity or reasoning by analogy"[2] in which the metaphor is founded on preexisting similarities between the source conceptual domain and the target, raising stipulations of further similarities. Similarity-based reasoning suffers from inductive inference problems that have already been discussed by many philosophers. According to Indurkhya, non-monotonous metaphors create similarities between the source and the target. The non-monotonous creative kind of metaphorical reasoning is the more significant one, being an engine of major cognition and practice shifts. To illustrate the non-monotonous creative kind, Indurkhya analyzes an example of problem solving through the adoption of a new metaphor: in manufacturing a nylon fiber paintbrush by chemists in product development, as presented in *Displacement of Concepts* by Donald Schon.[3] Schon's *Displacement of Concepts* was first published in 1963, proposing a conceptualist theory of metaphor. That book's definition of metaphor, its spirit, and its ideas (particularly that metaphors are conceptual in essence) would appear in later conceptual theories of metaphors. What is now described as "understanding the target conceptual domain in terms of the source domain" was referred to by Schon as the "displacement of concepts," with the source being the "old concept," and metaphor was characterized by Schon as seeing a new concept in terms of an old one. He describes the structure of metaphor in these words:

> new concepts emerge out of the interaction of old concepts and new situations, where the old concept is not simply re-applied unchanged to a new instance, but is that *in terms* of which the new instance is seen. This is what we have described as the displacement of concepts—a process in which old concepts, in order to function as projective models for new situations, come themselves to be seen in new ways[4] (emphasis in original)

The similarity between his conceptualist definition and the one which has prevailed since the 1980s is clear.

The example which Indurkhya uses is that of an improving a nylon fiber brush to smear the paint on a canvas as smoothly as a natural-bristle brush does. This is a corollary of the displacement of a "painting as smearing" metaphor with that of "painting as pumping." This displacement brought about a new perspective and design,

> ... when a member of the team had a flash of insight suggesting that the painting process be viewed as pumping. The concept of painting, as well as the role of a paintbrush in it, was completely transformed. Now the paint is sucked up in the space between the fibers by capillary action as the brush is dipped in the can of paint.[5]

As informed by Indurkhya, this observation provoked innovative suggestions for gradual-blending synthetic fibers, which resulted in smooth paint. That is to say,

> the very causal structure that determines how the paint sticks to the brush after it is dipped in the can, and how it is coated on the surface when the brush is moved back and forth across it, is different in each case. Moreover, the primitives underlying the structures are different. For example, the space between the fibers plays no role in the structure of painting-as-smearing model, but is a key factor in painting-as-pumping model.[6]

According to this depiction of product development, in conceptualizing painting as pumping the participant must mentally simulate the painting process. In this simulation, a cluster of properties of pumping is projected—this is what Indurkhya dubs "activated Gestalt." "This projection, which is partly constrained by the characteristics of the painting process—for the simulation invariably incorporates past perceptual associations—and partly by the structure of the pumping Gestalt, reorganizes the target in new ways, which in turn may result in the emergence of new features in the target."[7]

While Indurkhya offers a rich account of metaphors, this depiction of the situation is somewhat forced. It is just not the way designers and project developers' teams work. They try one thing, try another, work, think, work again… This creative, deliberative process is not derived from one abstract conceptual structure. Having worked with designers for a few years now, I found that not once has the concept retrospectively attached to the finalized project, not even in consulting with theoreticians to do so. The creative or planning process is material and visual more than anything—even when it initially includes what designers call a "brief"—and gains its substantiality and rightness, even Pygmalion power, due to it! When design students face their final project submission, telling them, "You are allowed to be formalist. Tell the judges that the work is supposed to be shown, or to speak for itself at most" is often met with a great relief and claims that this approach harmonizes with their work.

In his 2017 co-authored essay "Interpreting Visual Metaphors: Asymmetry and Reversibility," one can see that Indurkhya sometimes misses the visuality of metaphors—especially the visual ones. This shows in his emphasis on the asymmetry of verbal metaphors. Had he been cognizant of their nature as constructions, he would have seen that they are more symmetrical than he considers them to be—a point that Black disclosed in the early stages of the twentieth-century formulation of the interaction view of metaphors. It is true that the basic structure of metaphor is asymmetrical, or at least directional. But this clearly manifests in visual metaphors as well. What is more, the emergent part of metaphor, if not symmetrical, derives from a two-way operation. Padwa's pebble-shaped powermats, for instance, are introduced to the group of pebbles. But this logically, and ontologically, entails that among the pebbles there are a few powermats. This is not a symmetrical relation, but it is not an anti-symmetrical one either. No doubt memberships in both groups bring an ontological import of metaphors in enlarging and reorganizing categories. However, even though he comes bearing good tidings of the primary role of perception and experience of environment in creating metaphors, Indurkhya still attributes a paradigmatic status to linguistic metaphors. While in other essays he emphasizes the role of perception in metaphorical creativity, here he claims that even visual metaphor revolves around aboutness and the delivery of a message, contending that "the problem with visual metaphors is that because there is no explicit copula, or a word such as like, one essentially has to rely on the context to figure out what the metaphor is about and what message it is trying to convey."[8] Still, compared with most of the cognitivists, Indurkhya goes the furthest toward the realization of the visuality of metaphors.

This chapter takes a critical view of the relatively new but magisterial cognitivist modification of the linguistic, mainly semantic, view of metaphors. It presents the cognitivist "conceptual turn" that shifted the discussion from language to mental schemes and perception. In 1980 the cognitive approach, which contested the priority of the literal over the metaphorical, took an avowed conceptual turn inspired by the philosophy of mind. In their *Metaphors We Live By* (1993, 2003) and later writings, George Lakoff and Mark Johnson presented an internalist-conceptualist assertion that metaphor is "a cross-domain mapping in the conceptual system."[9] The conceptual mind is metaphorical in essence, they claim, because nearly every single concept cannot be understood except through a prism of other concepts: "most of our normal conceptual system is metaphorically structured; that is, most concepts are partially understood in terms of other concepts."[10] They claim all metaphors, linguistic or otherwise, are merely manifestations or externalizations, more accurately tokens, of metaphorical abstract thoughts. Thereby, due to their work in conjunction with the theories proposed by Kövecses, Gibbs, and others, the field of metaphor went through a conceptualist-cognitivist wave. According to them, their characterizations of metaphor are not only fundamental to human thought, but also serve as a conceptual foundational mental scheme that dictates external human conduct. The conceptual movement first targeted the then-magisterial linguistic model of metaphor, trying to prove that metaphors in language are merely entailments of the primarily internal conceptual ones. This movement soon became the leader of the field, and yielded numerous subfields of cognitive research, including metaphors in visual culture and film, anthropology and folklore, politics, economy, and advertisements, etc. Numerous studies conducted by different disciplines have been trying to track down the external entailments of internal, conceptual, abstract metaphors—that, according to conceptualism, are supposed to stand as the groundwork of almost every sort of metaphorical practice and substance.

Beate Hampe's recent description of the main idea of the conceptualist-cognitivist movement is accurate: "the first widely influential theory that rejected the traditional notion of metaphor as a poetic or rhetorical device, a figure of language in use." She rightly emphasizes the grand assumption of the conceptualist metaphor theory that metaphors create conventions, since it underlies a "shared tacit knowledge of speakers—not just within but to a considerable extent also across speech communities/languages." According to Hampe and the conceptual-cognitivists, external metaphorical tokens "reflect cross-domain connections at the conceptual level, allowing targets in abstract domains to be understood and hence also talked about in terms of their (more concrete or accessible) sources."[11]

As a visualist, I claim the opposite: *If we think metaphorically it is only as a result of speaking, behaving, creating or seeing things metaphorically.* Abstract thought is neither the origin of external metaphors, nor does an internalization of external metaphor ever reach full conceptual abstraction. I claim that the leap that the conceptualists take to prove the existence and rule of internal conceptual levels is ad hoc, based on a circular argument, and involves a glaring inconsistency. *The conceptualist line of inference, which advances from conventions to conceptual shared levels—which in their turn, according to conceptualism, allow us to understand the experiences which created the conventions to begin with—is hard to defend.* Conventions are external, belonging to social ontology, and both motivate shared experiences and are motivated by them. What is more, I maintain that the conceptualists are wrong in classifying the target to be understood by conceptual metaphors as originally an abstract entity, which metaphor is recruited to explicate. The Life Is Journey and Love Is Journey conceptual metaphors, which are often presented in the conceptualist literature, are key examples of this mistake. Life, the target of the metaphor, is anything but abstract. Is there anything more individual, ordinary, specific, full of particularities than life? If at all, given that life is so ordinary and rooted in the everyday, many try to relate it to abstract systems such as those of ethics, hierarchies, cosmological reasonings, religion, and other systems of "big meanings" as Menachem Mautner calls them.[12] As for the journey part of the metaphor: life is a journey given that we build lives so that we can walk in paths, because we are actually used to walking in paths in a concrete sense. I will elaborate on this in Chapters 4–6.

A related conceptualist account of metaphors held by Sam Glucksberg et al. (1982, 1990, 1993) is derived from empirical psychological studies of the comprehension of metaphors versus literal expressions. Still responding to contemporary linguistic theories of metaphors, Glucksberg is obliged to defend the internalist-conceptualist theory of metaphor. In doing so, he demonstrates that internal metaphorical meanings are not inferior or subsequent to literal meanings. According to him, the mind sometimes tends to metaphorical comprehension, which involves the perception of categories. Glucksberg's mind theory, however, is less radical than Lakoff and Johnson's; Glucksberg claims that metaphors are converted to similes, and thus the mind is not fundamentally metaphorical. An innovative development of Glucksberg's theory of categorization is presented by Yeshayahu Shen in his "Metaphor and Conceptual Structure," in the framework of a comprehensive investigation of the cognitive value of metaphors and the perception of categories. Shen looks at the conceptual theory of metaphor from unique angles, which I interpret as plausibly challenging its narrowness. In his more recent "Imposed Metaphoricity," he and Roy Porat explain away the semantic content of a linguistic expression as being unnecessary for metaphors. For example, comparing *This piece of metal is a magnet* with *This piece of metal is such a magnet*, he shows that while the former invites literal interpretation, the latter can only be interpreted metaphorically: "the minor change in form not only intensifies the metaphorical meaning of *magnet*, but also blocks the literal reference to the concrete metallic object, forcing a metaphorical interpretation. This example demonstrates the phenomenon of *imposed metaphoricity*, in which metaphorical processing is activated regardless of the semantic properties of the concept."[13] Thus, Shen's project has more explanatory power than Lakoff and Johnson's, given that it explains the various ways conceptual schemes and categories are arranged and metaphors are created. He claims that metaphorical mappings are constructed by ad hoc categorization, and furthermore: "in the context of metaphorical ad hoc category, the more prototypical member (the vehicle) is more accessible in memory than the less typical one (the topic)."[14]

3.1 Problems with the mentalist-cognitivist account of metaphors: the Crocodile Nutcracker example

Among the cognitivists, Christopher Peacocke (2009, 2010) takes the absolute most radical internalist approach. Contrary to the cognitivist mainstream, Peacocke formulates his theory of metaphor using a non-conceptualist philosophy—one which is endorsed by a school of thought that tries to prove the presence of mental contents that are not propositional in character, though nonetheless intentional and representational, such as fine-grained content, non-measured content, content that needs no concept to be specified, or ways of seeing. Within a framework of philosophy of mind, he considers what he classifies as "exploiting" one content metaphorically—as another—in such a manner that it is treated as a non-propositional, hence non-conceptual, content. However, though claiming that metaphor is essentially nonlinguistic, being supported by the non-conceptualists' main ideas, Peacocke does characterize metaphor as cognitive. He accordingly defines the "conception of metaphor as essentially nonlinguistic, as something cognitive that can be found in many different types of mental state and event."[15] Linguistic metaphors, as well as all other kinds, Peacocke insists, are nothing more than externalizations of the mental ones.

Consequently had he not endorsed a mentalist view, due to his non-conceptualist framework Peacocke would have opened a whole new path on the road to grasping the essence of metaphor. One of his most significant non-conceptualist propositions suggests the fine-grained character of both the big parts of the ontological sphere and their perceptions, which are not captured by concepts but whose mental images are intentional and representational.[16]

3.1.1 Pro non-conceptualism

These non-conceptualist propositions reconcile the fine-grained nature of metaphor as a composition with emerging relations and properties that sometimes cannot be conceptualized. See for instance *Sweetheart Nutcracker*, made by Jim Hannon-Tan in 2020—a relatively simple and elegant metaphor of a crocodile nutcracker, easy to recognize in all of its positions, closed or open, as a tool made to hold and crack a nut (Figure 12). Not only did its elegant, minimal, and still but kinetic elements not derive from concepts, but these elements and their internal relations also *resist* conceptualization. It is just impossible to preconceive the force that emerges from the minimalist body and head of the

Figure 12 Jim Hannon-Tan, *Sweetheart Nutcracker*, 2020. Reproduced by permission of Jim Hannon-Tan.

crocodile: its somewhat rigid appearance saturated with a tint of cuteness and humor, the face possessing an eye made from the top of a screw, its teeth and the serrated mouth, intended for small nuts, and the way the mouth opens once the body opens to collect a big nut—all these combine in such a rightness of reciprocal interrelation between form and function. I feel that these words, my own and any words, are a dull medium to describe this visual metaphor. In general, had the crocodile nutcracker metaphor not been a powerful composition, detailing it would have killed it—or at least would have frozen its livelihood. This *mass-produced* design object, actually a mass-produced metaphor, is not an externalization of "understanding a nutcracker through a crocodile" (it is funny to even suggest it!), nor does it entail this conceptualization. One has to see it! It gained its properties from the visual rendering of emergent properties of a crocodile which now can only be possessed by a nutcracker, and vice versa. Only this crocodile can have a crocodile mouth and body, made from steel and shaped to fit a nut, as well as possessing these very kinetic properties. It is the mouth of a crocodile—every single person I asked about it immediately recognized it, saying simply "it is a crocodile"—but of one that dwells in the suburbs of the group of crocodiles.

Still, crucially, the same resistance to conceptual-linguistic capture characterizes linguistic animal metaphors (and linguistic metaphors in general, of course). One can easily think of a situation in which a colleague complains "our boss is a crocodile," which before everything else is a construction of the boss as a scary, predatorial, employee-cracking creature, founded on an imagistic, aesthetic composition. This composition cannot be conceptualized either, nor is it accomplished by understanding one concept through other, but rather from the aesthetic *visual* shape and conduct of the crocodile reconstructing a person who is higher in the chain of command. Addressing a more common metaphor such as that of the "shark lawyer" or "busy bee" will result in an analogous analysis; the external visuality of a fast-moving, never-resting, small but fruitful, ever-buzzing bee is the constructing element of the latter metaphor.

3.1.2 Against mentalism

Peacocke's paradigmatic and significant non-conceptualism notwithstanding—covering visual, ontological, and perceptual areas that resist conceptualism—his affixed extreme internalist-mentalist definition misses out on the real, essential substance of metaphors. Non-conceptualism proves helpful in explaining how we can represent the reverberating, emergent, not preconceived properties of metaphors. But internalism cannot but fail to track metaphor's visual source, its power and the externality of the emergence of metaphorical properties. These properties have an ongoing dynamic existence, building metaphors long before mental representations may or may not reflect them. But for Peacocke mental representation, as he puts it "a correspondence between the mental representations of items in each domain," is the site in which metaphor is created by this procedure: "some representations of the metaphorically represented domain are copied to some special kind of storage binding them with their corresponding mental representations (of the representing domain) in the subpersonal state underlying an experience, imagining, or thought which has the metaphorical content. Thereby their content enters the metaphorical content of that mental state or event."[17]

The external-visual character of metaphors often demonstrates inconsistencies and cracks in internalist views of metaphor. On the one hand, speaking of sensuous metaphor, Peacocke admits: "often a piece of music succeeds in expressing a particular emotion by some of its features being perceived metaphorically-as having characteristics of this affect."[18] He acknowledges the fact that the metaphorical property of (music) being full of suffering or joy is an element in composition. On the other hand, his analysis of the Life Is Journey metaphor overlooks the substance of metaphors, claiming that metaphors both originate in "mental states whose contents involve metaphor" and take shape there. Peacocke argues that, when you think of life as a journey, various features of your representation of a journey are mapped onto your representation of a life. The mapping is exploited, rather than being thought about or represented. This is why, when you think or imagine or experience metaphorically, you appreciate the metaphor first. In more complex cases you may have to think hard about, and work out, what exactly the correspondence in question is if someone raises the issue.[19]

Later on, in his 2010 "Music and Experiencing Metaphorically-As," this neglect of metaphorical substance is manifested by a characterization of musical metaphor, this time about hearing a piece of music express a shift from suffering to joy. In ascribing this shift to mental activity rather than to the compositional features of the music, Peacocke proposes a reduction of both the aesthetic talent of the composer and the creative compositional medium to the mental content of the hearer. Moreover Peacocke, so it seems, tends to conceptualism after all. According to Peacocke, this perception of the metaphoricity of music is dependent on an "isomorphism between the musical features in question and a domain of mental states including suffering and joy," and with regard to visual metaphor he notes, "the isomorphism involved in the perception of Zurbaran's painting of pots maps the concept of those pots to the concept person."[20] Given that Peacocke is a traditional (internalist) cognitivist, his return from non-conceptualism to conceptualism suggests that the roots of the problems of the internalist view of metaphor lie in traditional cognitivism as much as in conceptualism.

3.2 Conceptualism and conventions: the basis of its inconsistency

The various approaches in the cognitivist school share a claim that the structure of metaphor consists of a conceptual source and target—along with a mapping, understanding or thinking of the target through the source. The same target may be mapped onto alternative targets and vice versa, as Lakoff and Johnson note. For instance, argument is usually mapped onto war, but it would not be a logical contradiction to map argument onto something else—to map argument onto a dance, for example. Mappings are akin to highlighters, focusing on some elements and ignoring others. The editors of the 2014 collection *The Power of Metaphor: Examining Its Influence on Social Life*, Landau, Robinson, and Meier, present metaphor through the commonly used example Love Is Journey vs. Love Is Plant as follows, "Thinking of love as a journey will highlight the fact that relationships should head somewhere, whereas thinking of love as a plant that needs to be nurtured will deemphasize movement but perhaps better capture the idea that relationships can wither to the extent that we do not water them (e.g., by periodic expressions of kindness)."[21] A mainstream conceptualist line of argument is that "alternate conceptual mappings can produce systematic changes in perceptions, inferences, and attitudes toward the target," that is to say, an internal conceptual schema motivates our external lives through conventions. For example,

> conceptualizing arguments in terms of war ("I cannot penetrate her defenses") should promote a hostile orientation in which one party is the victor and the other is the vanquished. By contrast, conceptualizing arguments in terms of locations that are far apart ("Are we on different planets?") should downplay hostility and even promote efforts toward finding a "common ground," or compromise, between arguing parties.[22]

The claim for conventions-based possibilities became so popular and useful that it yielded a dialectic, or at least twofold, result. One result is a major inconsistency (up to a partial refutation) in the internalist element of the conceptualist theory, regarding what it defines as the (internal) origin of metaphor. The other result led to an impressively wide deployment of the theory into various disciplines, a few of them originally unrelated to cognitive studies. On the one hand, the assertion that the metaphorical conceptual combination is based on conventions requires the assumption that metaphor originates in the external sphere—paraphrasing Hilary Putnam on meaning, convention just ain't in the head.[23] More accurately, conventions may be internalized, but they are definitely created by society in the external sphere. It is in social ontology that they gain their dynamic character, which allows the versatility of using different sources to reconstruct the same target. Additionally, in tracking conventions as the original locus of metaphors (as with the physical sphere and the body), the conceptual theory of metaphor points to an external stratum but at the same time ignores it—and for good reason, if we look at this external stratum from the conceptualist view which tries to preserve the picture of us as conceptual beings. The conceptualist theory of metaphor claims that conceptual metaphors both serve as a source of our understanding the world and dictate the conduct of our lives, our behavior and other external phenomena. Lakoff's support of Michael Reddy's contention that "our everyday behavior reflects our metaphorical understanding of experience" is but one manifestation of this inconsistent stance. But then, one may easily see that the delineation of the stages of metaphorical construction do not make sense: if it all begins with external ontology, social or bodily ontology included, which is conceptualized, then it does not make sense to claim that after the conventions were conceptualized, we go back to construct conventions as reflections of their own conceptualizations. Look at the problematic structure of Reddy's proposition: "our everyday behavior reflects our metaphorical understanding of experience."[24] Everyday behavior *is* experience. To have a metaphorical understanding of experience, we need an experience first to be the subject of understanding. Therefore, the claim that, first, we experience everyday conduct as a subject of a metaphorical understanding and, second, our experiences (among which include our everyday behaviors) are dictated by this understanding, is circular. Again, it seems that the price of circularity is one that conceptualism is willing to pay in order to preserve the internalist conception of ourselves.

3.2.1 "Relationship is journey": visualist opposition to the idea of entailments

Let us look at the materialization of this circularity in a conceptualist analysis of the very often discussed Relationship Is Journey metaphor—this time by Lakoff in his "The Contemporary Theory of Metaphor." In it, the back-and-forth conceptualist order is revealed. According to conceptualism, the metaphorical process progresses through these stages, which I extract from Lakoff's text and present in conjunction with his description:

1. A convention creates a prism, through which a relationship is perceived as a journey.
2. The mind joins the task, viz. an internal conceptualization begins: "imagine a love relationship described as follows: Our relationship has hit a dead-end street. Here love is being conceptualized as a journey with the implication that the relationship is stalled, that the lovers cannot keep going the way they've been going, that they must turn back, or abandon the relationship altogether."[25] In the framework of the conceptualization, the concept of relationship (classified as target) is *understood* through the concept of journey (classified as source). Understanding here is achieved by mapping of knowledge (the knowledge derives from experience, of course): "The Love-as-Journey mapping is a set of ontological correspondences that characterize epistemic correspondences by mapping knowledge about journeys onto knowledge about love."[26]

3. An abstract scheme is created: "There is a single general principle ... a general principle that is neither part of the grammar of English, nor the English lexicon. Rather, it is part of the conceptual system underlying English. It is a principle for understanding the domain of love in terms of the domain of journeys."[27]
4. Conventions regarding the characterization of particular life events, such as treating a specific marriage as reaching a crossroads, are entailed by the abstract scheme "relationship is journey"—a scheme which had been made due to the external convention:

    such correspondences permit us to reason about love using the knowledge we use to reason about journeys. Let us take an example. Consider the expression, "we're stuck," said by one lover to another about their relationship. How is this expression about travel to be understood as being about their relationship? "We're stuck" can be used of travel, and when it is, it evokes knowledge about travel.[28]

5. Conceptualism omits the first stage and its external nature from the account, addressing the particular ways to speak about the concept of relationship (or ways of experiencing relationships) as if these ways are entailed from the abstract conceptual scheme rather than the other way around. "This is not an isolated case. English has many everyday expressions that are based on a conceptualization of love as a journey, and they are used not just for talking about love, but for reasoning about it as well."[29]

From the third stage onward, Lakoff's description of the Love Is Journey metaphorical scheme and its entailments misrepresents what life events are, relationships included. Speaking about "relationships" or "journeys" as abstract concepts is senseless, given that we cannot even conceive of them without particular examples. First, the very idea of conceptualizing into schemes human ways of being—being so rich, full of particularities, full of idiosyncrasies, and consisting of actions and emotions—is ad hoc. One can rightly claim that they are conventions-dependent, as the conceptualists imply. But conventions are anything but abstract or stable. They are externally formed and reformed. We live relationships, experience them, and construct them, and the same goes for journeys. Second, we do not fall in love, have a fight, deepen friendships, grow bored, or become frustrated with the way things are going in relationships as an entailment of some internal, stable, abstract scheme. We first do any of these, whether we are influenced by conventions or not. Then we sometimes partially and temporarily conceptualize them, but not up to the point of forming a distinct scheme that serves as a source of so many elements and occurrences in relationships, such as: "Look how far we've come. It's been a long, bumpy road. We can't turn back now. We're at a crossroads. We may have to go our separate ways. The relationship isn't going anywhere. We're spinning our wheels. Our relationship is off the track. The marriage is on the rocks. We may have to bail out of this relationship."[30] These are entirely different experiences, involving ingredients from entirely different fields. For example, the experience of driving has very little to do with that of being a bystander standing at a crossroads. The visual qualities, textures, shapes, noises, the body positions and movements involved, the respective relationships with the environment—all are so different. Therefore, they lend very different properties to construct very different metaphors. "We're spinning our wheels" and "We're at a crossroads" do not originate from the same place. If a conceptualization is made at some point it is mixed with visual images, bodily sensations, feelings, and images. It is pretty messy.

3.2.2 Conceptualism endorsed by many disciplines

The second result of the claim for the conventions-based possibilities of mapping targets, which is conjoined with omitting the conventions' externality, is the following. As was already said, the first result, which is the problem of going back and forth between the external and the internal—namely, claiming that conventions and other ontological phenomena both serve as the starting point of many conceptual metaphors and are shaped by conceptual metaphors—is critical in the conceptual theory of metaphor. At the same time, this claim encouraged various disciplines to use the conceptual theory of metaphor as a *method* of research. Thereby, they embarked on tracking down the conceptualized (external) conventions, and subsequently to present the influence of this conceptualization on the conventions and ordinary practices of the different disciplines. Gibbs portrays this phenomenon well:

> Since 1980, several hundred cognitive linguistic projects have demonstrated how systematic patterns of conventional expressions reveal the presence of underlying conceptual metaphors. These studies have explored a large range of target concepts and domains (e.g., the mind, concepts of the self emotions, science, morality and ethics, economics, legal concepts, politics, mathematics, illness and death, education, psychoanalysis), within a vast number of languages (e.g., Spanish, Dutch, Chinese, Hungarian, Persian, Arabic, French, Japanese, Cora, Swedish), including sign languages and ancient languages (e.g., Latin, Ancient Greek), and have investigated the role of conceptual metaphors in

thinking and speaking/writing within many academic disciplines (e.g., education, philosophy, mathematics, theater arts, physics, chemistry, architecture, political science, economics, geography, nursing, religion, law, business and marketing, and film).³¹

Surely, Gibbs is right. It ought to be added from a more general-cultural point of view that the conceptual model of metaphor became so paradigmatic and harmonized with the Western post-linguistic turn, and the characterization of the human as conceptual, that it is taken to be both a theoretical groundwork and a research methodology. So much so, that different disciplines—endorsing conceptualism with open arms, no questions asked—use it as a method of analysis for their terminologies. They must believe that conceptualism as a method has the power to expose the deep structure of the discipline's reasoning and even its motivation. The influence of conceptualism stretched as far as, for instance, the analyses of business terminology. Primary metaphors such as Business Is War, and its derivations A Business Meeting / The Market Is a Battle on a Battlefield, Or Business Strategies Are War Strategies, are presented among other conceptual metaphors by Éva Kovács, in the framework of her 2006 analysis of business terminology and discourse, as dwelling in its founding ideas.³² Her "Conceptual Metaphors in Popular Business Discourse" is but one among numerous examples illustrating the magisterial status of the conceptual theory of metaphor, where the underlying metaphor Economy/Business Is a Human Body is described as follows: "the general well-being of an economy / a company is understood in economic terms as its economic health. There are also some threats to the economic health, which can be tackled or not. Thus, an economy/company can also suffer injuries or fall ill, undergo medical treatment, and recover or collapse."³³ Another example is a 2020 study of *visual* metaphors as constructing scientific arguments, favoring the conceptualist model of metaphor both as an obvious theoretical infrastructure and a research method, viz. as a filter for the scientific use of verbal and visual metaphors. In a paper titled "Non-Verbal and Multimodal Metaphors Bring Biology into the Picture," José Manuel Ureña Gómez-Moreno uses the conceptualist model to analyze the tree visual metaphor commonly used for typologies in science. Drawing upon Lakoff and Johnson's claim from 1980 that the perceptual process of portraying biological models tree "cognitively transformed into a *gestalt*," he shows a few examples of the visual tree metaphor, one of which is,

> fungus taxonomic reconstruction, taxonomies are trees dispenses with the roots, downplays the trunk, and focuses on the branches (e.g. *Chytridiomycota*) and

leaves (e.g. *Allocycles macrogynus*) ... the concrete-to-abstract metaphoric mappings involve the concrete source concepts tree branches and leaves being mapped onto the abstract target concepts phylum, subphylum, class, subclass and species, which are categories making up the hierarchical structure of biological kingdoms. By virtue of the tree metaphor, these abstract entities are conceptualized as, and visually organized into, an arboreal arrangement.[34]

3.2.3 Conventions and context

The idea that metaphors are conceptual, internal, built-in schemes is so entrenched in the field that *many theoreticians of metaphors overlook even their own admission of the external source of metaphors*. A telling example is the metaphor theory formulated by Gilles Fauconnier and Mark Turner, who present an important critique of the conceptualist assumption that the metaphorical conceptual scheme is well-ordered and consists of merely two distinct elements, which they describe as "bundles of pairwise bindings considered in recent theories of metaphor," offering instead a picture of networks. In the framework of their critique of what has become the mainstream conceptualist theory of metaphor, in "Rethinking Metaphor" they go against "the focus on single mapping,"[35] which omits the emergence of blending and integrations between mappings and successive conceptual structures, even of such fundamental metaphors as Space Is Time. In their more general book *The Way We Think: Conceptual Blending and the Mind's Hidden Complexities*, they use Lakoff and Kövecses's analysis of the metaphoric understandings of anger as a paradigmatic example of blending. This metaphor, entailed by "*He was steaming. She was filled with anger. I had reached the boiling point. I was fuming. He exploded. I blew my top*," is based on mapping between conventional models of heat and of anger: "a heated container maps to an angry individual, heat maps to anger, smoke and steam (signs of heat) map to signs of anger, explosion maps to uncontrolled rage."[36] To these are added "folk theory of physiological effects of anger: increased body heat, blood pressure, agitation, redness of face," which are manifested but metaphors like "She was red with anger." Thus, heat input, emotion input, body input are mapped onto each other in various crossing relations, producing a metaphorical blend with a "further emergent structure" to which "we can recruit other information to the inputs to facilitate its development. For example, we might say, He was so mad I could see smoke coming out of his ears."[37] According to Fauconnier and Turner, this blend of "smoke coming out of the ears" is produced by using ears in the body input and an orifice in the heat input and projecting them both to anger. We see here, then, a clear link to the idea of emergence and emergent properties as essential to metaphor.

On the one hand, Fauconnier and Turner support the established conceptualist assertion that metaphors are mental constructions that reside in the basis of all thought and action, arguing that "what we have come to call 'conceptual metaphors,' like time is money or time is space, turn out to be mental constructions involving many spaces and many mappings in elaborate integration networks constructed by means of overarching general principles."[38] On the other hand, they acknowledge the external cultural ontology in establishing the integration networks of metaphors. Accordingly, they inform us that: "integration networks underlying thought and action are always a mix ... cultures build networks over long periods of time that get transmitted over generations. Techniques for building particular networks are also transmitted. People are capable of innovating in any particular context."[39] Then again, progressing with their definition of metaphor, this crucial external origin of internal networks is omitted in favor of locating the roots of metaphor in mental content (albeit not in as stable and fixed a form as Lakoff and Johnson define it).

Fauconnier himself, interestingly, begins his linguistic study in theories of reference within the philosophy of language, as in his 1985 book *Mental Spaces: Aspects of Meaning Construction in Natural Language*. Together with the other philosophers of language in the 1980s, he shifted his line of research from formal logic to an internalist theory of mental activities and abilities to explain complex reference by mental blending. This shift is curious. One facet of the literature that sought to portray of the linguistic character of the human being was, at one point, the pragmatist philosophy of language. Realizing that logic and pure ostensive semantics would not suffice to cover the complexities and dynamic of language, this branch of the philosophy of language steered their analysis of linguistic meaning toward the external uses of language or semantic externalism. The other facet of theories of meaning was composed of those who joined the philosophy of mind and cognitivism in seeking the sources of meaning in mental contents.

A recent impressive step that continues Fauconnier and Turner's renunciation of conceptualist atomism is taken by a prominent theoretician of metaphor Zoltán Kövecses in his 2020 "An Extended View of Conceptual Metaphor Theory." We will soon see that parallel to them, though he formulates a contextualist theory of metaphor, Kövecses would not abandon the internalist vantage point. His contextualist step is combined with a criticism of the discrepancy between the conceptualists' inexplicit reliance on context and their omission of a clear reference to contexts of conventions. He argues, "though it is true that theories of metaphor comprehension make extensive use of context, theories of metaphor production within conceptual metaphor theory have almost completely ignored the notion." Kövecses, and rightly so, wishes to let go of the conceptualist atomism and to remodel it toward a conventional contextualism, and therefore takes it upon himself to check the possibility of proposing: "a theory of conceptual metaphors within the cognitive linguistic paradigm that could integrate the context of metaphor production into conceptual metaphor theory."[40] Under "metaphor production" he subsumes, like Fauconnier and Turner, metaphorical blend in mental spaces and networks which are created online in the communicative event.[41]

To develop the idea of metaphor production, Kövecses discusses the metaphorical expression "the 2005 hurricane capsized Domino's life," used by a journalist who interviewed the American rock musician Fats Domino following Hurricane Katrina in New Orleans. For Kövecses, this expression is a strong example of a combination of contextual elements gathered online to form a metaphor. Kövecses finds three types of metaphorical meaning of conceptual metaphor (he refers to proper ones, which he dubs "correlation-based metaphors," as well as others such as similarity-based metaphors): meaningfulness meaning, decontextualized meaning, and contextual meaning. The first are founded on image-schema, the second on conventions, and the third on the "individual level" of conceptualization, which "corresponds to the level of mental spaces in metaphorical schematicity hierarchies."[42] The individual level is the most personal, specific, and conceptually rich, according to Kövecses. Therefore, the capsize metaphor used to portray the formidable change in Domino's life focuses on one aspect of a whole rich context of a metaphorical sea journey, but also expanding on it. Kövecses explains that the contextual meaning of the capsize metaphor in this case is Domino's life,

> changing for the worse. But it (capsizing) has its own conceptual potential to expand by means of drawing out its implications, such as one's life being normal before it happens, the change being sudden and unexpected, uncertainty about the future following the change, the change for the worse evoking empathy and compassion, and others. It can be suggested that a particular contextual meaning is introduced in order to enable a variety of social, pragmatic, emotive, rhetorical, etc. functions and effects.[43]

Kövecses's criticism of the one-dimensionality of the conceptualist theory of metaphor notwithstanding, he still does not break the internalist framework.

Certainly, he acknowledges both the personal, particular level and the constitutive role that a whole external net plays in making the capsize metaphor so rich, as well as its emergent features. But he still points to mental activity as the site of the work of the contextual elements in shaping the metaphor. According to him, the uniqueness and newness of the ruinous life event is enabled by conceptual transgressions: "it is this last type of meaning construction (i.e., the one on the level of mental spaces) that is the true 'element' of conceptual integration; it is here that conceptual integration can break up conventional conceptual structures, reassemble them in new ways, and can construct novel meanings."[44] We see nonetheless that the external intensity of having a boat overturned and being thrown to the water being applied to the life-changing event of a storm, to so sensuously experience—a hurricane!—that caused life to never be the same again, Kövecses contends that the real, metaphorical blend takes place in the conceptual-mental space. Even if we merely point to a small boat, a kayak, flipping upside down as the source of a metaphor, this event gains its character by possessing an external sensuous character, with a very salient composition, the elements of which are the ones that construct life to then capsize.

Curiously, however, conceptualism still tends to internalism. Even a moderate, contextualist, conceptualist approach to metaphor such as Kövecses's, while allocating a slot in the theory to the *personal, particular experience*, still attributes a privileged status to the conceptual meta-schema, believing that the conceptual abstraction of "capsizing" is in charge of shaping the experience of an irreversible and traumatic life event. But doubtlessly, the metaphor dwells in the original external experience of being overturned and thrown to the water, possessing all of its visual and compositional properties—and this, rather than a concept, is the source of the metaphor as well as the big schema it might belong to.

The priority of the external medium of metaphor to the mental image-schema applies also to similarity-based metaphors which Kövecses contends ought to be included under the conceptual kind. According to him, image-schema underlie similarity-based metaphors, which are more abstract and less contextual than what the mental space metaphors are based on. The example here is "to gut a building" which is supposed to be renovated.[45] Here, too, I claim that the image-schema is not prior to the metaphor, but rather follows it. We see a gutted animal and apply it to buildings, more accurately we reconstruct buildings to have a body. In particular, there is no level of abstraction in the middle. Controversies notwithstanding, Kövecses's rich account of metaphor is innovative and impressively self-reflective. Paul Hopper's emergent grammar theory (which I will say more about in the following subchapters and in Chapter 3) presents a claim about this inversion within language, drawing on Ludwig Wittgenstein's meaning as use idea: "the emergent grammar theory postulates an inversion of the usual relationship between a rule and a practice ... In this analysis, rather than speakers' practice being governed by rules, it would be more accurate to say that rules are created and sustained by agreement among speakers during acts of communication."[46]

In this context, it is very instructive to look at the theoretical moves taken by Gibbs, who exercises the same theoretical walk back and forth, from the external to the conceptual-mental contents and back again. He refuses, so it seems, to accept the primary role of ontology in metaphor. He further defies the externality of human character and existence. His emphasis, though, is on language, taking us back to the mainstream of the linguistic turn. Gibbs reminds us that language is ever-present in metaphorical experiences, that conceptual metaphors can be deduced from the study of language, and that Lakoff and Johnson's primary argument for conceptual metaphor theory was derived from a methodical study of the ways people talk about their life experiences. These inconsistent moves back and forth, from defining metaphors as conceptualizations of external experience to characterizing external experience as taking shape and coherence due to conceptual schemes, appear in Gibbs's *Metaphor Wars: Conceptual Metaphors in Human Life*, in which he argues: "metaphor pervades our meaningful understandings of many mundane and artistic life moments, and enables us to make sense of what is otherwise inchoate. This is not just a matter of providing linguistic labels to organize certain vague experiences, but a continual, instinctual impulse to conceptualize what is happening now in terms of what we already understand more directly."[47] We see here that Gibbs describes the human being as conceptually motivated, all the way down to their "instinctual impulse" to conceptualize even the post-present, particular moments of life.

Gibbs continues to exercise this internalist approach in his significant extended study, one that covers the ways different nonlinguistic multimodal experiences embody conceptual metaphors along the recent conceptualist line of thought. "Conceptual metaphors are not just evident within language," he claims, "but also structure the creation and understanding of many life events, including those pertaining to categorization, memory, emotion, and different social judgments, as well as our experiences of static images, film, gestures, music, dance, and other forms of material culture."[48] He finds an illustration of his conceptualist stance in an experiment that reveals a correlation between creativity or creative cognition and embodiment of metaphors—in this case, the metaphor "thinking outside of the box"—and novel and atypical problem solving. I think Gibbs's conclusions from this experiment are not the right ones. He asks if physically thinking outside of a real, adjacent box (namely, a big box standing in the middle of the room) enhances creativity.

> One test of this idea had participants sit comfortably inside a five-foot square box, sit outside of the box, or sit in a room without any box, and then complete a 10-item Remote Associates Test (RAT). The RAT presented people with three clue words (e.g., "room," "blood," "salts") and asked them to think of a word (e.g., "bath") that was related to each one of the clues. Participants who were physically sitting outside the box generated more correct associates to the clue words than did people who sat either inside the box, or in a room without a box."[49]

Gibbs's analysis of the results is surprising, given that clearly the idea of thinking outside of a box was born from an experience of getting out of a familiar environment and freeing oneself from a closed place. Now, this is exactly what the experiment shows! The very visuality and composition of sitting outside of a box enhanced the participants' creativity. If anything, the external setting pushed the cognition forward, rather than the other way around.

3.3 Criticism from within: back to language

What I pointed to as a denial of the external source of metaphors by the conceptualist theories, which caused a few of them to go to and fro between conceptual-mental content and ontology and external experience, is partially implied by Gibbs himself. Nonetheless, and its rigid conceptualism aside, among its peer theories, Gibbs's philosophy is one of the most (if not the most) ontologically oriented—or, more accurately, the least internalist due to its wide scope of kinds of metaphors. In light of this, he bravely faces challenges that would otherwise affect the obviousness of the conceptualist theory's ruling status.

In the 2014 anthology *The Power of Metaphor*, Gibbs outlines a chain of concerns that have been raised by critics of the conceptual metaphor theory throughout its development. The most significant among these addresses the circularity of the account of the sources of linguistic metaphors—a significant critique, indeed one that I find helpful for my attempt to show the conceptualist mis-tracking of the external motivation of metaphors in general, as I have mentioned in different formulations above and before, and will again shortly.[50] The conceptualist circularity is described by Gibbs in this manner: "a traditional analysis may start with an examination of different conventional expressions that in turn suggest the existence of an underlying conceptual metaphor. However, the final step in making the existence proof for any conceptual metaphor is to go back to the language to find other linguistic expressions that fit the same conceptual metaphor schema."[51] That is to say, according to the methodical duplicity revealed by Gibbs, from external findings (linguistic expressions) the existence of an internal schema is inferred (the metaphorical structure of thought); but then, to prove the effect of the internal schema, external findings (linguistic expressions) are searched for again.

3.3.1 The first visualist critique: exposition of the conceptualist circularity

I find the conceptualist circularity essential rather than merely methodical, therefore my critique is stricter than Gibbs's. The conceptualist theory of metaphor not only returns to external expressions as evidence of the existence of abstract primary metaphor induced by the external expression. The same theory also considers the external expressions to be tokens of types, or embodiments of abstract mental content. Let us revisit once more the often-analyzed Relationship Is Journey metaphor: our relationship has hit a dead-end street; it's been a long, bumpy road; we're spinning our wheels; our relationship is off-track; the marriage is on the rocks; look how far we've come; we may have to go our separate ways. All these expressions, though they are experienced so differently and emerge from such different external visual pieces, are presented by Lakoff and Johnson in a few texts as dependent entailments, or tokens, of one abstract mental content of "love is journey."[52] To the questions "Is there a general principle governing how these linguistic expressions about journeys are used to characterize love? Is there a general principle governing how our patterns of inference about journeys are used to reason about love when expressions such as these are used?," Lakoff answers positively, claiming there is a single general conceptual principle for understanding the domain of love through the domain of journeys—which is, in fact, the conceptual internal mapping of journey onto love.

This generalizing argument or model of subsuming various metaphors under a single, abstract, big metaphor is one of the most problematic and indefensible parts of the conceptualist theory of metaphor. It is also one of the main indications of what is seen by externalists and visualists as an erroneous characterization of the human being. First, linguistic metaphors, just like visual ones, are autonomous and independent. They are not embodiments, entailments or tokens of preconceived metaphors, but are the medium of metaphor itself, that in its turn may motivate the conceptual metaphor. Considering their deeply different properties, compositions, and descriptions of elements in relationships as but entailments of an abstract scheme of metaphor miss out both what relationships are and what it is to be human. First, relationships are very real, sensual, substantial, and particular; they involve feelings and urges, behaviors and actions, and are very diverse. Different elements of relationships have their own compositions and aesthetic structures. Claiming that they are perceived, understood or dictated by an internal, abstract, conceptual meta-structure is close to absurd. Second, the sources—the experiences, compositions, and visuality of hitting a dead-end street; walking on a long bumpy road; being inside a car, the wheels of which spin in vain; going off the track; walking along the road, and then stopping to look back and see "how far we've come"; going separate ways— are so visual and so diverse! The visuality of a static, blocked street, in which you need to turn back to wherever you came from, constructs one of the metaphorical elements of relationships. The visuality of the kinetic composition of wheels spinning and spinning, leaving the car stuck, constructs a whole different element of relationships. Additionally, these metaphorical structures are very visual, very sensuous, and have their own compositions, forms, and aesthetic qualities. Each of these elements given in the whole creates the third part of metaphor: the emergent properties borrowed from the source, which can be newly possessed only by the target. Just as only the *Sweetheart* (figure 12) crocodile nutcracker can have nutcracker crocodileness—namely, being made of metal, with a top of a screw eye and serrated mouth aimed to crack small nuts, etc.—a blocked street of relationships can only be of relationships. It is a blocked path *of a relationship*, on which friends or couples can no longer continue in the same manner. Emergent properties, with their ontological, aesthetic, sensuous properties, just cannot be preconceived abstractly and conceptually. Indeed, these properties are what make the structure metaphorical.

If I am right, Gibbs understands this. In his 2013 "Conceptual Metaphor in Thought and Social Action," he refers to President Barack Obama's 2009 address, in which Obama described the nation's economic challenges using metaphorical expression: "in this winter of our hardships let us brave once more the icy currents, and endure what storms may come; let it be said by our children's children that when we were tested we refused to let this journey end."[53] Above this address, says Gibbs, stands the general metaphor that life is a journey. Nonetheless, Gibbs is aware that even though the speech with its different tropes "necessarily reflects enduring patterns of metaphoric thought," it is possible that

Obama chose the specific metaphors for their rhetorical power and communicative character for the American public. In his 2017 *Metaphors Wars*, Gibbs refers to *Hardball* American political television show host Chris Matthews's preliminary analysis of the then-forthcoming first presidential debate between Barack Obama and Mitt Romney. The host, Gibbs notes, used expressions that "convey metaphorical meanings," such as "Romney will take some hard shots," will be "blasting away at the President," and "I think Obama will play with him, parry the assaults, block the blows, try to keep his head clear so he can avoid getting hurt."[54] Yet again, Gibbs argues that beyond these expressions a foundational, abstract, enduring metaphor stands: that political debates are boxing matches. This is a central, typical conceptualist analysis.

But at the same time, Gibbs himself raises doubts regarding the preconceptions enduring in patterns of metaphoric thought that motivate, consciously or unconsciously, linguistic metaphors. Interestingly, he tries to combine conceptuality with a philosophy of the ordinary, arguing that the most significant contribution of the conceptualist theory of metaphor is the fact that it addresses ordinary metaphors, characterizing them as primary above and beyond poetic metaphors. The combination of the emphasis on abstract conceptuality and ordinary life is indeed forced, given that Gibbs himself admits that "the move from viewing metaphor as a linguistic entity to a fundamental aspect of thought" led his conceptualist peers to disregard the social role of metaphor. However, Gibbs calls for expanding the theory of conceptual metaphor, believing that it is entrenched in social customs, and that the very study of the ways people think metaphorically shows that metaphor is "a pervasive social action." Gibbs hopes that this approach will dissolve the distinction between thought, language, and communication, and show that metaphor is a context-specific daily tool.[55] He rightly argues, "metaphor does not signify an unworldly transcendence from ordinary language, thought, or reality. Instead, what is most clichéd and conventional about reality are those aspects of experience that are primarily constituted by metaphorical thought."[56] In this respect, Gibbs's approach is related to that of everyday aesthetics, along with its wish to address the particular, concrete, and aesthetic experiences. While he does hold the conceptualists' basic stance, claiming that metaphorical thought constitutes experience rather than the other way around, his theory is helpful in progressing toward a characterization of metaphorical practice as integral to our particular and external being living in visuality, or visual ontology, more than anything else.

Interestingly, Gibbs's (and others') recent refocus on language shows that conceptualism, after downplaying language as merely a token of abstract mental content, may converge with the current visual turn. My reasoning for this is the following. Language is, at least partially, external; it often serves as an aesthetic medium, whose substantial syntactic composition and qualitative traits are its essence. Returning to language *as medium* helps to open a vent to the visual medium, on whose imagistic character aesthetic language relies. Sensitive to language as medium, Gibbs bravely published a critical essay challenging his own conceptualist discipline. Among the list of points of critique, he claims that the conceptual theory of metaphor might be too reductionist. Furthermore, he draws our attention to the aesthetic motivation and interpretation of metaphors, both for creators and for what I would like to call "the viewers of metaphors." These were disregarded in metaphorical discussion since the early 1990s:

> Many metaphor scholars seek to understand the consciously produced aesthetic, poetic qualities of metaphors, which they believe have little to do with the possible embodied and conceptual foundations of metaphor... much traditional research on metaphor focuses on how people interpret the novel, emergent meanings of classic "A is B" metaphors, such as "My love is a red, red rose" and see this activity as being related to artistic intentions and deliberate metaphor use on the part of speakers and writers. Conceptual Metaphor Theory rarely considers any of these other possible constraints on why people produce metaphors in the ways they do or how we interpret verbal metaphors as having specific, poetic meanings.[57]

The fact that even conceptualists return to the downplayed linguistic metaphors is helpful in proving that, rather than being internal conceptual infrastructure, metaphor is an external aesthetic autonomous medium that furnishes impressive chunks of our visual ontology.

The new linguistic-conceptualists still do not realize that the visual basis and origin of metaphor ought to be covered by metaphor theory as the basis for the very possibility of metaphorical constructions. Nonetheless, they have moved toward a cognizance of body and physicality in cognition, which is promising. The next subchapter addresses this move.

3.3.2 Deliberation, embodiment and communicativism—stepping toward externalism

The reattribution of an autonomous status to linguistic metaphors, and to language as a metaphorical medium, brings out another interesting recent development in the linguistic-cognitivist metaphor research that challenges the conceptualist claim for internal, abstract metaphorical infrastructure. That is deliberate metaphor theory, which has been formulated mainly by Gibbs, Gerard Steen, Cornelia Müller, and from the side of applied theory mainly by Lynne Cameron. Though deliberate metaphor theory focuses on verbal metaphors and is founded on the cognitivist view of the human being as an essentially linguistic-cognitive creature, one can analyze it as implying a cognizance of metaphor as an external medium. Steen explains that this school's motivation is to expand the theory to explain metaphorical diversity instead of unity, that is to say, "the reason why people use metaphor in diverging ways within and between various domains of discourse [in education, politics, religion, and so on]."[58]

The main challenge that deliberate metaphor theory sets for the conceptual metaphors model is in regarding the focus on the internal pre-action scheme that underlies metaphors. These transcendental schemes, so it is claimed in deliberate metaphor theory, apply only to the use of non-deliberate metaphors. Indeed, these schemes oversee parts of our thought and language, namely of thinking or speaking of one concept in terms of another. But there is a second kind of metaphor that the research must address: deliberate metaphors, being metaphors intentionally used as metaphors. Deliberate metaphors are not merely entailments of a built-in unconscious scheme, such as treating a collaborator in an argument as a rival, while not being aware of an abstract Argument Is War metaphor that arranges things as they are (this is the picture many conceptualists paint). Deliberate metaphors, so this cognitivist school claims, are chosen, and then used while both the sender and the addressee acknowledge the classification of their use. Steen explains this by pitting "Juliet is the sun" against "relationship is a journey." The former, Steen remarks, "is a deliberate invitation for the addressee to adopt a different perspective of Juliet from a truly alien domain that is consciously introduced as a source for reviewing the target."[59] The latter, Steen argues, which is manifested for example by a speaker uttering *we have come a long way* to talk about his relationship, does not ask the addressee to actually change their perspective on the topic of the sentence, which is the speaker's relationship. In his 2017 "Deliberate Metaphor Theory," Steen explains that the awareness of using metaphor focuses mainly on the source: "this definition minimally implies that language users, in production or reception, pay distinct attention to the source domain as a separate domain of reference."[60]

I am not sure that the distinction between non-deliberate and deliberate metaphors holds water or is even as sharp as this movement describes it. I do not think that there are unconscious metaphors—in any case, they do not dwell in some basic abstract cellar. Additionally, contrary to deliberate metaphor theory, metaphors, even the conscious or deliberate ones, are not so intentionally well-organized. In any case the intention is not the most important parameter to look at, since metaphors are aesthetic, inspire creative and productive or emergent imagery, provide insight, etc., which cannot be fully intentional. This is the case with fully aesthetic metaphors such as Picasso's *The King* and *The Queen* (Figure 13), *Ship Building* (Figure 8), or the description of the forthcoming Obama–Romney debate as a boxing match. Picturing the two candidates as boxing rivals carries a lot of drama in a spatial-temporal composition of the debate-boxing-match. What is more, the deliberate metaphors theoreticians explicitly, and curiously, claim that metaphor dwells only in the land of thought, language, and communication, thereby neglecting the huge fields of visual and material metaphors. In this case, quantity turns into quality, and no general metaphor theory can ever capture what metaphor is with too small an extension of "metaphor." However, in acknowledging the deliberate character of metaphors, we are referring here to the use of metaphors as a rhetorical communicative means of speech and discourse. That is to say, the deliberate theory of metaphors takes on itself a pragmatic, rather than epistemological, subject of research. In this respect, deliberate metaphor theory undermines the status of the internalist paradigm which considers internal conceptual metaphors as paradigmatic.

Figure 13 Pablo Picasso, *The King* and *The Queen*, 1952, 1953. Reproduced by permission of the Landau traveling exhibition.

A related critical approach that challenges abstract internalism from within the conceptualist school of metaphors is proposed by Beate Hampe's interesting convergences of linguistic and communicative approaches. "Metaphor scholars used to debate over the 'conceptual' or 'linguistic' nature of metaphor. More recently, they have been considering whether metaphor is 'embodied' or 'discursive.' Despite the shift in focus implied by this terminological change, the divide between communication-oriented and cognition-oriented approaches to metaphor has not disappeared."[61] Hampe offers to bring together the perspectives of the social sciences with those of the cognitive sciences, on metaphor and on multiple methodologies. Like deliberate metaphor theory, hers sees the arena of multimodal and interactive communication between speakers and addresses in society as the right one to study metaphors: "Examining real-life discourse offers significant insights into the dynamics of metaphor in social life that may also lead to a more social, discursive view of metaphor, one that still sees metaphor as part of thought, but as socially emergent cognition, not just as private concepts buried inside people's heads."[62] Cornelia Müller supports the communicativist approach to metaphors as well, claiming that metaphors should be analyzed by how shared they are, viz. by a criterion of the level of collaboration between the user of the metaphor and the addressee.[63]

3.3.3 Emergent grammar: against the conceptualist stable purism

Another linguistic approach that points to the dynamic structures created by active linguistic discourse as the actual sphere of language is the "emergent grammar" theory. I have a similar motivation for my visualist approach to that of emergent grammar's externalist approach to language and meaning. Indeed, I find emergent grammar theory helpful for the visualist metaphor theory I am trying to formulate here, given that it results from a disapproval of theories that attribute a stable internal scheme to language, the various linguistic expressions of which are considered as proofs for its existence.

The motivation of the emergent grammar approach was formulated in 1987 by Paul J. Hopper, one of its main thinkers and a prominent critic of the purist conceptualist approach. Hopper expressed his worries about the "fundamental problem of the assumption of an abstract, mentally represented rule system which is somehow implemented when we speak. It is an assumption which is very deeply entrenched in our field, and indeed is virtually an official dogma."[64] Hopper supports the view that discourse comprises a significant part of the actual use of language, and accordingly goes against the "sentence grammar" viewpoint for which an "abstract mental system" is implemented in all uses of language. After all, the elevation of such a system would overlook language's actual inexhaustibly dynamic character, capable of creating new linguistic events. I find a similar dogma in the field of metaphor theory, motivated by the same Western wish to assume that we possess a well-ordered mind, whose mental contents are really what we are.

This conceptualist wish is revealed for example by the fact, as Hopper reminds us, that even discourse linguistics commonly assumes "[a] dualistic structure in discourse, the notion that structure pre-exists discourse and that discourse is mimetically related to a logically prior abstract organization, formulated this time in terms of paragraphs, episodes, events, and other such macro-units."[65] This tendency is also found in various theories of visual studies, aesthetics, and art, not least in the rich field of the study of metaphor, regardless of metaphor's wide range of media and forms, different levels of complexity, and its lively, aesthetically creative nature.

It is no wonder, then, that the source of inspiration for emergent grammar is cultural anthropology. Hopper informs us that he borrowed the term "emergent" from the cultural anthropologist James Clifford, who "remarks that 'Culture is temporal, emergent, and disputed,'" to apply the same notion to "grammar." Hopper explains that "the same is true of grammar, which like speech itself must be viewed as a real-time, social phenomenon, and therefore is temporal; its structure is always deferred, always in a process but never arriving, and therefore emergent."[66] Moreover, this discipline is founded on a formalist epistemology. Hopper's well-formulated assertion that "grammar is always in a process but never arriving" means that structures of language are constructed, often anew, in external, particular interactions between individual speakers in discourse, bringing their linguistic experiences to the present. Thus, emergent grammar theory suggests a new hypothesis that seems obvious to me, but nonetheless must be emphasized time and again: that structures of culture, expression, thought, creativity, visual and material things, behavior, and conduct are often newly formed by actual, particular, external happenings. It is the external experiential sphere that houses these, rather than some well-ordered, *a priori* scheme of thought. In a 2012 chapter with the same title, "Emergent Grammar," Hopper retrospectively surveys the motivation and development of this approach. He explains:

> linguistic structure is a process that unfolds in real time. Emergent grammar therefore aims its projector to the ongoing structuration of language and

unfolding events of speech communication as they happen. The fundamental temporality of spoken language implies the paradox that structure itself is unstable, intrinsically incomplete, and is constantly being created and recreated in the course of each occasion of use.[67]

The gap is very wide between conceptualist-cognitivism and emergent grammar regarding the characterization of language and its motivation. The conceptualist dedication to the *a priori* generalization of language is clearly stated by Lakoff, in his 1990 delineation of the "the generalization commitment of cognitive linguistics" as "a commitment to characterizing the general principles governing all aspects of human language." Lakoff further details the generalization commitment of syntax, semantics, and pragmatics: "In syntax: Generalizations about the distribution of grammatical morphemes, categories, and constructions."[68] What is more, Lakoff, who quit the then-magisterial school of generative grammar of Chomsky and his followers—who claimed the creativity of language—to co-inaugurate the conceptualist school of metaphors, stresses the *a priori*, abstract order that his cognitivist school attributes to grammar. As informed by Lakoff, conceptualism expects categories to possess: "one of the various kinds of prototype and to be organized in terms of basic-level, superordinate and subordinate levels."[69] The discovery of conceptual metaphor, Lakoff notifies us, helped to clarify this assumption of basic-level abstract types.

Against this picture of a transcendent, somewhat rigid, predetermined, and well-ordered pre-language scheme, Hopper offers his emergent grammar account. He explicitly defies theories that define language as being secondary to an internal, *a priori*, stable grammatical system. Renouncing the idea that "rules generated grammatical sentences, and sentence-level grammaticality justified the rules," emergent grammar endorses the line of functionalist reasoning that sees "the possibility for discourse explanations of grammatical facts established on the basis of isolated sentences." If we look at it from a philosophical vantage point: the emergent grammar line of ideas shifted from the internalist model of language, which portrays the human as a conceptual being, to an externalist view of the human as a creator and performer in particular events. Given that conceptualist-cognitivism in metaphor theory followed cognitivist linguistic approaches, of the kind that Hopper opposes, his account of language is helpful in demonstrating the plausibility of the externalist view of metaphors as constructions in the ontological sphere. Emergent grammar theory has an explanatory power with regard to the real location of metaphors, their concreteness or specificity, as well as their status as an external medium. This school's understanding that syntactic rules neither exhaust nor cover all the facts about linguistic expression, and that one should look at the public living discourse in which they are reconstructed, sheds light on the essence of conceptual and linguistic metaphors, and then on visual ones. It obviously supports the proposition that different kinds of metaphors, among those the omnipresent, paradigmatic visual ones—which as we already found in the first chapter, we can see just about everywhere—cannot be exhaustively covered by the conceptualist model, given that it classifies as paradigmatic the internal, primary, abstract metaphors that are constituted by two abstract concepts.

Furthermore, emergent grammar theory may be used as a proof that metaphor doesn't consist of merely two parts, but an emergent third part as well. The emergent part oversees metaphor's livelihood and aesthetic import created by the unexpected results of the metaphorical composition. The metaphorical properties that emerge from the mutual relations of the elements are always borrowed from, and are best demonstrated in, visual compositions. These properties also help us see that metaphor is neither abstract mental content, as conceptualist-cognitivism argues, nor aimed mainly at communication, as cognitivist communicativism claims. To have a nutcracker be communicative, one would not design it to be a crocodile but would simply leave its function transparent and ready for service. The aesthetic emergence and experience of the relations between the object's two basic metaphorical parts, the source-crocodile and the target-nutcracker, promotes the third element—which is neither abstract on the one hand, nor communicative on the other. The third element is a paradigmatic metaphor, which is a visual aesthetic composition.

3.3.4 Body cognition: the last step toward the visual turn of metaphor theory

Though conceptualism is blind to the rich visualist literature on metaphor as well as the ubiquity of visual metaphors, it did not shut its eyes to the critique from within and the general visual revolution. After all, the visual revolution resulted in every single person being turned into a cellphone photographer and interfaces of user and external visuality taking over collective conduct. Thus, the second decade of the twenty-first century saw a body-oriented path being paved by the conceptualist-cognitivist movement. The acknowledged motivating factors are the adoption of phenomenology by the philosophy of mind, the rise of philosophical theories of body and, not least, the inauguration of the visual and material turn in culture and philosophy. Does the Western crisis of rationalism and of enlightenment ideas have something to do with this? No doubt it does. Democracy is founded on the rationalist inspiration and trust in the citizen to extract a pure internal wisdom and inference while voting, as well as in the legislator to wear John Rawls's veil of ignorance, excluding external sectorial considerations while voting for a constitution based on universal justice.

In light of the rationalist crisis, even under the framework of conceptualist-cognitivism in metaphors, we see a rise in awareness of the fact that the visualists—Arnheim, Gombrich, and others—pointed to all along: that cognition is not owned entirely by the mind, but the body and external experience may house cognition and even knowledge. Johnson's 2017 book *Embodied Mind, Meaning, and Reason: How Our Bodies Give Rise to Understanding* is devoted to these ideas. Johnson, Lakoff's collaborator in the 1980s' inauguration of internalist conceptualism, in 2017 presents his anti-dualist proposal as innovative and bold, though this idea had been aptly represented by work in phenomenology and in the visualist analyses of cognition, thought, and metaphor, for example by Arnheim in his *Visual Thinking*. The difficulties in the progress toward externalism, and in overcoming the prevalent Western picture of human being as essentially characterized by a pure disembodied mind, are presented by Johnson in the following words:

> Our embodiment shapes both what and how we experience, think, mean, imagine, reason, and communicate. This claim is a bold one, and it challenges our received wisdom that what we call "mind" and "body" are not one and the same, but rather are somehow fundamentally different in kind. From a philosophical point of view, one of the hardest tasks you'll ever face is coming to grips with the fact of your embodiment. What makes this task so very difficult is the omnipresent idea of disembodied mind and thought that shows itself throughout our intellectual tradition, from claims about pure logical form to ideas of noncorporeal thought, to spectator views of knowledge, to correspondence theories of truth.[70]

Set aside the fact that the visualist, externalist ideas of cognition as dwelling in the body, actions, and the visual and material sphere did not receive their due credit in the recent conceptualist-cognitivist discussion of embodiment. Instead, I would prefer to direct the reader to the threshold that conceptualism fortunately reached, but unfortunately did not cross over. The early conceptualist model of metaphor—inaugurated in the 1980s—presented an inconsistent and circular structure of metaphor. At the same time, it attributed a privileged status to the *a priori* conceptual mind as the base and foundation of metaphor, and tracks the sources of its scheme to our external ontology—mountains, food, and social lives, for example, are included. On the one hand, Lakoff presents the famous Love Is Journey metaphor in this manner: "the ontological correspondences that constitute the love is a journey metaphor map the *ontology* of travel onto the *ontology* of love" (my emphasis). On the other hand, he argues,

> what constitutes the love as journey metaphor is not any particular word or expression. It is the *ontological mapping across conceptual* domains, from the source domain of journeys to the target domain of love. The metaphor is not just a matter of language, but *of thought and reason*. The language is secondary. The mapping is primary, in that it sanctions the use of source domain language and inference patterns for target domain concepts. The mapping is conventional, that is, it is a fixed part of our conceptual system, one of our conventional ways of conceptualizing love relationships.[71]

On the way to the body cognition theory, using the expression "conventional ways of conceptualizing," Lakoff reveals the inconsistencies embedded in the conceptual theory of metaphor. The internality of conceptualization is confounded with the externality of conventions. Conventions are formed by societies or sub-societies, by definition, and are much less ordered with many fewer clear contours than those of the internal schemes that Lakoff attributes to the mind and the foundation of metaphor. The conceptual theory of metaphor thus confuses apriority and order with the particularity of relationships, experiences, and pieces of ontology. As the argument about circularity showed before: if conceptualization is conventions-dependent, then its source is external; it makes no sense to claim that metaphors originate in conventions, climb up to well-ordered conceptual schemes, and again construct conventional behaviors, especially if body cognition is now inserted to the picture. The expression "conventional conceptualization" discloses the simultaneous cognizance of the external-social-ontological nature of us and the denial of it in favor of characterizing us as conceptual beings.

Then again, about thirty years after their model had been set, the conceptualist-cognitivists fathom that their account of metaphor and thought overlooks a foundational part of our being. During a visual turn, they are reaching an understanding that locating metaphor in a disembodied mind and an internal conceptual scheme not only does not suffice to capture metaphor's livelihood, creativity, and particularity, but also would not make do during a turn to the visual as *the* sphere of analyses of us. In the age of screens and media, it is no longer possible to ignore how effective and aggressive the visual sphere is—in particular, how seeing a commercial sign while waiting for the light to turn green affects our thought much more than an alleged internal abstract concept affects our behavior. When Susan Sontag wrote about the aggressiveness of the camera and photography in her brilliant 1973 *On Photography*, saying that "photographed images do not seem to be statements about the world so much as pieces of it, miniatures of reality that anyone can make or acquire," she did not know she was being just as much a clairvoyant as a philosopher of visual culture.[72]

The refreshing embodied cognition approach, which aims cognitive-conceptualism toward an understanding that our physical existence contains thought, reason, and essence, is but one step in the road to a deep theory of metaphor. I fear the cognitivist may never walk that road to its end. The good point is that the embodied cognition approach does share a few assumptions with what is called in the philosophy of mind literature "the extended mind theory," also labeled as "active externalism," first formulated by David Chalmers and Andy Clark in 1998. Active externalism is different from the content externalist approach formulated by Hilary Putnam and Taylor Burge, which conditions mental contents on passive, distal, external features that "play no role in driving the cognitive process."[73] Clark and Chalmers deem a category of epistemic action to be a cognitive process, undertaken by parts of the world (the body included); they claim, "cognitive processes ain't all the head ... In these cases, the relevant parts of the world are in the loop, not dangling at the other end of a long causal chain." Actions, such as choosing or rearranging words, are (according to Clark and Chalmers) the outcome of an extended cognitive process. Clark and Chalmers even go as far as characterizing the very activities we make as saturated with thoughts: "in a very real sense, the re-arrangement of tiles on the tray is not part of action; it is part of thought."[74] Clearly this externalist characterization of cognition is closely related to, or more accurately it follows, the preceding definitions of visual thinking offered by Arnheim (his canonical book of the same name is often quoted here), Aldrich, Gombrich, Hausman, and even Goodman and Rorty.

We ought to note that the embodied cognition school is more conservative than the externalist, given that its main idea is still based on the assumption that the mind is our main operator, and the bodily actions mere embodiments. It is no wonder that while they discover the body in the embodied cognition theories, they have no cognizance of the visualist theories of thought, cognition, and culture, which supplied the description of thought as dwelling in the visual sphere long before the cognitivists grasped this insight. The visual sphere is deemed inferior even in the new embodied cognition theories, which sees the crux of our being in the contents of the mind and the human being as a conceptual creature first and foremost. This explains why cognitivism approached metaphor from a vantage point that is indifferent to metaphor's aesthetic infrastructure, aesthetic creativity, motivation, and effect. We could say what we mean in many ways, but our formalist immersion in forms, compositions, and visuality motivates us to use a figurative medium such as metaphor. It is our compositional nature that drives us to be attached to forms and to apply them to various things: to see faces on cars, buildings or kitchenware (everywhere!); to shape a pencil holder as a sharpener and a pouffe as a muffin (Figures 3 and 5); to crazily use emoji; to use visual, spatial, and temporal compositions to reconstruct non-sensuous things like theories as buildings and sadness as a deep water; to experience an enormous joy in encountering established forms preserved for a new function.

Then again, Johnson does not go all the way to elevate the status of the external up to a denunciation of the privileged status of the mind in his school, the depth and richness of his embodied cognition theory notwithstanding. Nor does he denounce what he himself dubs "[the] unsatisfactory notion of understanding as merely an abstract intellectual grasping of concepts and their relations." He would not admit that we are external, visual beings. In his 2015 "Embodied Understanding," Johnson bravely acknowledges the failure of the conceptualist-cognitive project of metaphor and human nature, which he was one of the first to embark on in his and Lakoff's mind-praising 1980 *Metaphors We Live By*: "Western culture has inherited a view of understanding as an intellectual cognitive operation of grasping of concepts and their relations. However, cognitive science research has shown that this received intellectualist conception is substantially out of touch with how humans actually make and experience meaning."[75] Still Johnson cannot, and would not, desert the concept of "understanding" as central in our character, and his use of the concept of "embodiment" betrays his apparatus as revolving around the subject of embodiment of mental content. Rather than stepping toward real life, real experience, and ontology, with their diversity, particularities, and their visual and aesthetic drives, his ideas center around "experience of meaning." His promise is "to counteract our inherited cultural habit of conceiving of mind as disembodied" and "to show some of the ways that meaning, concepts, logic, and inferential patterns are grounded in our bodies and in bodily activities."[76] However, he continues by once again wishing for internal abstract conceptual schemes to have the highest priority; he says, "body-based meaning is extended, via imaginative processes like conceptual metaphor, to structure our abstract concepts. Conceptual metaphors allow us to understand and reason about abstract entities and domains, without losing the bodily grounding of meaning ... our bodily experience thus provides a pre-reflective fund of meaning that makes it possible for us to think abstractly."[77] That is to say, Johnson realizes that the origin of cognition is our physicality and externality. Physical and external structures and experiences are particular and concrete, and their interaction with the world is not well-ordered. But the genuine article for him, at the end of the day, is abstract thought, rather than real life, reality, culture, and society, which are the spheres of describing human beings—and our metaphors.

Maybe I am too suspicious regarding the ability of conceptualism to let go of the picture of us as finding ourselves in internal, pure, well-organized abstract schemes, in place of the real us. After all, Johnson's critique of the Western love of the disembodied mind is brave, and his theoretical turn is very significant in the field of metaphor studies. But then again, let us look at how material culture scholars, such as Christopher Tilley and Kate Cameron-Daum, describe the body or physicality, and the cognition embedded in them, in their recent *An Anthropology of Landscape*—which allows them to capture so well what metaphors really are, that they are external things. Let us see how we can at last understand the "journey" that constructs life or relationships in those famous metaphors.

Tilley, who made a very rich study of material metaphors, or more accurately of metaphors and material culture, theorizes with Cameron-Daum in this book about the various relationships between persons and their environments. Among these relationships are embodied action and bodily knowledge which is fused with the knowledge of the operated tools or things, or toured landscapes. One of their topics is bike riding, viz. a movement across the landscape, that creates mobile relationships "in which encounter and perception unfold as part of a journey."[78] They note that the riding is mediated by the bike and its technology—along with the way it is used, which forms mobile relationships. A praxis approach for mountain bikers, for example, "could include factors such as the sensual and emotional; the memories each bike may encapsulate for the rider; the creation of identity that has been shaped, perhaps, by the embodied material culture of the biker; the transforming of space into a place embodied in movement; and the meaning silently conveyed by choice of bike and clothing worn."[79] We see here a deep grasp of the levels of ontology and experience, and of the mutual influence of persons and things. The cognition, they claim, dwells in the particularity of the action (riding), with an object (bike), in the environment, the specific landscape,

> their mutual interaction, and how this relates to a mobile relationship to the landscape: what bicycles do for people and what people do to them. This is an embodied relationship in which the bicycle becomes part of the body of the cyclist. In relationship to the landscape this involves ways of knowing, sensing and interacting with the world that differ significantly from those experienced by other groups such as walkers or horse riders.[80]

Therefore, in realizing the accuracy of this characterization of us, we understand how external and non-abstract cognition is, and how it is shaped and reshaped in external composition—in the case of bike riding we speak of temporal compositions, but spatial compositions are of course common as well, such as looking at a building and recognizing it as a ship (*Ship Building*, Figure 8), or applying external physical depth to a thought. The blending between categories which the conceptualist-cognitivists locate in the mind, anthropological material culture scholars locate in the relationship between us and our external environments. Or more accurately, material culture scholars locate this blending in the external things and the mutual effect between us and them. This stance has its import on the characterization of metaphors as external, which manifests in the power of things. In his *Metaphor and Material Culture* and *Anthropology of Landscape*, Tilley beautifully explains how the mutual relationships between us and things create metaphors: "artefacts can possess a silent form of communicative agency: 'It follows that without an exploration of the metaphorical power of things and the effects that these things have on people's lives we cannot adequately know or understand ourselves or others, what makes up our identity and culture, past or future.'"[81]

The material culture view of metaphors as an ontological medium, focusing on the metaphorical power of things, surely brings us right into Gombrich's analysis of Pygmalion power and the visualist idea of active perception, dynamic objects, and visual thinking. Moreover, it shows us, like the visualist view of metaphor, that visual (or material) metaphors are the paradigmatic ones. This is the right moment to go back to where the visualist theories of metaphor began, which is also the place from which it ought to proceed.

4

The Advent of the Visual Perspective of Metaphors

The description "ours is a visual age" was offered in the 1970s by Gombrich who, just like the current visual-turn scholars, sets an imperative for philosophy, art theory, and theories of perception to devote better attention to the fact of the visual. In his 1972 "The Visual Image," he details what makes an era visual:

> We are bombarded with pictures from morning till night. Opening our newspaper at breakfast, we see photographs of men and women in the news, and raising our eyes from the paper, we encounter the picture on the cereal package. The mail arrives and one envelope after the other discloses glossy folders with pictures of alluring landscapes and sunbathing girls to entice us to take a holiday cruise, or of elegant menswear to tempt us to have a suit made to measure. Leaving our house, we pass billboards along the road that try to catch our eye and play on our desire to smoke, drink or eat. At work it is more than likely that we have to deal with some kind of pictorial information: photographs, sketches, catalogues, blueprints, maps or at least graphs. Relaxing in the evening, we sit in front of the television set, the new window on the world, and watch moving images of pleasures and horrors flit by.[1]

4.1 Against language

Gombrich's proposition, its ontological accuracy notwithstanding, was asserted in the midst of a linguistic century in which numerous disciplines considered language and cognition, rather than the visual, to be the main spheres of research of ontology, culture, and humanity. Unlike Gombrich, current proponents of the visual turn can point both to a reality that became yet more visual and to theories that began to incorporate the visual in their analyses: to screen-based big chunks of ontology and the daily practice of picture-taking, as well as new studies of the visual, material, and body. It is therefore fascinating to follow the line of thought that the visualists such as Gombrich, Arnheim, and Aldrich bravely developed—both along a linguistic century and in spite of it. It is through their early visualist theories that the current visual turn can take place. They had acknowledged the status of the visual sphere in our ontology, in our lives, and in our visual nature, opening up theories of cognition and thinking to externalist approaches.

Arnheim's systematic approach dissolves the distinction between thinking and seeing. In his 1980 "A Plea for Visual Thinking," Arnheim presents a harsh critique of the linguistic turn, since due to it "language has been designated as the place of refuge from the problems incurred in direct perceptual experience; this in spite of the fact that language, although a powerful help to our thinking, does not offer in and by itself an arena in which thinking can take place."[2] This externalist reframing, placing thought in the external visual sphere, is foundational to the visual turn. The deep commitment here is not merely to re-present the visual ontology as worthy of analysis. It is rather to characterize the visual as the foundation of thought and cognition, and the origin of the forms of both perception and mental content.

Gombrich was one of the first (1963) to extend the discussion of metaphors *to include objects and images*, endowing it with an ontological aspect. As he claimed in the 1970s, images are everywhere: "picture books, picture postcards and color slides accumulate in our homes as souvenirs of travel, as do the private mementos of our family snapshots." He, therefore, predicted that the visual would overcome the verbal, and accordingly calls for an analysis of the visual's unique capabilities. "No wonder it has been asserted that we are entering a historical epoch in which the image will take over from the written word," Gombrich argues, "in view of this claim it is all the more important to clarify the potentialities of the image in communication, to ask what it can and what it cannot do better than spoken or written language. In comparison with the importance of the question the amount of attention devoted to it is disappointingly small."[3]

Along these lines, in the mid-twentieth century the visualists embarked on a project opposed to the linguistic turn *of aesthetics* (which began later than the linguistic turn proper, given that formalist aesthetics was dominant in the first half of the twentieth century). During these decades, the twentieth-century aesthetics gathered its efforts to prove the visual sphere language-dependent, and accordingly visual artworks and metaphors as mere symbols or embodiments of internal preconceived meanings. The visualists, on the contrary, tried to prove the visual is not only independent of language, but also precedes language, intentions, and meaning, and possesses an autonomous and substantial ontological status that invites perceptual attention and visual cognition. As

Verstegen, a scholar of visualism, rightly contends, "it is characteristic of Arnheim's thinking that the notion of a symbol is completely perceptual, and he dispenses completely with any kind of logical semiotic classification."[4] That is to say, even linguistic elements of our being are based more on sensuality than referentiality. Accordingly, the various visualist accounts of visual metaphors are in opposition to those that consider these metaphors as being founded on verbal or conceptual metaphors.

In light of the visualist progress, parallel to the linguistic age, Aldrich voiced an explicit need to define nonlinguistic metaphor, and "how it occurs outside language, not only in the visual arts but also in the perception of almost anything."[5] In his essay "Visual Metaphor" from 1968, he informs us that one of his main aims in defining what he calls "seen metaphors" or "visible metaphor" is to establish their status as omnipresent external things, which are commonly experienced, and to refute "the old prejudice ... to the effect that aesthetic experience, with the metaphorical twists it gives things, is a 'subjective' affair, tainting aesthetic judgments with its subjectivity—as if the metaphorical is an inner interpretive or imaginative response to external things."[6]

In his quest for affirming the autonomous status of visual metaphors—an autonomy later disenfranchised by the linguistic turn theories, such as Noël Carroll's in his "Visual Metaphors"[7]—Aldrich makes a point to clarify that visual metaphors are not conditioned upon linguistic ones, nor are they linguistic metaphors wearing a visible dress. One of the expected ways to prove the autonomy of visual metaphors is to argue against the common proposition, that of semantic theoreticians of metaphors such as Black, that a metaphor gains its metaphorical meaning by widening the semantic extension of the source of the metaphor. Namely, "this lawyer is a shark" widens "shark" to apply to humans as well. The extension of "shark" is widened all right, but this widening is far from getting at the metaphorical mechanism. The sharkness that emerges from the metaphor adjusted to include humans presents a new, third, property and metaphorical element to accompany the source and target, even more so when the case of sharkness is a caricature presenting a lawyer as a shark. Both metaphors are compositions, enabled thanks to visuality. What is more, while the linguistic metaphor is based on the imagistic composition of the perceptual properties of the shark reconstructing the lawyer, the visual metaphor is free of language. For Aldrich, a visual metaphor is unparaphrasable in words, because it involves what he calls "metaphorical seeing." That is to say, for Aldrich the aesthetic creativity that metaphor embodies is internally linked to metaphorical creative experience, or even depends on it.

Metaphor is defined by Aldrich as seeing one thing as another, which "involves a fundamentally or irreducibly triadic relation":

1. The thing whatsoever there to be seen, one way or another (M, material).
2. What M is seen as, the subject-matter (A).
3. The "content" (B) of M seen as the subject-matter (A) bodied forth by the material (M), namely, the image of A (what M is seen as) embodied by M.

The important condition in this definition is that both M and A are transfigured in the third factor, and cannot be extracted or distinguished separately. For example, in the pebble-powermat (Figure 1), the powermat (M) is seen as pebble (A), and the metaphor is actually B—the pebble-powermat, where the pebble and powermat actually cannot be perceived separately. The image of the pebble is bodied forth by the powermat. In *Ship Building* (Figure 8), the image of the ship is bodied forth by the building, and they are fused in one another. This fusion, the content of the metaphor, is actually *the* metaphor. Aldrich calls it "a reciprocal transfiguration of M in B—an interanimation of M and A that presents prehension in the form of the 'content' B which is soul of this affair."[8]

These relations are beyond the reach of language. Obviously, since Aldrich believes that visuality is the real foundation of metaphors, this point is crucial in his account. Aldrich thereby asserts:

> what must be brought to light is the fact that figurative expression is linked with figurative perception at base, and that this is why any attempt to translate it literally and thus to refer it to nonfigurative, "observational" experience at base, must fail to preserve the "sense" of the original, though such "reduction" may serve other purposes—may even assist one finally to get the figurative sense without any equivalent, literal reformulation.[9]

Visualism grasps and addresses the deep qualities which only visuality can possess—mainly its own expressivity, which allows for creations of metaphor. According to the visualists, the visual "has both unlearned and acquired reactions," and artists and critics are often concerned with the former, and "interested in the expressive character of shapes and colours as such. There are 'loud' and 'subdued' colours and 'violent' or 'melodious' lines. Hard as it may be to test the validity of such metaphorical descriptions, there is no doubt that they could not be swapped round at will."[10] These, Gombrich claims in "Tradition and Expression in Western Still Life," invite natural "reactions to forms" combined with cultural expectations.

Contrary to Wollheim and Danto, two main initiators of the linguistic turn of aesthetics who define visual metaphors as symbols that are drawn upon linguistic metaphors, in his "Visual Metaphors and Values in Art" Gombrich marks out a clear distinction between symbol, which he names "code-sign," and metaphor. He defines symbols in art as "signs which form something like a code laid down by tradition, and in the case of allegories, in painter's manual. They become visual labels often derived from the residue of an illustrative context—Jupiter carries the thunderbolt, because he is recognizable as the thunderer."[11] Studying the *Lion of Lucerne* (*The Lion Monument*, 1820–1, by Bertel Thorvaldsen), which stands for the fallen Swiss soldiers in the French Revolution, Gombrich formulates a definite characterization of metaphor as based on visual affordance (a concept which will be analyzed in Chapter 6). He argues that "in contrast to use of these images as labels, the lion ... is not a code-sign." The image of a lion rather lends itself to various visual uses depending on the context. Gombrich names this affordance of uses "the area of metaphor." It is detailed as follows: "traditional lore about the lion as is crystallized in bestiaries and fable. It is this lore which defines what may be called the area of metaphor. Which of these qualities we decide to use, however, depends largely on our wish and whim."[12] Gombrich specifies that these could be, for example, the idea of nobility in association with the King of Beasts, ferocity, or some humoristic idea. "Each of these qualities ... can be isolated and 'transferred' to another object. Returning to Thorvaldsen therefore, we are entitled to say: this is not a code-symbol of the type 'the lion in art means courage'. Rather should we say, 'because of its alleged courage the lion lends itself to being used as a symbol (or metaphor) for heroes.'" Visual metaphors, for Gombrich, are paradigmatic in this respect. Therefore, he proceeds by asserting "a simple example of what I shall call a visual metaphor is the use of the color red in certain cultural contexts." His proposal is that red offers itself as a metaphor for anything strident or violent, due to it being the color of flames and blood. But this net of possibilities is diverse and cannot be predetermined, and even though red was selected for the stop traffic sign as a code-sign, "the color itself has no fixed meaning."[13] Language, therefore, neither establishes nor captures the affordance of the visual, especially visual metaphors.

Arnheim draws a similar depiction of the right relation between language and the visual. The visual may not be utterly indescribable by language, he claims, *but the visual is definitely in charge of its own categorizations* that are sometimes later expressed by language, rather than the other way around. "It often happens that we see and feel certain qualities in a work of art but cannot express them in words," Arnheim asserts in the introduction to his brilliant *Art and Visual*

Perception: A Psychology of the Creative Eye, "the reason for our failure is not that we use language, but that we have not yet succeeded in casting those perceived qualities into suitable categories."[14] We see, then, that the visualists refused to go along with the utmost admiration of language that characterized the linguistic turn in philosophy. Their approach explains why defining visual metaphors through verbal metaphors and artworks through text is misleading to begin with: language lacks the right tools to absorb the world and its properties. One cannot stress enough the significance of Arnheim's declaration of the preeminence of perception over language, in his 1954 book *Art and Visual Perception*, in the midst of linguistic turn and at the very moment in which aesthetics joined it by defining art as language. Arnheim's parameters are intimacy with reality, finesse, and the primacy of perceptual categorization over description or naming:

> Language cannot do the job directly because it is no direct avenue for sensory contact with reality; it serves only to name what we have seen or heard or thought. By no means is it an alien medium, unsuitable for perceptual things; on the contrary, it refers to nothing but perceptual experiences. These experiences, however, must be coded by perceptual analysis before they can be named. Fortunately, perceptual analysis is very subtle and can go far. It sharpens our vision for the task of penetrating a work of art to the limits of the ultimately impenetrable.[15]

Thus, parallel to the cognitivist-conceptualist line of thought, the contemporary ongoing development of theories of *the visual sphere and visuality* since the second half of the twentieth century has its own influence on the philosophical research of the ubiquitous cultural phenomenon of metaphors. Rorty, who coined the term "linguistic turn," and Donald Davidson explicitly went against the cognitivist theories of metaphor. Davidson refuted "the thesis that associated with a metaphor is a cognitive content that its author wishes to convey, and that the interpreter must grasp if he is to get the message," stressing that there is no such thing as metaphorical meaning beyond the literal meaning.[16] For him, metaphor belongs to the realm of pragmatics, and the result of metaphor is not an enhanced semantic charge, but a metaphorical effect. Following Davidson, Rorty classifies metaphor as an *imaginative* means of "speaking differently," which is the chief instrument of cultural transformations. For him, we ought to consider the intellectual history "of language, and thus of the arts, the sciences, and the moral sense, as the history of metaphor."[17] While not aesthetics per se, their work is sufficient to analyze the visuality of metaphors.

Even though he was a philosopher of language and mind rather than an art theorist, Davidson went so far as to close his famous essay on metaphor by speaking about the unparaphrasable nature of pictures:

> when we try to say what metaphors "means", we soon realize that there is no end to what we want to mention. If someone... mentions the beauty and deftness of a line in a Picasso etching, how many things are drawn into your attention? ... Bad question. A picture is not worth a thousand words, or any other number. Words are the wrong currency for a picture.[18]

One can see right away that the visualist critique of the linguistic turn of philosophy would also apply to the subsequent conceptualist turn, and to a much bigger extent. While the linguistic turn saw pragmatist, externalist paths (not all of them, of course; the meaning-as-intention school is internalist) and even some behaviorist theories of language, conceptualism concerned itself solely with mental content for a lengthened period, disregarding the external visual sphere. As mentioned in the previous chapter, even embodied cognition theories of metaphor considered bodily actions as nothing but an entailment of internal, abstract, superior conceptual schemes. Across from these developments, as if waiting for the visual turn, the visualist defied the attribution of primacy to the mind and internal content. Thus Gombrich claims in his famous 1963 "Meditations on the Hobby Horse or the Roots of Artistic Form" that the hobbyhorse which a kid reconstructs by applying rideability to it is not a symbol of an internal concept of a horse:

> the hobby horse does not portray our idea of a horse. The fearsome monster or funny face we may doodle on our blotting pad is not projected out of our mind as paint is "ex-pressed" out of a paint tube. Of course any image will be in some way symptomatic of its maker, but to think of it as of a photograph of a pre-existing reality is to misunderstand the whole process of image-making.[19]

Gombrich published this essay in 1963, a year before Danto's "The Artworld"[20] almost completely drove aesthetics to define art as language and later on to define the artwork as an embodiment of its maker's ideas. So we see that two counterpart aesthetic movements were progressing side by side. But while Danto, Wollheim, and other aestheticians deemed the mind to be independent and primary to the visual, and thereby missed the thorough impact the visual has on us before the mind could even process it, Gombrich and Arnheim saw the status of visuality all along. Their theories of wide cognition preceded the current theories of embodied cognition, of Lakoff and Johnson for example, which realize that much of our cognition does not dwell in the mind and is much more external than they assumed it to be when they formulated the conceptualist theory of metaphor. It is Arnheim in his *Visual Thinking* who defined "visual categories" or "visual concepts" as a perceptual fit of the stimulus material with simple shapes: "The full moon is indeed round to the best of our viewing powers. But most of the things we see as round do not embody roundness literally; they are mere approximations. Nevertheless the perceiver does not only compare them with roundness but does indeed see roundness in them."[21] According to Arnheim, perception provides the infrastructure of concept formation, rather than the other way around. The categories to which percepts fit are visual and structural. They are really seen.

The gap between the linguistic or conceptualist and the visualist lines of thought is surely also manifested in theories of metaphors. While semanticist and conceptualist-cognitivists theoretically denote two distinct parts of metaphor, the visualist emphasizes that metaphor is an emerging unified whole, possessing emergent properties, the original elements of which are less significant for its creation and perception. The following point will be elaborated in Chapter 5, but ought to be mentioned here as well given that it is one of the main qualities of early visualism, and shows how visual metaphors are paradigmatic. In visual metaphor we can only speculatively point to its (formerly distinct) elements. In reality, these elements are fused to one entity. We may see that the recently designed *White Tree* building in Montpellier is both a tree and a building, but these properties cannot be discerned separately (Figure 14). This is also why the linguistic or conceptual metaphor does not merely consist of two parts working in tandem with one another, but rather consists in the imagistic-aesthetic character of the concepts or the words amalgamated into a composition.

Some support to this view of linguistic metaphor could be found in the Paul Hopper's theory of emergent grammar. In his instructive 2012 essay carrying the same title, Hopper opposes attempts to catalog a complete, all-inclusive, inventory of rules and forms in a single language, describing this as a futile task. While not saying it in so many words, Hopper characterizes language as a *qualitative medium*. Language is very rarely liberated from the context of situations, possessing only "very limited provisional cognitive stability" or "fixed grammar." According to Hopper's portrayal, language is composed of particular parts and uses. What he labels as "real language" is "distributed over space and over occasions of use."[22] Language has very few forms shared by all linguistic events. It instead produces emergent uses varying by styles, genres, places, situations, and groups of speakers.

Figure 14 Nicolas Laisné and Manal Rachdi, *The White Tree*, Montpellier, 2019. © Alamy Image ID: 2G12M1A.

Famously claiming that "visual perception is visual thinking," Arnheim attributes the emergent amalgamation to the mutual effect visual properties may have on each other while perceived in composition. He sometimes names this effect "blending"—a term to be used later by the conceptualists as well. This idea has its roots in the Gestalt theories that Arnheim endorsed. To blending he adds the concepts of "ception" and "scanning" that refer to the internal link between perception and conception. In a chapter in *Visual Thinking* named "Thinking With Pure Shapes," where he analyses thinking with relatively abstract perceptual imagery, Arnheim claims that even scientific or philosophical theories cannot be detached from perceptual imagery, and even abstract images or pure shapes have "properties of their own, not necessarily applicable to the facts to which the concepts are applied." They consequently often "neglect aspects or quantitative or spatial relations considered vital under certain cultural conditions."[23] For example, deciding how many people can accommodate a certain space cannot rely on purely numerical relations; working hours from eight in the morning to two in the afternoon cannot be equated with working from two in the afternoon to eight in the morning. It is true in practical situations and all the more in artistic compositions. In those, too, numbers are not arbitrary.

> A sonata consisting of three movements or a temple front with seven columns has a centerpiece, which an even number of components does not provide ... The 5-7-5 syllable form of the Japanese haiku poems makes the second line the center of a vertical symmetry and also produces an open, more dynamic sound structure than lines with even numbers of syllables would.[24]

In the frame of this analysis, he argues that by scanning a painting an observer perceives its various elements, shapes, colors, their interrelations, and their mutual effects. The total image that the observer receives stems from the perceptual influence the elements exert on one another and their interactions. It is obvious that metaphors work exactly like that. The blend of the treeness of the *White Tree* (Figure 14) with the structure of porches as abstract branches and foliage is the nucleus of this metaphor. "Tree" is not a rare source in metaphors, given the reconstruction of various targets anew. But it appears so differently in each of them! René Descartes's philosophy tree, the tree of knowledge "of which the roots are Metaphysics, the trunk is Physics, and the branches, emerging from this trunk are all the other branches of knowledge," which is presented in the preface to the French edition of *Principles of Philosophy*, is given in a different blend to that of the *White Tree*.[25] Its affordance allows specific properties (a hierarchical structure of growing) to merge with knowledge, which emerges differently than in the *White Tree* (having an impressive height and width). Acknowledging the potency of the (external) medium in composition suffices to prove both that neither the pre-ontological (internal) concept nor pure semantic verbality can even serve as origins for metaphor, let alone cover the real part of metaphor. The emerging blend can be fully captured only visually.

One of the largest projects about visuality is of course Mitchell's *Iconology*. A central aim of Mitchell, like Goodman, is to dissolve the accepted distinction between visual and verbal languages. Images, Mitchell claims, are to be found in language parallel to visual media.

> Texts and speech-acts are, after all, not simply affairs of "consciousness," but are public expressions that belong right out there with all the other kinds of material representations we create—pictures, statues, graphs, maps, etc. We don't have to say that a descriptive paragraph is exactly like a picture to see that they do have similar functions as public symbols that project states of affairs about which we can reach rough, provisional agreements.[26]

His utmost respect for visuality notwithstanding, Mitchell, like Goodman and Danto, is captured by the privileged status attributed to language by the West. He therefore tries to elevate the picture to the level of text. Then again, the very theoretical juxtaposition of the visual media with linguistic media is promising, given that the dissolution of the distinction between picture and text goes both ways. *Thus, we may begin to think about imagistic verbality and about visual verbality.* This goes beyond the Wittgensteinian proposal that propositions depict, and are pictures of, states of affairs based on isomorphism and structural homology. What renders verbal expression figurative is a compositional character, some architecture, which emerges from the visual charge of the words, together with their load, that are arranged in a specific way. "Figurative language, on the other hand, is what we ordinarily mean when we talk about verbal imagery. The phrase, 'verbal imagery', in other words, seems to be a metaphor for metaphor itself!"[27] I do not mean here that the imagistic and visual character of verbal metaphors emerges from the visual association, but that the words, loaded with their content, reference, etc., and their interrelations combine to form a composition. There we find the metaphor. Our ability to absorb these compositions emanates from our experience of visual compositions.

As aforesaid in Chapter 3.3, cognitivism gradually reached some visualist ideas toward the end of the twentieth century. The concept of "blending" was broadly analyzed by Fauconnier and Turner in a number of essays. They understand that the two-domain model of metaphor is too parsimonious, neglects various aspects of metaphors, and is merely a part of a wider model of conceptual projection, which they named the "many-space" model. The very aspects of metaphors that were ignored by the conceptualist-cognitivists gained a thorough analysis and definition by the visualists from the 1960s and on. But at the turn of the twenty-first century Fauconnier and Turner presented their model as new. They claimed that their model revealed "previously unrecognized aspects of even the most familiar basic metaphors." Furthermore, "structure from two or more input mental spaces is projected onto a separate 'blended' space, which inherits partial structure from the inputs, and has emergent structure of its own."[28] The original parts of the metaphor emerge in a new concept, losing their separate meanings within the new imaginary space. The intended structure, they say, can emerge only within the metaphorical blend. In their 2002 book *The Way We Think*, they note that their theory of conceptual blending is revealed thanks to the fact that "we live in the age of the triumph of form. In mathematics, physics, music, the arts, and the social sciences, human knowledge and its progress seem to have been reduced in startling and powerful ways to a matter of essential formal structures and their transformations."[29] Just like the visualists before them, who pointed to the dynamic character of the composition, and explained and exemplified it thoroughly in many a text, Fauconnier and Turner acknowledge the power of composition. They present very similar propositions about composition to the ones Arnheim and Gombrich formulated, as well as Goodman and Beardsley later on and recently also Indurkhya: "the blend develops emergent structure that is not in the inputs. First, *composition* of elements from the inputs makes relations available in the blend that do not exist in the separate inputs."[30]

Establishing that the emergent fusion of the metaphorical elements is the third, but most essential, part of metaphor naturally leads us to grasp that the metaphorical mechanism is first and foremost visual. It is only in visuality, or in the sensuous plane, that these compositional blends can and do happen. They definitely do not happen in the conceptual realm, which allows the elements to be fused at a second stage. Quite the opposite! This is very clear in visual metaphors. *Ship Building* (Figure 8) does not separately consist of a ship and a building, its shipness is not distinct from its being a building. The emergent metaphorical property, which Indurkhya and Beardsley define well, the unpredictable "metaphorical twist" is the constitutive part of the metaphor. It is not that we conceptualize "ship" and then "building," fuse them conceptually in our mind, and the see the building's shipness. Right away we see them together as one. The same goes with the one we argue with and the metaphor of Argument

Is War. How could an argument be war? Because in an argument our opponent is really a rival to win over. We want to *win* the argument. One sometimes wins the argument, or in losing it experiences a real defeat. We experience the composition of argument externally—we speak, we are stopped by our opponent, we stop them abruptly, we refute them and are being refuted... Then we may enlarge our conceptual system by thinking about argument as war. But the conceptual system does not produce these fusions. They are created under the realm of compositions.

Consequently, the scholars who inaugurated the visualist school of metaphor found the Gestalt model of perception very useful.[31] In *Art and Visual Perception*, Arnheim notes that Gestalt is natural for the creative disciplines. While the artist has always been aware of the fact that "a whole cannot be attained by the accretion of isolated parts," the scientist often needs to be reminded that "most natural phenomena are not described adequately if they are analyzed piece by piece."[32] Accordingly, metaphors are based on grasping integrated structures as wholes, as much as reasoning involves "grasping of significant structural patterns." Like Gombrich in his *Meditations on the Hobby Horse*,[33] Arnheim claims that perceptual and cognitive development progresses from the general to the particular—but the general is a matter of form, of composition, rather of conceptual-mental content: "Eyesight is insight," he claims, and "overall structural features are the primary data of perception."[34] This relation, between the eyesight as insight and the structural features as the data to be perceived by the eye, is addressed in the following subchapter.

4.2 The load of the eye, the power of the object

Arnheim, Gombrich, and their follower Nelson Goodman went against the model of the innocent eye in favor of active perception and projection, which are interconnected to the properties the thing lends itself to acquire. Gombrich claims that metaphor is a projection of a required functionality onto a thing, which transfigures it into another thing (be it a stain of color transfigured to a horse image, a stick transfigured to be a hobbyhorse, a snowman, or an artistic sculptor). The projection is related to the schema that load the eye and mind, which sometimes originate in an external, intrasensory, primordial, material, and perceptual sphere. Gombrich contends that "it adds to the interest of these categories that they are so often intrasensory: the smile belongs to the category of warm, bright, sweet experiences; the frown is cold, dark, and bitter in this primeval world where all things host."³⁵ In his review of Gombrich's theory of representation in *Art and Illusion,* Arnheim notes that this primary load of the seeing eye is influenced by culture, and accordingly the source of representation is external—namely in education, conventions, habits, or history. Mental sets are also created by an epoch:

> Gombrich is not mainly interested in the goal of pictorial representation but rather in the ways it is accomplished. In his opinion, representation becomes acceptable when it fits the schemata of realization to which the perceiver is accustomed. The artist paints what the reservoirs of his experience offer him as the proper form for his subject. These reservoirs contain the schemata supplied by the artist's teachers and by other models of the past. Beyond that, they equip him with the expectations necessary to see anything at all: We see what we assume is "out there."³⁶

Indeed, in *Art and Illusion* Gombrich harshly criticized Ruskin's campaign for the mimetic model of art. Ruskin fully supported J. M. W. Turner's "truth to nature" ideology and endorsement of the then-contemporary empiricist science, which he manifested in romanticist-impressionist painting. As we are told in another review of Gombrich's *The Image and the Eye,*

> Ruskin's theory of the "innocent eye" dictated that a picture best copies nature when the artist attends only to what he sees, not to what he knows about the scene he depicts. Painting in an almost literal sense mirrors reality, when the artist produces a canvas whose reflected light rays correspond at every point to the light rays one would see reflected from the actual scene. Gombrich's *Art and Illusion* played a central role in exposing the fallacies inherent in the notion of the "innocent eye" and the empiricist reduction of perception to sensation which underlies it.³⁷

We should mention here that, his support of the innocent eye model and the privileged status he attributed to fact-dependent depiction notwithstanding, Ruskin's mimetic theory classified visual mimesis as partially conceptual and even as narrative. Truthful thought is one of the conditions of mimesis, and pictures are composed of thoughts and tell the stories of the depicted objects, on the word of Ruskin. Realistic work—the iconic imitation of reality—is based on a conceptual comprehension of reality. In other words, it is based on ideas. Furthermore, beyond a mere imitation of the symbolized, Ruskin thickens the characterization of artistic mimesis by ascribing a dimension of literality to good mimetic work—even of still life. According to Ruskin, the more historical truths are, i.e., the more truths tell us "about the past and future state of the object to which they belong," the more valuable they are. Consider how narrativity might be embodied in landscape painting: in a depiction of a tree,

> it is more important to give the appearance of energy and elasticity in the limbs, which is indicative of growth and life, than any particular character of leaf, or texture of bough. It is more important that we should feel that the uppermost sprays are creeping higher and higher into the sky, and be impressed with the current of life and motion which is animating every fiber, than that we should know the exact pitch of relief with which those fibers are thrown out against the sky.[38]

Along these lines, the literal dimensions of the painting and narration are endowed with the status of being the main artistic referents of the work, beyond the immediate-direct objects that are represented. According to this characterization of mimesis a painting, even of still life, is supposed to tell a story. Ruskin is therefore not more of a visualist than Gombrich, coining the term "talkative facts," and claiming that "the first truths tell us tales about the tree, about what it has been, and will be, while the last are characteristic of it only in its present state, and are in no way talkative about themselves. Talkative facts are always more interesting and more important than silent ones."[39]

In *The Image and The Eye* Gombrich softens his critique of Ruskin, due to the progress of the twentieth century in cognitive science. As stated in a review of the book, "trust in the deliverances of science has been restored, and the results of its experiments surely now have put scientific art criticism on a firm foundation."[40] Still, significantly, the schema which Gombrich ascribes to the eyes either of the creator or the viewer, which do the making and matching or perceiving the medium, *are acquired from the external*. Arnheim concisely puts it in his effusive review of Gombrich's *Art and Illusion*: true "expectation creates illusion and knowledge gaps. Incomplete shapes are supplemented by the holder's 'projections,' which presuppose a mental set and a sufficiently empty screen";[41] the origin of these projections is external. While attributing an epistemological significance to the cognitive-conceptual mental elements in grasping the world or gaining familiarity with categories and objects, Gombrich ought to be considered to hold an externalist view, albeit one more moderate than Arnheim's. Gombrich promotes a theory of expression based on social-cultural forms to replace the self-centered one. Gombrich names these forms cultural lore and the area of metaphor. Thus, Arnheim points out that in line with Gombrich, "mental sets created by an epoch make the works of a particular style understandable to its public ... A work of art 'comes to life', not by its actual faithfulness, but meeting the needs and expectations of the period." This is the very motivation of art—an ontological motivation to add a real thing to reality—as Arnheim tells us, "the artist is rarely concerned with making things look real. He wants them to come alive."[42]

A formalist proposition about the load of the eye and perception is expressed by Arnheim in 2001 in an educational interview titled "The Intelligence of Vision"—a reference to the "Intelligence of Visual Perception" chapter in his *Visual Thinking*. The status of form in our understanding of the world is formulated as follows: "we have to realize that perception organizes the forms that it receives as optical projections in the eye. Without form, an image cannot carry a visual message into consciousness. Thus it is the organized forms that deliver the visual concept that makes an image legible, not conventionally established signs." Like Gombrich and Goodman, Arnheim holds that our perception is constructive—shaping the form of the perceived world. "Vision and perception," he says in the interview, "are not processes that passively register or reproduce what happens in reality. Vision and perception are active, creative understanding."[43]

What is more, and this is significant to our understanding of metaphors, Arnheim's theory of active perception is sheerly externalist and empiricist. For him, the forms with which reality is shaped derive from our sensuous realm, saturated with their interactions with reality:

> you have to imagine the following: When we observe something, then we reach for it; we move through space, touch things, feel their surfaces and contours. And our perception structures and orders the information given by things into determinable forms. We understand because this structuring and ordering is a part of our relationship with reality. Without order we couldn't understand at all. Thus in my opinion the world is not raw material; it is already ordered merely by being observed.[44]

4.2.1 Use of visual knowledge

Parallel to stressing the interrelations between the creative load carried by the perceiving eye and the external forms that shape reality, Arnheim stresses *the constructive force of the perceived things—the objects themselves*. This force is possessed thanks to the emergent qualities of compositions that arrange their elements in an intra-influential order—all parts of a whole which is bigger than their sum. In his 1974 revised version of the canonical 1954 *Art and Visual Perception: A Psychology of the Creative Eye*, Arnheim names this force the "dynamic character of precepts," shifting the focus from the mind to ontological structures and to visual categories, and showing structural relations and formal and principal mechanisms at work. The perceived thing, argues Arnheim,

> is not only an arrangement of objects, of colors and shapes, of movements and sizes. It is, perhaps first of all, an interplay of directed tensions. These tensions are not something the observer adds, for reasons of his own, to static images. *Rather, these tensions are as inherent in any percept as size, shape, location, or color.* Because they have magnitude and direction, these tensions can be described as psychological forces.[45] (my italics)

Arnheim's idea about forces is that the dynamic character and import of forms— artworks and metaphors are paradigmatic here—emanate from tension and contrast and their respective experiences.

The structure of the perceived object or phenomenon is an "induced structure" as named by Arnheim, the product of dynamics in the field of vision beyond the simple characters that meet the retina in the eye. In visual metaphor, I would like to add, emergent properties are among the induced structures. Here is one of Arnheim's examples of this force:

> [an] incompletely drawn circle looks like a complete circle with a gap. In a picture done in central perspective the vanishing point may be established by the convergent lines even though no actual point of meeting can be seen. In a melody one may "hear" by induction the regular beat from which a syncopated tone deviates, as our disk deviates from the center.[46]

Arnheim emphasizes the distinction between logical inferences and perceptual inductions. Inferences, in this case, are thought operations that interpret visual fact. "Perceptual inductions are sometimes interpolations based on previously acquired knowledge. More typically, however, they are completions deriving spontaneously during perception from the given configuration of the pattern."[47] One may claim that metaphors are easily recognized thanks to perceptual inductions. Given that only a few of the properties of the source are transferred to the target, the ability to induce the target of metaphor thanks to former perceptual knowledge is foundational in metaphors. The resultant completion is actually the emerging properties and reconstruction of the target, namely, the third part of metaphor. Where the upper part of *Muffin Pouffe* (Figure 5) is the seatable head of a muffin, the muffin shape induces a specific seatable structure and this seatability induces structural properties of size, texture, and softness which are infused with the head of the muffin. Though different elements of being a tree are not transferred to the *White Tree* (Figure 14), the building is constructed as a tree, and the porches are completed as branches thanks to the emergent properties of tree-building that can only exist in this metaphor. The very same perceptual mechanism operates in conceptual and verbal metaphors. Building a solid theory, or alternatively collapsing one, results from a perceptual induction that fills the gap between theories and buildings.

A current supporter of theories of active perception is Yuriko Saito, who names the perceiver the "active agent" within the framework of her everyday aesthetics project. Saito explicitly stresses that "even as a 'spectator' or 'receiver,' we are never a sitting duck, so to speak, but rather an active agent of creative engagement with what we are perceiving. In short, we are never passive and inactive when it comes to aesthetic experience."[48] Saito aspires to prove that engagement with both familiar and the unfamiliar art is a form of activity. At the end of the day, she claims, this activity has a lot to do with the practices of the good life, given that "there is no separation between and among the aesthetic (via artistic activities), the moral, the spiritual, and the practical." She continues:

> Even within a typical 'spectator's' experience, some writers in the Western aesthetic discourse have pointed out that it is never a passive, receptive experience and that it involves the 'spectator' in actively creating the aesthetic experience. Dewey, for example, points out that the aesthetic should not be interpreted solely as characterizing the receiving end of perception. A common assumption, according to Dewey, is that the perceiver or appreciator "merely takes in what is there in finished form." However, he stresses that "perception is an act of the going-out of energy in order to receive, not a withholding of energy. To steep ourselves in a subject-matter we have first to plunge into it." The role of a perceiver thus includes that of a creator because "to perceive, a beholder must create his own experience. And his creation must include relations comparable to those which the original producer underwent." Thus, for him, in aesthetically experiencing something, "doing" and "making" are inseparable from "undergoing" and "receiving."[49]

The visualist movement of metaphor led the opposition to the model of the innocent eye, as that model related to active perception, to induced structures, to emergent properties, and to expressivity as well. Expression is loaded with the history of perception, and it is actively perceived accordingly. Expressivity also gains its character from a choice made from various possible alternatives of composition. Arnheim notes this when he describes Gombrich's theory: "the expression of shapes and colors is not absolute. It can only be when the range of alternatives is known … cast into historically determined categories and modified further by the artist."[50] Danto, a historicist himself, is impressed by Gombrich's meta-level version of art history, namely his theory of art history itself, specifically a theory of how art has a history. In a 1983 retrospective essay on Gombrich, Danto argues that this question drove Gombrich "to seek for answers in perceptual psychology and in postpositivistic epistemology."[51] Danto refers here to Gombrich's renouncement of the innocent eye model, a renouncement that defies the naïve realism of the given in favor of active and constructive perception. It is interesting to see that historicity is one of the mechanisms that produces metaphors. Active perception is a mechanism of progress, and metaphor is one of its main tools. Danto emphasizes that Gombrich relates the motivation for the history of art to his history of perception, "which explains why it is important to face the fact that in this respect the history of figurative art differs radically from that of decorative design." He therefore quotes Gombrich sharing his motivation:

> in *Art and Illusion* I have tried to show "why art has a history". I gave psychological reasons for the fact that the rendering of nature cannot be achieved by any untutored individual, however gifted, without the support of a tradition. I found the reasons in the psychology of perception, which explains why we cannot simply "transcribe" what we see and have to resort to methods of trial and error in the slow process of "making and matching", "schema and correction".[52]

An analogous description of the history of art is proposed by Arnheim, who points to *visual intelligence* as the source of perceptual memory and visual or perceptual inference. Arnheim indeed gestures at the internal parts of percepts, such as the typewriter residing under its cover, as a means to show our dependence on visual knowledge:

> Much of what is known about the hidden inside of things presents itself as a bona fide aspect of their outside appearance. I see the typewriter cover as containing my typewriter; I see the Peruvian pot on the shelf as empty. *This knowledge is entirely visual. Visual acquisitions of the past are lodged in the appropriate places of the present perceptual field, completing it most usefully.* The typewriter is not only known to be under the cover but seen as being there— seen, in fact, in the appropriate position defined by the spatial orientation of the cover.... The intelligence of these perceptual complements becomes particularly evident when one remembers that not everything an observer knows automatically becomes a part of his visual field.[53] (my italics)

This assertion, supported by numerous experiments and daily experience, explains the visual essence of metaphors. All kinds of metaphors exploit visual intelligence and acquired visual knowledge as part of their structure. For instance, examining "theories are buildings" (a frequently invoked example of a conceptual metaphor) we see that our acquired visual knowledge of the structure of buildings in different conditions allows us to reconstruct theories as buildings. We do not have to see the foundations of a solid theory at the very moment we encounter this metaphor. We use our visual knowledge of the foundations of buildings, and of what makes a building solid, and apply it by means of visual completion and induced structure. The same goes with using our visual knowledge of a collapsing building for a collapsing theory and completing its structure. Arnheim explains it well:

> given the visual nature of such knowledge, there is no break between what is known and what is seen. The inside fits snugly into the outside. This continuity extends perception beyond what is depicted on the retina. The mind is not held back by the surfaces of things. They are seen either as containers, or their inside appears simply as a homogeneous continuation of the outside.[54]

Arnheim adds that visual knowledge is also responsible for the perception of absent parts of different objects or phenomena. The "absence of something functions as an active component of a percept," he claims, quoting Alberto Giacometti's report that he sees the emptiness caused by the absence of a formerly removed object.[55] Emptiness, gaps, just like the invisible content of an object, may all be charged with no longer existing properties, or alternatively one may place into the larger object a missing element whose absence endows negative properties. Goodman's description of metaphor in this context is appropriate. He notes that metaphor always involves a conflict, since the metaphorical application is "contra-indicated"; "a picture is sad rather than gay even though it is insentient and hence neither sad nor gay." Accordingly, Goodman typifies metaphor as "an affair between a predicate with a past and an object that yields while protesting ... Metaphorical application of a label to an object defies an explicit or tacit prior denial of that label to that object."[56]

Arnheim's examples for the properties emerging from the absence of a property, a contra-indication, are: a setting which looks motionless after a lively action that took place in it ended; a wine bottle next to a fireplace, looking forlorn in a room that seems quieter after a guest did not show up. My examples of this phenomenon are redesigned objects or buildings whose original functions were removed in favor of new ones. The Musée d'Orsay in Paris is saturated with the absence of its former function as a railway station; the Tate Modern museum in London is charged with the absence of its former function as a power station.

Applying a new function (which is more than an accidental use) to an object is also common in daily life—in which a glass is transformed into a flower vase and a car tire into a swing. These examples share the trait of metaphors of transferring only a few of the properties of the source, merging them with only some of the properties of the target, or having emergent properties as a result. Mainly, they share with metaphors the dialectic structure of the power of the traits that are accepted by the target, but not completely, adjoined with the hinted absent properties which did not manage to go through and take part in the reconstruction of the target. This is why the metaphorical, newly constructed, thing joins a new group, but as a peripheral member. To these absent properties, reverberating through negation, belong: the stone material that is not a property of the pebble-powermat; anything edible that is not present in the hot dog sofa or the muffin stool; the sand or asphalt not present in a path of life; the ability of a tree to grow or decay that does not take place in the building of the *White Tree*; the ability to sail that does not transfer to the *Ship Building*. This is part of the magic of composition, and part of what allocates metaphor within the aesthetic sphere, along with its aesthetic effect of conviction—that which makes metaphors ontologically influential. This reality effect of metaphors will be discussed next.

4.3 Metaphor and the realist effect

The reality effect of metaphors, referring not only to their convincing power but also to their becoming pieces of our ontology, is internally linked to metaphor's aesthetic import and its visuality. This issue was addressed in Chapter 1, yet it ought to be readdressed as part of the inauguration of the visualist movement of metaphor, which is reemerging now thanks to the general visual turn. The first visualist argued that the visual is better suited to the realist effect than the verbal or conceptual, and it is visuality which is in charge of metaphorical success. Gombrich, as mentioned earlier, names this success, which he sees as ontological, "Pygmalion power." As Gombrich indicates, "try to say the sentence to a child and then show him the pictures and your respect for the image will soon be restored. The sentence will leave the child unmoved; the image may delight him almost as much as the real."[57] The force of visuality explains the primacy of visual metaphors. Even Danto, though he would be rightly labeled a linguistic aesthetician, supports Gombrich's approach here, claiming in his review of Gombrich's oeuvre that he "is correct in saying that it is a matter of perceptual psychology to explain why certain schemata of pictorial representation are optically convincing."[58]

This applies to linguistic and conceptual metaphors as well, and Gombrich claims that they are founded on imagery, given that "language carries old and new figures of speech that are rightly described as images: 'The sands are running out,' 'The pump must be primed,' 'Wages should be pegged,' 'The dollar should be allowed to float.' The literal illustration of these metaphors offers untold possibilities for that special branch of symbolic imagery, the art of the cartoonist."[59] The visuality of cartoons as acquired perceptually, for example, serves as the infrastructure of the above-mentioned metaphors as well as an explanation for their success.

Gombrich draws a distinction between a realist copying of the external object and allowing an image to come alive as a result of fit between the mode of representation and the visual load the viewers are adapted to. Goodman later called this coming alive the "realist effect," arguing after Gombrich that what is considered a realist depiction is not really based on similarity. Such a "realist" depiction actually produces the reality effect, caused by a high level of readability or conviction, which in turn stems from the depiction's fit with the conventional systems of representation.

Goodman's exposition of Gombrich's theory of representation-as-creation in his review of *Art and Illusion* is instructive and worth reading. Goodman focuses on the innovative explanation that Gombrich proposes for the mechanism underlying the accumulation of visual vocabulary and schema, which Arnheim names "visual knowledge": "Our whole edifice of visual schemata and representational vocabulary functions much like a scientific theory, put to the test by the experiment of picture-making. In comparing our pictures with what they represent, we discover inadequacies." Being a functionalist himself, Goodman is sensitive to the significance that Gombrich attributes to practice in epistemology and ontology. While the Popperian influence is explicit, the empiricist element is not often mentioned. Goodman therefore proceeds:

> This may lead us to revise not only our way of painting but also our way of seeing: not only our representational vocabulary but also our visual schema. We learn to see by looking and to represent by painting; but we also learn to represent by looking and to see by painting. By repeated experimentation and consequent modification of our perception and of our methods of conveying what we perceive, we gradually achieve more and more effective representations.[60]

I would like to claim that the idea of realistic effect of visuality over other media is a main corollary of the emergent properties of metaphor, which are the most apparent in the visual kind of metaphors. Realistic effect stems from rightness of form—from the working arrangement. Rightness of compositions and forms is aesthetic in kind. Otherwise, one cannot explain why certain compositions succeed and join a new group and our ontology, but others do not. Metaphor is internally linked to the practice of making a thing come alive rather than just look like another thing. It is a constructive thing that has a bearing on reality, from shaking up categories to rebuilding things. In simpler words, a realistic effect is created when the transferred property sticks to the target and emerges as possessed by it. Having a path sticks to life and reconstructs it as a real journey, albeit one that is peripheral in the group of journeys. The ability to reach a road with no exit, a dead-end, sticks to relationships, reconstructing them as excursions or journeys as well. Temporary metaphors, in which we see faces everywhere, belong to this realistically effective group, and possess what Gombrich titles "Pygmalion power" in his *Art and Illusion*. It has real ontological import.

In yet another review of Gombrich's *Art and Illusion*, this time by Arnheim, he criticizes Gombrich's choice of "illusion" as his central concept, since illusion does not fully capture the difference between images and reality, nor does it capture the difference between liveliness and existence. According to Arnheim, "nowhere in the arts, except for the few episodes of extreme illusionism, can 'to be alive' have meant to be like living beings; because the difference between nature and simulacrum must have always been obvious. Works of art not only are equivalences—to use Gombrich's term—they also have always been seen as such."[61] Apparently Arnheim overlooked the fact that Gombrich's analysis of Pygmalion power was close to his own notion of the dynamic force of the visual. However, it might be true that Gombrich's ontology was more pluralist than Arnheim's. The difference is that Gombrich attributes Pygmalion-like ontological abilities to the visual: abilities to create new things and enlarge categories. On the other hand, Arnheim considers the visual to be ontologically substantial to begin with. Arnheim therefore proceeds by stressing: " 'To be alive' meant to display the perceptual quality of liveliness. Since this quality can be found in animate or inanimate objects, in physical objects as well as in their images, the artistic distinction between lifeless and alive is strictly perceptual, not epistemological."[62] Arnheim, one may claim, is more of a visualist than Gombrich, and disagrees with Gombrich's proposal that "all art is conceptual in that it relies on traditional schemata rather than on mere perception." Gombrich actually refers to what

Arnheim classifies as "visual concepts," and for him the mental is dependent on the external. But for Arnheim, this model is not inclusive—after all the Egyptian may draw what she knows, but the Greek draws what is seen.[63]

Still, both Arnheim and Gombrich are (moderate) realists in the sense that for them the external is partially autonomous, not wholly dependent on internal contents, and has a power and affordance of its own. Moreover, the active part of our perception is built up by accumulating visual knowledge and experience of the external. As Arnheim puts it, with regard to Gombrich, "a work of art will 'come to life', not by its actual faithfulness, but by meeting the needs and expectation of the period."[64] Even Goodman, the antirealist (but still externalist, given that his theory of symbols relies on the conventions and rightness of rendering), partially agrees with the assertion that the external sets some limits on representations, and definitely on relativism. He accordingly agrees with the limits Gombrich set for representation and for likeness, as stated here:

> Though vision is relative to imposed schemata, and representation further relative to conventions employed, Gombrich nevertheless holds that there are objective standards of representation. Relativism can be overdone, he says; and he speaks repeatedly of testing, correction, adjustment, and even progress in representation—all implying some objectivity. We must recognize that things may be seen in various ways and depicted in terms of different vocabularies; but we must not be forced to conclude that a child's drawing is as accurate a representation of Wivenhoe Park as is Constable's painting, or that the painting is quite as much a representation of a pink elephant as of the Park.[65]

We see, then, that while Gombrich is a moderate realist and Goodman is an avowed antirealist, their ways cross at externalism, constructivism, and the idea of realistic effect as resulting from a fit to a system. This leads to a deep correspondence between their theories of metaphors. Goodman's proposition in his acknowledged "Seven Strictures on Similarity" from 1972—that metaphors are not dependent on similarity, but create similarities—explains the livelihood of metaphors. Goodman argues that "saying that certain sounds are soft is sometimes interpreted as saying in effect that these sounds are like soft materials. Metaphor is thus construed as elliptical simile, and metaphorical truths as elliptical literal truths. But to proclaim that certain tones are soft because they are like soft materials, or blue because they are like blue colors, explains nothing."[66] To present similarity as a vacuous base of metaphors and to offer a constructivist alternative Goodman trusts the logic of similarity, according to which any two things are similar in countless ways. Therefore, for him (and the other visualists), metaphor creates similarities and "the fact that a term applies, literally or metaphorically, to certain objects may itself constitute rather than arise from a particular similarity among those objects. Metaphorical use may serve to explain the similarity better than—or at least as well as—the similarity explains the metaphor."[67] Constitution of similarities is yet one more formulation of metaphor's constructivist essence, ontological import, emerging properties, Pygmalion power, or realist effect. In each case, the upshot is that metaphors belong to the ontological sphere. So, let us proceed to the chapter that addresses metaphor and ontology.

5

Metaphors and Ontology

In the following paragraph, Gombrich presents an illustrative example of metaphors in music, explaining how a piece of music may acquire the metaphorical property of being noble:

> The phenomenon here characterized in such pleasantly untechnical language would probably be called "ego control" by the psycho-analyst. It is a quality that is particularly well exemplified in the art of the musical performer with its temptations and the possibility of rational checks. When we are told, for instance, that Toscanini "never overpaints a phrase" we understand that he never yields to the allurement of a moment, as minor performers do, that he renounces the "cheap effects" that may provide immediate gratification but disrupt the architecture of the whole, and that the gain from this austerity in the presence of intense emotion is the "divine simplicity" that becomes a musical metaphor of highest values.[1]

The restraint in music described above (ego control, avoiding the effects of immediate gratification) endows it with its own nobility (which is applicable only to music). It is an emergent property, perceived through what Gombrich refers to as "metaphorical experience." These emergent properties, which we will refer to as the metaphorical properties, are the third and central part of metaphor. This third part is created by the fusion of the properties of the source and target belonging only to the whole composition: in the case of *Muffin Pouffe* (figure 5), the special kind of muffinness which can be possessed only by the pouffe; in the case of *Sweetheart Nutcracker* (figure 12), the property of being a crocodile possessed only by the nutcracker; in Relationship Is Journey, a path which can only be toured in relationships; in the case of the *White Tree* (figure 14), the treeness that can only be applied to the building; a different sort of treeness that can be possessed only by knowledge as conceived in Descartes's metaphor. They are the properties that add the metaphorical thing to its new group: the muffin pouffe to the group of muffins, *Sweetheart Nutcracker* to the group of crocodiles, relationships to the group of journeys, or knowledge to the group of trees in the case of Descartes's metaphor. Thereby, they are responsible for the ontological import, constructions, and ultimately the success, of metaphor. Metaphorical success, for example in the nobility of music resulting from a structure of overall control of the passionate elements of expectation and arrest, is adjoined by the "intuition that great art is sincere," according to Gombrich in his essay "Visual Metaphors." "Great art has given to many the feeling that they are in the presence of 'truth.'"[2] Since the ontological argument about the emerging third, essential, part of the metaphor is one of the most significant to the visualist theory of metaphor, and to my definition, we will address it further.

5.1 The third part of metaphor: emergent properties

The emergent metaphorical properties are described by Arnheim as the product of formal relations that serve as context to different elements. The very apposition of two not naturally, but potentially, related things may lead to this emergence in the different media, he claims: "the pairing of two images throws into relief a common quality and thereby accomplishes a perceptual abstraction without relinquishing the contexts from which the singled-out quality draws its life."[3] The pairing of images of the sea and the turning of pages in a poetic phrase from *To the Reader* by Denise Levertov is the example Arnheim presents for the mechanism that generates the metaphoric property: "and as you read / the sea is turning its dark pages, / turning / its dark pages."[4]

As analyzed by Arnheim, the sea and the page-turning converge in a rhythmic movement, even though they do not initially seem fit to be fused together. But this apparent clash of figures creates the aesthetic element of metaphor: "the motion of waves and the turning of pages cannot be fitted in a unitary perceptual situation. Confrontation, however, presses for relation, and under this pressure the common element, the rhythmic turning, comes to the fore in its purity, conveying a sense of elementary nature to the pages of the book and of readability to the waves of the ocean."[5] Arnheim shows here that a linguistic metaphor, found in a sensuous sphere, brings about a reciprocal influence between the source (book, turning pages) and the target (the sea), which together serve as the metaphorical source of reading. The emerging properties, though operated by linguistic metaphors, are also based on perceptual experience, imagistic and visual, within a composition. Arnheim proceeds by formulating this mechanism accurately: "relation, then, far from leaving the related items untouched, works as a condition of the total context of which the items are parts and produces changes that are in keeping with the structure of that context."[6] Interpreting Arnheim's *Visual Thinking*, Verstegen accurately presents the central status of imagery in metaphor: "when a metaphor is active, it plays with levels of abstraction in order to lay bare a deeper structural affinity between two perceptual images."[7]

The emergent property of the composition of metaphor appears clearly in Aldrich's theory as well: as the third part of metaphor, named by him "the content of seeing as" (as mentioned briefly in Chapter 4). He demonstrates its role by analyzing visual metaphors, which he sees as crucial to our understanding of the whole phenomenon of metaphors. He does not use the term "emergence" explicitly here, but does so in other texts, such as " 'Expresses' and 'Expressive,' " where he analyses "the emergent quality of the music," asking a rhetorical question: "if 'the music is sad' is a metaphor, are we to suppose the emergent quality of the composition, denoted here by 'sad,' is not there in the music for objective notice? Only the local or part qualities literally qualify the composition?"[8] Surely the answer is "no," and it ought to be added that Aldrich criticizes Beardsley here for not realizing that a metaphorical property such as "sad" with regard to a piece of music is more than merely applied to it, but also emerges from the composition. Beardsley actually does realize that metaphor properties are emergent in kind, subsuming their emergence under what he dubs a "metaphorical twist." However, Aldrich thinks that Beardsley's (as well as Goodman's) physicalism and nominalism prevent him from grasping the productive nature of metaphorical compositions. Aldrich, like Arnheim, Gombrich, and Hausman, attributes a dynamic productive power to composition. He explains this power well in his "Form in the Visual Arts" from 1971, through the fact that materials of artworks which, for example, are made to exhibit the shapes of mountains are endowed with an emergent power thanks to the composition.

Seeing stains of colors as mountains reveals "the character both of the mountain and of the art-materials, the latter embodying the former." The same applies to a "paint-patch coming alive as face" thanks to color having a resonance, which it lacks in a different thing. "A composition, in this view of it, is expressive *both* of (shows) the character of its materials and of its subject-matter or what it represents. This 'character of the art materials', come alive and thus shown in the composition, I call 'the medium of art'." [9]

Aldrich rightly attributes his characterization of the power of composition, to enliven an element to be reconstructed anew, to metaphors as well. He mainly does this to explain the emergent transfigurative element of metaphor. Unlike most metaphor theories, Aldrich's definition explicitly characterizes metaphor as comprising three ingredients, which are given in a "triadic relation": the material (M); the content of the seeing-as experience (B); the subject-matter (A), which M is seen as. The content B is the material M seen as the subject-matter A, or conversely, the content B is the subject-matter A bodied forth by the material. Look at how Aldrich describes B, the emergent part of metaphor, as its constitutive element, that which makes a thing a metaphor, as well as what makes it aesthetically successful:

> The third factor is the elusive one, hard to differentiate from M and from A in the perception of M as A. But this is the crucial one for such perception, and whether or not it is "aesthetic" depends mainly on the prominence of this factor and on how it functions. The reason that distinguishing it from either A or M is a delicate job is that it is a "function" of both. Both M and A are transfigured (transformed) 'expressively portrayed' in this third factor, though in different senses ...
>
> ... In view of this, the subject-matter as such (A) and the material as such (M) drop from notice, in favor of the content (B)—the embodied image in which M and A are transfigured "expressively portrayed."[10]

Using Aldrich's theory, the charger-powermat is transfigured through a pebble (Figure 1), but ends up with the content of pebble-powermat—which is the third ingredient of the visual metaphor, "the content of seeing as." Both of the main elements of the metaphor, what are today called the source and the target, the powermat and the pebble, disappear in favor of the "embodied presentation" of the content of the metaphor: "a content (B), which emerges for prehension, a fusion of A and M."[11] The powermat which is constructed as a pebble, not a mere powermat nor a pebble, is the content which is expressively portrayed. The third ingredient of metaphor is what makes the metaphor cohesive.

Aldrich thus explains not only visual metaphors, but the figurative and imagistic character of all metaphors, as well as their fitting in the sphere of the aesthetic. Moreover, Aldrich extends the use of the third part of the metaphor, its content, to draw a distinction between metaphor and reference. He does so by differentiating visual simile from visual metaphor, which is helpful to grasp the depth of the emergent, irreducible third part of metaphor, which similes lack. Seeing a cloud as a woman's head (metaphor) is crucially different from seeing that a cloud is similar to a woman's head (simile). In the former, the noticed head is not at all apart from the content (B) which is realized in the cloud. But noting a similarity between a cloud and a woman's head (M is like A) implies a reference to (description of) something external to M—an element which happens to be like the cloud in some respect. The attention accordingly is directed "to this A as the referent of M"—to the woman as referred to by the cloud. "Thus, B as content is liquidated."[12] Additionally, the more stable the content (B, M seen as A), the more stable and self-standing the metaphor.

Aldrich's meticulous analysis of the range of metaphorical perceptions is impressive. It stretches from noticing similarities between kinds of seeing, such as the simile kind of seeing and semi-metaphorical seeing—namely seeing something as something else where the third part (the content) is unstable—to metaphorical construction. His line converges with Gombrich's and Arnheim's— both accounting for the scale going from the metaphorical seeing and practice of daily encounters, such as Gombrich's hobbyhorse, to stable metaphorical constructions such as Picasso's *The King* and *The Queen* (1952, 1953; Figure 13).

This third part of metaphor, that which is actually the metaphor itself, may also be explained by Arnheim's delineation of the mutual effects of parts on the whole, as well as the perceptual status gained by the different parts in different contexts along with relations of dominance or subservience. To show that these mutual effects exist, Arnheim refers to experiments whose results show that a given shape is absorbed, or dismembered, by the structure of the pattern that surrounds it. Depending on the pattern that shape may be indiscernible, or alternatively if its structure is independent of its surroundings it could be detached from that pattern. Additionally, when the same feature is placed, or functions, in two different contexts "when it dominates the one but is subordinate in the other may be hard to discover even though it is of exactly the same shape and detaches itself fairly well from its surroundings."[13]

The main point, which sharply opposes the two-elements conceptualist theory of metaphor, is that the emergent third element is the core of a real metaphor. By a "real metaphor" Aldrich means one that is *fully aesthetic*: a planned metaphor that is "arranged under the control of what is going to appear as the content B of the experience of seeing the arranged material M as its subject-matter." Clearly, this mechanism of emergence is characteristic of art, and Aldrich tells us that

> Picasso said that when Matisse draws a line on a piece of white paper ... it doesn't remain just that; it becomes something more—A and M are at the "mercy" of B ... The material (M) and subject-matter (A) meet in the content (B) where they in some sense fuse and lose their separate identities in favor of the fusion.[14]

The more stable the metaphor (i.e., the more the metaphor is a construction rather than a temporary seeing-as experience), the more aesthetic it is, since it must be well-arranged and successfully composed. "A master artist pre-visions the content to be realized by the appropriate manipulation of the material that is to be seen as something."[15] Aldrich explains that in a real metaphor the planned appearance of the material, today called the "source," is the arranging factor of the material. This arrangement is made within the ontological sphere, thereby enlarging categories and creating new properties and things. I would like to allocate a subsection to a specific theory, formulated by Carl R. Hausman, which proposes an interesting take on the ontological corollary of metaphors. Though it focuses on linguistic metaphors, and is not entirely unproblematic, it does shed a light on the essence of emergence shared by each of the various kinds of metaphors, and it breaks the wall between metaphors and reality.

5.2 Emerging ontology

Hausman was maybe the first to explicitly point to the ontological productivity of metaphors. His ontological theory further develops Black's interactionist theory combined with a theory of reference—this all adds up to a very interesting and unique theory. It might seem too heterodox to fit in the current conceptualist sphere, but it definitely touches the essence of metaphor. In his 1989 *Metaphor and Art* and his 1991 "Language and Metaphysics: The Ontology of Metaphors," Hausman presents a comprehensive theory of metaphor. He stresses that metaphors do things due to their interactive character adjoined by their illocutionary force. The general purpose of his ontological picture has been to explore the relation between metaphorical expressions and their *newly made referents-objects*. He stresses "that metaphors not only create new meanings but also have new and unique objects or referents that function in the world by interacting with one another in contexts that are structurally like those found in linguistic metaphors."[16] His referential-interaction theory of metaphor, he promises, allows a depiction of this ontology.

Hausman argues that the referent of the interaction made by the two terms that compose the (linguistic) metaphor are distinct from the original referents of each original term before it joined the metaphor. One of Hausman's examples is the mind–computer metaphor. He claims that the referent of "the mind is a computer" or "mental activity is a computer processing" is neither the mind or mental activity, nor a computer as had been referred to or "understood before the metaphor." The referent is also not the combination of these former referents. Rather, this metaphor has *a new referent* which is a specification of "mind," "mental activity," or "computer," "as these conspire to enable the creative designation to refer to a new referent." That is to say, the new referents under the context of the new metaphor enable the referentiality of the metaphorical expression: "creative metaphors refer to referents that are new."[17] The idea is that the productivity of language, dubbed as "significance" by Hausman, extends all the way to creating new referents, and thus to the realm of ontology—as he himself proclaims. He sets two conditions for a metaphorical referent: "the created referent is both an extralinguistic and a unique object. This extralinguisticality adds an ontological dimension to the uniqueness."[18]

Hausman, by these means, draws on the interactions theory of metaphors; he formulates "metaphorical referential interactionism," which characterizes creative functions of language and production of new significance. Significance is the meaning plus the referents, which in its turn sets limits to interpretation. "In the case of instances of metaphorical language," Hausman explicates, "the idea that one may find significance in such an instance is crucial, because it indicates not only that there are sometimes interactions of established meanings that, according to all interaction theories, may yield new meanings, but that there are objects referred to by those new meanings." The point, he emphasizes, is that metaphors that create new meaning also create emergent referents, different from the original referents and the terms that took part in the interaction, and that they are in the ontological sphere. In "man is a wolf," each of the two terms in interaction "has a referent independently of the metaphor, neither of which is the referent of the metaphor as a whole. The metaphor as a whole refers to a new focal condition of constraints that can be understood only by means of metaphor itself."[19] So, we see, Hausman's theory may be classified as a theory of emergence, like the visualist ones.

However, endorsing theories of reference, Hausman still stays in the realm of language and sees linguistic metaphors as paradigmatic of metaphor, or at least treats metaphor as essentially symbolic rather than a medium of its own. This is the main difference between my claims about metaphor and his. While Hausman characterizes metaphors as creating referents that "participate" in the world, I think that metaphors themselves are *in* the world. They do not have referents, but rather could be referents of different symbolic systems or mental contents. I prefer Gombrich's approach that the stick which is constructed to be a horse by a kid "is neither a sign signifying the concept 'horse' nor is it a portrait of an individual horse. By its capacity to serve as a 'substitute' the stick becomes a horse in its own right."[20]

Hausman, on the contrary, explicitly asserts that the kind of referent he denotes ought not to be "understood as something existent in any ordinary sense

... an object in a reference need not exist as something physical or spatial." By an "object" Hausman refers to any discrete thing, physical or intentional, an occurrence or even a law, "a locus for the senses."[21] Moreover, he considers nonverbal metaphors to have the same structure as verbal ones, and that "the function of the components of nonverbal artworks is isomorphic with the interaction found in verbal metaphors."[22] These functions are analyzed in terms of meaning and semantic relations. I would prefer to go all the way to externalism. Therefore, my aim is to join theories that see visual metaphors as the roots of all metaphors, serving as the model of the linguistic and conceptual ones, and accordingly adapt the externalist position to portray these relations within the metaphorical field. I will therefore take one step further to an explicit presentation of the externalist conception of metaphor in the framework of visualism.

5.3 Metaphors and externalism: categorization

The core of the conflict between the conceptualist and the visualist theories of metaphor revolves around the question of the source of metaphors, which is essentially related to the source of categorizations and prototypical forms, that in their turn allow for recognitions to take place. Obviously, visualism points to all of these sources as located in the external world. Speaking of the mechanism of recognition and classification, Arnheim—who I believe to be the most externalist among the visualists—criticizes the excessive flexibility that theoreticians of the visual, even Gombrich, attribute to a projection of forms on the world. Though our perception is active, the world has a shape of its own, Arnheim believes; he joins Jerome Bruner, one of the fathers of cognitive psychology and theories of perception and categorization, by claiming that "the mind cannot give shape to the shapeless."[23] As is well known, Bruner's theory of categorization and learning points to the origins of the three stages of categorization in perceptions of the external world: encountering the object (for the enactive stage), visual imagery (for the iconic stage), and representation (for the symbolic stage). In the literature Bruner is sometimes even explicitly labeled as externalist, given the primacy he attributes to culture in the design of the self (though he emphasizes the inner world as essential as well).[24] In any case, it is no wonder that Arnheim, as well as Goodman and Gombrich, were in discourse with Bruner. Notwithstanding Bruner's part in the inauguration of what he calls the "cognitive revolution,"[25] he stresses the formative role that culture plays in thoughts and meaning-making, and accordingly promotes a "cultural psychology."[26]

Still, the current strand of cognitivism tends to internalism, and I find the cognitivist gaze at the relationships between humans and their reality to be misdirected. Charles Forceville, one of the main and significant voices in the visual and multimodal metaphors field, notes in the recent *Current Approaches to Metaphor Analysis in Discourse* that "healthy strong, and growing, a body of work analyzing visual, gestural, and multimodal expressions of metaphor and metonymy" has been added to the study of the verbal manifestation of the conceptual theory of metaphors.[27] Forceville himself has been formulating a theory of multimodal metaphors, namely, "metaphors whose target and source are each represented exclusively or predominantly in different modes," such as visual source and auditory target.[28] We see, here and in other texts, that the cognitivist field of metaphor theory does acknowledge that, alongside language and conceptual schemes, metaphor comes in various kinds of visual media, of spatial or temporal kinds, and that these media ought not to be dismissed. This rich study of visual and material metaphor notwithstanding, conceptual schemes are still endowed with a primary privileged position in making metaphor. The endorsement of conceptualism is curiously manifested even in the most recent embodied cognition theories, those which are the most progressive with regard to the visuality of metaphors. Gibbs, a prominent scholar of embodied cognition asserts that "the main upshot of this varied research is that recurring patterns of conceptual metaphors have influence in people's thinking, speaking, and understanding." According to him, primary conceptual metaphors are universal,

> because they reflect pervasive correlations in embodied experience typically shared by all people, such as *understanding is seeing* ("I can't see what you are saying in that article"), *intimacy is closeness* (e.g., "We have a close relationship"), *important is big* (e.g., "Tomorrow is a big day"), *more is up* (e.g., "Prices are high") ... In this way, basic metaphoric schemes of thought are grounded in embodied experience, one reason why conceptual theory of metaphor is often linked to new developments in the embodied cognition movement in cognitive science.[29]

Look, then, at how Arnheim explains the very status of what Gibbs classifies as the universally shared bodily primary metaphors. While Arnheim joins the line of thought that distinguishes between universality and particularity, he claims that it is the particular experience that leads us to the universal: "one aspect of the wisdom that belongs to a genuine culture is the constant awareness of the symbolic meaning expressed in a concrete happening, the sensing of the universal in the particular. This gives significance and dignity to all daily pursuits and prepares the ground on which the arts can grow."[30]

Arnheim's visualist definition of cognition is very helpful here. He explicitly notes that he is in conflict with cognitivist psychology. The extension of the meaning of "cognition" and "cognitive," as stated by Arnheim in *Visual Thinking*, ought to apply to "the activity of the senses" as well as perception.[31] In *Art and Visual Perception*, he therefore focuses on what he names "the psychology of the creative eye" which is equivalent to Gombrich's "study in the psychology of pictorial representation" in his canonical *Art and Illusion*.

The apparatus of Arnheim's visualism clarifies the idea that metaphor cannot be paraphrased to a metaphorical semantic meaning, the analysis of which, according to the semanticists, would bring us to the real core of metaphor. Arnheim explicitly tries to refute the main idea of the linguistic age, that which sees the human being as a linguistic creature first and foremost. In the infrastructure of his theory we first find not only a dissolution of the distinction between perception and thinking, both in artistic and extra-artistic practices: "my earlier work had taught me that artistic activity is a form of reasoning, in which perceiving and thinking are indivisibly intertwined. A person who paints, writes, composes, dances. I felt compelled to say thinks with his senses." It does not end here for Arnheim. He advances to a full reversal of the linguistic-turn hierarchy which ranks cognition and ordinary language as superior to visuality, with linguistic meaning capable of representing visual forms. "Inversely," he argues about cognitivism, "there was much evidence that truly productive thinking in whatever area of cognition takes place in the realm of imagery."[32] Blaming the linguistic theoreticians for placing language as originating in the mind and in charge of the expression of reasoning, on the one hand, and modernism for guiding art to stay secluded on the other hand, Arnheim, like Aldrich, Gombrich, Mitchell, and other visualists, sees visual creativity, visual thinking, and reasoning as taking place in the realm of the public. All these, indeed, operate in the realm of the visual and perception. This, I believe, is one of Arnheim's main contributions to ontology—yes, ontology—opening us up to the idea that humanity takes place outside. In this respect, he is more of an externalist than Gombrich and Goodman. For him, reconstructions of objects, phenomena, and categories are made by the visual, due to its dynamic forces, which emanate from the composition.

However, by characterizing the human being as a conceptualizer rather than as a beholder and builder of composition, cognitivism misses the sources of the ontological order as perceived by us. Following are two recent examples that I find typical to the cognitivist line of thought and etiological reasoning, which externalist visualism proves fundamentally problematic. Under a discussion entitled "conceptual metaphor in categorization and creativity," in his comprehensive and somewhat retrospective *Metaphor Wars: Conceptual Metaphors in Human Life* from 2017, Gibbs scrutinizes the depth of our ordinary and everyday categorizing kind of judgment, such as "tomatoes are members of the category of fruits." Gibbs contends that, by and large, categorization is understood through the concept of containing. His trust is in experiments, with the participants of these experiments using what he calls "the bodily idea of containment" to categorize nonlinguistic phenomena. As Gibbs informs us,

> one study asked participants to judge as quickly as possible whether two pictures were from the same or different categories (animals and vehicles). *The picture contained a rectangle form that bounded either one item or both items.* On some trials, the two items from the same category were completely within the rectangle, and in other cases, the two items were positioned within different rectangles.[33] (my emphasis)

The speed of categorizations was clearly influenced by the rectangular frames, even though the shape of the frames was unrelated to the categorizing decisions the participants were asked to make. Judging two items as belonging to the same category was much faster when both of them were presented inside the same rectangle. Gibbs sees the rectangles as "containers" and concludes that "these findings are consistent with claims that the *concept* of 'categories' is metaphorically represented in terms of containers, as seen in the conceptual metaphor categories are containers" (my italics).[34] That is to say, the results appear to Gibbs as follows: what promoted the participants in the experiment to classify things as joined together in the same category when they were presented in the bounds of a rectangle, or alternatively to classify them as disjoint when they were not in the same rectangle, is *an internal conceptual structure* of a category understood through a container. This conceptual scheme was subsequently presented by the external drawn rectangle.

But this linearity is not plausible! The practice of the participants in the experiment, in my view, was actually what Arnheim calls "perceptual classification." The participants were quick to group together items presented within the boundaries of the same rectangular due to a simple cause: the items were *physically* located and *seen* together in the same frame! Moreover, in our ontological sphere things that are closely located, that dwell within the same boundaries, usually belong to some same category (as well as to other ones, of course). Categorization does *not* progress as follows: we see some items together, create the concept, the concept becomes entrenched in our mind and then accompanies us from now on. No. The things affect how we *see* them—due to their properties, affordances, and perceptual contexts. The items presented inside the same rectangular frame are *seen* as members of the same category, they invite us to see them as such, their *visuality* guides us to see them as such (surely, the same but inversely applies to the items that were located outside of the rectangular frame).

Samuel Guttenplan's 2005 work *Objects of Metaphors* offers a distinctive shift from language to objects in defining metaphorical predication by arguing that a nonverbal object, an exemplar of a metaphorical predicate, can itself be of predicative use in characterizing the subject of the metaphor.[35] Thus, understanding metaphor goes through grasping objects first. The role that the perceived things play in their own categorization, under the practice of perceptual classification, is explained by Arnheim in the following instructive account on their expressivity:

> When we go by the perceived patterns of forces, some objects and events resemble each other; others do not. On the basis of their expressive appearance, our eye spontaneously creates a kind of Linnean classification of all existing things. This perceptual classification cuts across the order suggested by other kinds of categories. Particularly in our modern Western civilization we are accustomed to distinguishing between animate and inanimate things, human and nonhuman creatures, the mental and the physical. But in terms of expressive qualities, the character of a given person may resemble that of a particular tree more closely than that of another person. The state of affairs in a human society may be similar to the tension in the skies just before the outbreak of a thunderstorm. Poets use such analogies, and so do other unspoiled people.[36]

Visualism, we see, rightly pays close attention to the *variety of qualities of appearance that effect categorization*, among which are expressive qualities. These are influential in the reconstruction of pieces of ontology, definitely in metaphorical practices, but they cannot be informed by the conceptualist model of metaphor. Visuality, rather than conceptualization, attends to these qualities.

Among the recent conceptualist-cognitivist theories of metaphor, Bipin Indurkhya's later body of work supports a relatively empirical approach—one which considers the external ontological sphere and empirical data as crucial in understanding the mechanism of metaphor. Indurkhya is aware of the constraints and possibilities that are offered by the external sphere, criticizing the interactionist accounts of cognition and metaphor for omitting objectivity from their account. Metaphor theory ought to reach out to the external in order to capture both metaphorical possibility and success, he submits. Construction of the world through internal theories is not arbitrary, but rather dependent on the properties of the external. Already in 1994, in an essay that examines "the thesis that all knowledge is metaphorical," Indurkhya betrays some support of externalist views, such as the semantic ones formulated by Earl Mac Cormac and Hilary Putnam who suggest that the theories and structure we are seeking "are out there in the objective world," and that "there is at least some mind-independent, objective structure in the world to which any conceptual system must conform."[37] The engineering discipline serves as a paradigmatic example of our compliance with the external and dependence on it for different lines of progress: "pre-history of flight, construction of bridges, electronic circuits, internal combustion engines, and so on—to find numerous examples that show that just to have an internally consistent theory that is carefully worked out, and the strong belief and commitment of the designer are not sufficient to ensure that it will actually work."[38]

This direction of mechanism applies to metaphorical fit and success, Indurkhya adds, drawing attention to metaphorical success as externally rooted: "for metaphors, this is evidenced by the fact that some metaphors appear more appropriate and more powerful than others, and this cannot be explained by the internal representations or coherence of the concepts alone."[39]

This is a crucial argument for externalism. Clearly, metaphorical success (viz., a reconstruction of targets by new emergent properties, which are added to the ontological sphere) is reached by the extramental, external, emergent part of the relation between the metaphorical parts within the metaphorical composition. These, as even Indurkhya the cognitivist realizes, do not, cannot, appear in the mind. It is only out in the ontological sphere that a building can be reconstructed as a white tree (Figure 14), a theory can be reconstructed as a building, and a thought can gain depth. As noted in the first chapter, Arnheim the aesthetician stresses that it is only with respect to a physical depth, and the experience of it, that thought may be reconstructed to possess depth (as well as different grades of depth). This aesthetic and imagistic emergence is external and exhibited to the viewing eye. We see, then, that the neglect of aesthetics, theories of composition, and aesthetic emergence, as well as the lack of understanding of the role of imagistic action in our being, was harmful to the conceptualist-cognitivist study of metaphor.

Indurkhya is not a sheer externalist like Arnheim or Putnam, hence he does not go all the way to acknowledge that metaphors are *out there*, in the ontological sphere. As a cognitivist, he also overlooks the imagistic-aesthetic-visual nature of metaphors. One may notice it in his conceptualist account of metaphors in fashion as well as the fairly recent distinction he draws between linguistic and visual metaphors (from 2013).[40] But he does realize the ontological significance of metaphors, mainly the ones which he classifies as creating similarities rather than based on similarities, as he submits in his "Rationality and Reasoning with Metaphors." For example, speaking on legal reasoning, he exposes its ontological productivity of similarity or dissimilarity between cases, given that it "sometimes requires the creation of new categories, or a change of ontology, especially when unconventional and creative arguments are being made. The created categories can make the facts of two different cases seem similar, or they can distinguish between cases that would otherwise seem similar. Here a new ontology was created."[41]

An example of created similarities, given by Indurkhya, is Darwin's image of an irregularly branching tree recurring in his thoughts, serving as the primal metaphor for his natural selection principle. Several excerpts from Darwin's notebooks show that it was not some existing similarities between the tree image and whatever was known about evolution at that time that kept Darwin searching for similarities. On the contrary, it was an emotional drive that kept up his intellectual commitment to articulate an account of evolution that matched the tree image. Darwin was not searching for similarities, but formulating them. Another example is Wegener's revolutionary 1915 use of the iceberg analogy to suggest the theory of continental drift, which was not accepted up until the mid-1960s. The analogy was not based on the known similarities between the continents and the polar icebergs. Wegener's strong attraction to the drift theory partly emanates from the fact that he was not trained as a geologist. Indurkhya's propositions are equivalent to Hausman's, whose linearity goes from language acts to ontology, and still endows some privileged status to language over reality.

Indurkhya, so I see in his writing, confounds ontology and representations, things and concepts, and like Hausman he holds too flexible an ontology. Thereby, his analysis of ontological shifts resulting from metaphors is mixed in with talk of concept shifts and what he calls "ontologies of representations," defining representations as our "representation," a meta-level term that refers to the internal states of the cognitive agent. A confusion of ontology with mental schemes is expressed in his assertion, on the one hand, that "when the cognitive agent has internal states, the set of states constitutes the ontology of the representation, and the state transition functions make up the structure," and on the other hand, that "every structure presupposes an ontology. When a cognitive agent interacts with an object, the result is a representation of the object that is internal to the agent." On the one hand, he argues that "representation is determined in part by the agent and in part by the autonomous nature of the object. The agent gets to play a role in giving an ontology to the object," and that "the agent can choose a different ontology, and thereby affect the structure of the object as internally represented." On the other hand, he claims that "the object gets to play a role by endowing this agent-determined ontology with a structure. Thus, the structure of the object always seems autonomous (external) to the agent."[42] Thus, Indurkhya sticks to the conceptualist view which gives concepts, rather than form or visuality, the prime role in arranging our ontology. This is why his theory of metaphor is not immune to the back-and-forth theoretical loop, between the external and the internal, drawn by Lakoff and Johnson. As said above, their line of reasoning progresses from the abstract conceptual system to the external tokens, but the requirement to track the source of the conceptual system is met by pointing to the external physical environment. Then again, this environment stays hidden in their definition of metaphor, whose consecutive stages are: (external world), then the conceptual system, then the external world. Indurkhya follows Goodman's externalist constructivism (and like Goodman, attributes truth values to metaphorical propositions: "the use of 'The sky is crying' to describe a clear sunny day could be described either as false or incorrect," he claims in *Metaphor and Cognition*[43]) but does not endorse his conventionalist, nominalist view. Thus, he characterizes "projection" as conceptual, explaining that "projection, derived from the Piagetian notion of assimilation, is used in applying a concept network to a phenomenon to which it does not normally apply."[44]

It is important to note that Indurkhya's theory of metaphor is nonetheless one of the richest and most progressive within the conceptualist-cognitivist school. He does betray an inclination toward the recognition that the ontological sphere is the real setting of metaphorical practice, and his line of reasoning indicates that that externalism is the right theoretical framework for defining metaphor. Indurkhya sums up with the significant proposition that "metaphors can radically alter the ontology of the target, thereby creating a new perspective on it that includes information not contained in the old representation."[45] Hence, Indurkhya and his collaborators reach an externalist conclusion out of their rich experiments with metaphors: "the effect of any such movement on changing one stimulus on my retina into another, possibly different, stimulus is determined by the structure of the external world. It is precisely in this sense that reality, while owing its form (as experienced by me) to my sensorimotor apparatus, nonetheless appears as an autonomous external entity to me."[46] Asserting this opens us to the end of the conceptualist rule of theories of metaphor.

A surprising step in this direction is made by one of the inaugurators of the conceptualist theory of metaphor, Mark Johnson, in his *Embodied Mind, Meaning, and Reason: How Our Bodies Give Rise to Understanding* (2017). Through a discussion of the nature of daily life experiences, Johnson supplies an outlet for a reversal of the conceptualist hierarchy. He appreciates two major, interrelated, facts: first, the internalist attribution of the privileged status of the mental content of the disembodied mind makes no sense in the discussion of our life experiences. Second, an understanding of our own life experiences is closely tied to an understanding of our bodily experiences. This is a first step in letting go of the chain of stages delineated by conceptual metaphor theory, that which assumes that the production of metaphors starts with our conceptual schema, in the internal metaphorical mind the mechanism of which is of each concept being thought through another. But what, according to conceptualism, causes a specific concept to be the filter of the conception of another? These, conceptualism admits, are the cultural conventions, material environments, and structures of experiences. Yet the conceptual schema is attributed with the status of the primary chassis of the external, which enables us to understand our experiences and label them. The external is pushed again to be considered as secondary to the conceptual mind. And rather than acknowledging the conceptualized body, the conceptualist theory, its cognizance of both the chronological and necessary status of the body notwithstanding, still holds the "embodied mind" as a key concept. This clearly does not make sense.

Johnson's step is not wide enough to reach the externalist, ontological theory of metaphor. Nonetheless, it is significant in its inversion of the conceptualist linearity, setting the body as primary in the activity of our being. He summarizes his book by explaining that "the nature of our bodies, as they interact with our structured environments, shape what things and events are meaningful to us and how we make sense of and reason about them. In other words, our embodiment is constitutive of the structure of our concepts and our reason." Our bodies, according to Johnson in his late theory, are more than conduits for sensory input leading to independent mental contents and schemes. They rather enable us to have experiences and meaning, as well as to self-reflect and communicate. "That is why we need to investigate our body-based meaning processes as a starting point for any further philosophical reflection."[47]

While embodied cognition is a much-needed phase for the development of conceptualism, the extension of this theory ought to be widened beyond the body, all the way to ontology. Visualism aspired to do it and reached impressive accomplishments about forty years before body theories, the adoption of phenomenology by the philosophy of mind, and most importantly the visual turn, addressed physicality and visuality as crucial for theories about the human being, its reality and culture. Returning to discussing categorization in terms of ontology and visuality, which is relevant now more than ever given the current visual turn, requires an account of the challenges that the emergent ontology of metaphor sets before us. The case of metaphorical reconstructions of readymades is a good place to start, so I will devote the next subchapter to it.

5.4 Metaphorical seeing and ontology: the case of readymades

The ontological import of metaphors, that which is based on visuality, is explained well under Aldrich's correct distinction between simile and metaphor, which actually stretches along a range that includes weak and strong cases of seeing-as. Simile involves reference to the non-exhibited similar thing. For example, the simile "the cloud is like a face" denotes a referent, a face, which is external to the cloud. Therefore, the third element of metaphor, which Aldrich names "the content," is not created. On the contrary, in metaphor, a self-standing construction is created, which is not dependent on any external reference but yields a new piece of ontology thanks to the fusion of the two parts of the metaphor (what Aldrich names "the content, B"). Aldrich describes this as follows:

> in such cases [metaphorical cases], M [cloud] and A [face] are in principle "at the mercy" of B [cloud with a face]. The main point, however, that emerges out of these considerations is that material (M) and subject-matter (A) meet in the content (B) where they in some sense fuse and lose their original distinct identities in favor of the fusion. This is why, in such an aesthetic case of seeing M as A, the report of the perceptual experience not only has the form of metaphor: "M is A," as does the report of any seeing-as experience; but involves, in addition, the subservience of A (subject-matter) to B (the content).[48]

Furthermore, Aldrich rightly claims that in metaphor, even if the material of metaphor (M, the target) and the subject-matter (A, the source) are noticed separately, the standards of considering them is through the prism of their fulfillment "in which they are expressively portrayed." They cannot be considered unless the emergent B—the face-possessing-cloud—is grasped. In other words, *the metaphor, the fusion, the third emergent part, is ontologically and perceptually prior to its original parts*. This most significant contention is opposed to the conceptualist model.

For Aldrich it is clear that even though the content, the third part of the metaphor, is not visibly distinguished as a self-standing ingredient, it is nonetheless involved in visual perception of the kind he names "prehension": "I suggest seeing something (M) as something else (A) is certainly a sort of visual perception. One must look at M to prehend the content ... One sees M-as-A while 'prehending' the content."[49] However, I refer to the ontological element of the visual metaphor, and claim that neither aspect-seeing alone nor what Aldrich dubs "a transfigurative seeing" will suffice by itself to create a metaphor, let alone a work of art. Being as constructivist as Gombrich, Arnheim, and Goodman, Aldrich argues that Picasso's *La Venus du Gaz* (Figure 15), which is a gas stove

Figure 15 Pablo Picasso, *La Venus du Gaz (The Venus of Gas)*, 1945. Photograph by Michalle Gal.

burner stuck on a block of wood—a readymade—is neither a metaphorical work of art, nor a work of art at all. One might only see it as a woman based on its title. Picasso's piece does not consist of a transfiguration of one thing borrowing properties from another. Even if the piece may be seen as a woman, Aldrich insists that "in such a case, however, the material is certainly not arranged for the sake of the content (B) that, with title, emerges for prehension."[50]

It is easy to approve the classification of intact readymades as merely borderline metaphors—since no real reconstruction is done here. However, a critique may show here that an artistic hierarchy of artifactuality, whose lower stage contains whole and untouched objects that went through no transfiguration but merely some relocation or gaining a new title, is implausible. One may claim that measuring the level of artifactuality or reconstruction is pointless. Thierry de Duve quotes Marcel Duchamp claiming in a 1961 interview with Katherine Kuh that tubes of paint are readymades chosen by an artist just like any other artifact: "let's say you use a tube of paint; you didn't make it. You bought it and used it as a readymade. Even if you mix two vermilions together, it's still a mixing of two readymades. So man can never expect to start from scratch; he must start from ready-made things like even his own mother and father."[51] Across from it, Danto quotes Marcel Duchamp describing his own work *Fountain* in *The Blind Man* (which Duchamp himself published): "Mr. Mutt ... took an ordinary article of life, placed it so that its useful significance disappeared under the new title and point of view—created a new thought for that object." According to Danto, the conceptualist, "the 'thought' must concert the power of titles to exsubstantiate objects as resistant to sublation as urinals must be." However, what remained of the object of consciousness is a urinal, not a fountain, and "it is not clear that the power in question extends quite that far."[52] So, at least some level of artifactual reconstruction is needed after all.

Aldrich is aware of the significance of practicing metaphorical seeing, and of Picasso's eye—experiencing what he beautifully formulates as a "triumph over the gross material by a transfiguring look at its shape—in a way that makes it become 'something more' than a mere shape of a gas burner."[53] And this may be accomplished without a wholesale reconstruction of the artifact in question. It is an integral part of our constructivist, creative nature, which is realized artistically but also in our interactions with the everyday.

Nevertheless, the difference between metaphor and seeing-as practice or aspect-seeing is crucial. The transfigurative look could not be accomplished merely by noticing similarities, nor by being dependent on them. A transfigurative gaze, or active perception, requires a well-informed visual load. Grasping this gaze helps us grasp the ontological foundation of metaphors. I find that delving into seeing-as epistemology and practice is unnecessary here, given that it is so well analyzed, and I would like to move on to the essential ontological structure of metaphors. Indeed, metaphors are advanced by the transfigurative gaze—we see a cloud as a woman's head, car lights as eyes, a relationship as a journey, a bird as a nag lecturing her flock. We apply faces to almost everything and personify inanimate objects. Aren't we all, and not only the poet, guilty of falling into the ordinary pathetic fallacy? For Ruskin, who coined this term, "there is no greater baseness in literature than the habit of using these metaphorical expressions in cold blood," while "the highest power of a writer is to keep his eyes fixed firmly on the pure facts."[54] Though Ruskin disparages what he described as the ubiquity of the "pathetic fallacy" among second-grade artists and ordinary people, most visualists deem it one of our positive creative characteristics—namely, metaphors are just natural ways of being and seeing. Our visual character and attachment to iconic forms is its motivating mechanism.

5.5 Everyday aesthetics, design and metaphors: the cloud coffee table

The habit of using metaphors is, without a doubt, deeply rooted in ourselves and our everyday being. Indeed, metaphor reaches great heights within the framework of art, but also is deeply saturated in ordinary ontology and perception. Georges Braque, as Arnheim tells us in his *Art and Visual Perception*, advises the artist to seek the common in the dissimilar, "thus the poet can say: the swallow knifes the sky, and thereby makes a knife out of a swallow." But this practice is common in the ordinary visual sphere as well, and Arnheim emphasizes it by calling for an everyday kind of gaze:

> it is the function of the metaphor to make the reader penetrate the conventional shell of the world of things by juxtaposing objects that have little in common but the underlying pattern. Such a device, however, works only if the reader of poetry is still alive, in his own daily experience, to the symbolic or metaphoric connotation of all appearance and activity.[55]

Arnheim's examples include: the overtone of attack and destruction evoked by hitting or breaking things; the fact that activities of ascension, including climbing a staircase, bring about a feeling of conquest and achievement; that pulling up the shades in the morning is more than a mere illumination, as the room becomes flooded with light. For visualism, "the poetical habit of uniting practically disparate objects by metaphor is not a sophisticated invention of artists, but derives from and relies on the universal and spontaneous way of approaching the world of experience."[56] Indeed, stressing the everyday naturalness of metaphor is crucial for the visualist project, being based on characterizing the human as a visual being first and foremost.

Parallel to the highlighting of everyday metaphoric creativity by Arnheim, Gombrich's visualist theory of metaphor could be interpreted to go so far as to present the metaphorical tendency as not only natural but also conservative. As noted in the discussion of face metaphors in Chapter 1.5, conservative tendencies sometimes motivate us to apply properties borrowed from known and close-by categories to further ones, thus making them closer to us. This explains the ubiquity of personification as a kind of temporary projection on almost everything: faces and body shapes are applied to clouds, buildings, kitchen tools, etc.; human feelings and emotions are applied to trees, animals, etc. After all, the ubiquity of personification established metaphors.

Arnheim's theory is an explanatory advance on Gombrich's, given that it lays the perceptual base of what he names "egocentric way of experiencing the visual environment." That is the foundational human visual tendency to see the self as central in the perceptual sphere. Arnheim details it in his brilliant *The Power of the Center* as follows:

> It is the primary way suggested spontaneously by what our eyes see. The world we see before our eyes exhibits a particular perspective, centered upon the self. It takes time and effort to learn to compensate for the one-sidedness of the egocentric view; and throughout a person's life there persists a tendency to reserve to the self the largest possible share of the power to organize the surroundings around itself as the center.[57]

The physiognomic kind of perception, which both Arnheim and Gombrich consider to be central in seeing the different kinds of phenomena, sensuous and non-sensuous, provides the groundwork for the immediacy of the visual over language, and the primary status of visual metaphors and the external visual source of other kinds of metaphors. We see buildings, we experience their material solidity, we see their foundations, and then we may reconstruct theories as buildings. We walk in different paths and absorb their shapes and vibes, and then we may conceive of relationships as having paths. But then, one must stress, the metaphorical structure is continuous. This is the character of the emergence: a path in life is built into it, fused in it, and can be possessed only by it.

The recent development of everyday aesthetics and the philosophy of design is very helpful for supporting my intuition that aesthetics is mainly an ontological practice. What is more, we do not need the force of conceptualism, and the leap to the conceptual, to realize that metaphors dwell in our everyday environment as well as in our poetic spheres. Indeed, aesthetics is undergoing an ongoing reassessment of aesthetic objects that furnish our daily lives and actions, with an increased understanding that the subject of aesthetics ought to widen accordingly.

In her recent *Aesthetics of Design*, Jane Forsey classifies design as "immanent," i.e., absorbed in our everyday being.[58] Indeed, design is to be discussed in our current context. Contrary to art, design objects and daily objects are mostly mass-produced and are made by teams. Hence, they are not usually attributed to a specific creator. Interestingly, this is also the case with regard to what in the discipline of design is called "one-offs"—a single object of design, usually handmade. It leads us to understand that those objects are aesthetically significant by themselves. If we take this thought further, they are significant independently of the mental contents of their creators, such as intentions, plans, motivations, or conceptual schemes. One can even claim that their significance is not related to any creator. Using Jan Mukařovský's terminology, their aesthetic function is socially determined. This is not to say that they do not have semantic content, political influence, etc. Surely, they do. But all of these markers are public and external, rather than internal.[59] Gombrich reminds the reader in his "Visual Metaphors of Value in Art" of the shift from the dark Victorian to the modernist design metaphor of light and brightness. These are metaphorical qualities, he claims, since they apply newness, clean and hygienic values, and traits to modernist design objects. The metaphorical shifts in modernist design are presented in a more recent externalist-visualist account of the metaphorical construction of modernism and modernity offered by Judith Attfield, a theoretician and historian of design and material culture. Analyzing the progress of the design of the coffee table during the modernist era, she formulates the ways that design, a visual-material practice within the world of consumption, creates "group identity and self-construction through the production of spaces and objects stimulated by the possibility of change offered by modernity through consumption."[60] One of the significant points in Attfield's fascinating account is her grasp of the primary status of a visual practice such as design in constructing schemes and ideas, rather than the other way around, for which the modernist coffee table is a typical example. In the frame of modernist design, Attfield conveys, the coffee table defined a new kind of real-living aimed at domestic space, as "a vehicle for socializing," and thus an operator of social reforms. The modernist coffee table "is advanced as an instance of design as a practice of modernity within the spatial/social context of the modern household, situated against the background of two themes—utility and leisure."[61]

Design is a substantial and central discipline of material culture, and as such accommodates and evokes, rather than embodies, social meanings and social changes—which may further produce and promote ideas and concepts. The British post-war coffee table appeared in various organic, sometimes metaphorical, shapes such as "boomerangs, amoebas, kidneys and blobs, to guitars, clouds and artists' palettes," pushing for "non-hierarchical open-plan life-style, where it provided the main focus of the living room and replaced the dining table for informal eating in front of the television."[62] According to Attfield, it created casualness, bringing out a positive attitude to leisure culture, which up until the modern era was practiced only by those of higher social status.

There are quite a few impressive examples of what Attfield beautifully calls the modernist "vehicle of socializing." In my view, Neil Morris's canonical *Cloud Table*, designed for Morris & Co, Glasgow in 1947, is a paradigmatic example of a metaphorical design piece (Figure 16). Morris designed this type of table using laminated wood which affords a lightweight style and used to refer to it as *Amoeboid*, but the table has become known as the *Cloud Table* for obvious reasons. Clearly (and contrary to the conceptualist stance), this table is *not* an entailment of an abstract conceptual scheme of tables or furniture which is thought or understood through clouds. This is as senseless as it sounds. *Cloud*

Figure 16 Neil Morris, *Cloud Table (Ameboid Table)*, 1947. Photograph by Michalle Gal.

Table—its title, which refers to its metaphorical nature, has been used by the public—constructs a table as some sort of cloud, being the amalgamation of a table with cloudness, external upper celestial views, and lightness. Sitting at the table, guests could enjoy the new possibilities it invited them to enjoy—of a table with no clear order, with no chain of ranks embodied by its sitting arrangement, making the gathering around it informal. It shapes social ontology, which may in turn entail fresh concepts of hierarchies and modes of life. This is the direction of the metaphorical medium.

This goes further to everyday things and actions that are not subsumed under art and design. Everyday aesthetics brings back good old traditional ontology to the discussion of aesthetics, as well as new kinds of realism—especially, in what seems to be an oxymoron, constructivist realism. The aesthetic objects and environments are made by us and saturated by human contents, but they are out there in the external sphere. They start and end there. Those are their ontological boundaries. The ubiquity of aesthetic everyday objects, and their external presence, their visual-material presence, reveals that that visuality is the basis of aesthetic compositions. This is a substantial phenomenon, an infrastructure of our lives. It is there all the time. Visual metaphors capture big segments of this. Even when we see facial features in car lights, an electrical outlet, or a door lock, it is an aesthetic attribution of form.

Richard Shusterman's approach to aesthetics, defining art as dramatization, within his pragmatist aesthetics and his subsequent theory of somaesthetics, is insightful for us in this context: he "not at all aimed at perfect wrapper coverage of the extension of art but instead to highlight two crucial aspects of art—the intensity of presence and formal framing—that have generated conflicting theories that divide contemporary aesthetics." Shusterman's work, at least in what it aspires to achieve, "connotes both intensity of meaningful appearance, action, or experience (which generates theories that define art in terms of immediate, captivating presence or experience). But it also connotes the formal framing of an action, appearance, or experience through a historically established conventional framework that differentiates what is framed from the ordinary flow of life."[63]

Reading Shusterman's cogent propositions of formal framing makes one think yet again how valuable for philosophy, and surely for a theory of metaphor, it is to reach out to the visual sphere, its practices, its appearances, and their entailed conceptualizations and conceptual schemes. While according to Shusterman art is endowed with dramatic formal framing, some everyday moments of formal framing are worth theoretical notice as well—in particular when perception reconstructs clouds as having faces, or when one sits at a coffee table of a sort that brings cloudness into the living room. The prominent Everyday Aesthetics scholar Yuriko Saito often voices her concern caused by the neglect of the familiar and commonly shared dimensions of our lives and their significance by aesthetics, nonetheless "our aesthetic life is rich and multifaceted," and "the realm of 'the aesthetic' includes any reactions we form toward the sensuous and/or design qualities of any object, phenomenon, or activity."[64]

Look at Attfield's study of the power of forms of textile craft and design in constructing forms of social and personal identities, claiming that "focus on textile might yield in the search for an understanding of how individuality is embedded into the material culture of everyday life." She draws the readers' attention to the fact that textiles are "remarkably resilient," surviving for decades, "withstanding years of wear, laundering and change of use from coat to clip rug and from curtain to patchwork quilt." The history of textiles and dress thereby reveals values and identities. Most important for us here is Attfield's claim that "dress and textile terms such as mask and veil are often used in a metaphorical sense to refer to the subtle interface between the interior self and the outside world."[65] These metaphors are brought about from social and personal values and identities, and created at the material-visual level. For example a veil, possessing a specific textile fabric, texture, and shape, is more of an operator of covering and oppression than an embodiment or a symbol for an idea or ideology. It is the history of the use of textile: the intense experience of wearing it, or rather seeing others wear it, and sometimes being forced to wear it; it is the history of textiles creating separation, segregation, and covering that constructs the metaphor in which veil is the target.

The approach presented by Tilley is close to Attfield's account of ordinary, material artifacts. Tilley impressively describes the complexity and role of objects or artifacts in constructing big parts of our ontological sphere, acknowledging their ability to create identities as well. Tilley claims that "through creating, exchanging and ordering a world of artefacts people create an ordering of the world of social relations. Such a process of objectification is about the construction of meaning and values, about social relationships, and self-understandings of those meaning and values through material forms. Social images are constructed through the material media of artefacts."[66] His vantage point is one of social objectification, presenting the world of artifacts as analogous and complementary to language.

On the one hand, Tilley still considers the conceptualist stance as a reliable model, stressing the meaning of objects and their communicative significance, which are objectified and to which the visuality is subjugated. "To be human," he asserts, "is to think through metaphors and express these thoughts through linguistic utterances and objectify them in material forms."[67] Rather than taking full cognizance of the essential visuality of metaphor, and its being a real structure, it is somewhat disappointing to find that Tilley attributes a telos to metaphor "to work from the unknown to the known" and to understand the world. Thus, Tilley devotes many arguments to elevate materiality to the level of verbality, and to elevate artifacts to the level of words. In his 2006 essay "Objectification" he offers that "another way to understand the relationship between speech or language and material forms is to suggest that metaphor is central to both, to the manner in which particular meanings are communicated and synaesthetic links are established between seemingly disparate social and material domains."[68]

On the other hand, Tilley's research is inspiring, in light of his deep anthropological projects, which aim to track the status of the external world in constituting the metaphor as a medium, along with his grasp of the autonomous primary status of materiality and visuality. "If material culture simply reified in a material medium that which could be communicated in words it would be quite redundant. The nonverbal materiality of the medium is thus of central importance."[69] One of his studies analyzes the Melanesian canoes as a central, ubiquitous, material metaphor, which enables people, so he claims, to express themselves and their social relations in un-discursive ways: being "dynamic forms articulating space-time and mediating social ties. They link opposed metaphorical qualities of land and sea, maleness and femaleness rootedness and journeying." After all, he rightly claims, the artifact is "is a multiple site for the inscription and negotiation of social relations, power and social dynamics. The artefact is both interwoven with and recursively engaged in the production and constitution society."[70] Tilley's grasp of the prominence and productivity of material metaphors is crucial to the new vision of metaphor studies in the current visual turn. His study proved the paradigmatic status of visual metaphors over the other kinds—conceptual or linguistic. His formulation of this status in his essay "Metaphor, Materiality and Interpretation" is precise: "The meanings created through artefacts and words cannot be exchanged for each other, and thus the material object forms a powerful metaphorical medium through which people may reflect on their world in a way simply not possible with words alone."[71] I will proceed with the second part of Tilley's words in the next subchapter, concerning visual metaphors as being paradigmatic of all metaphors.

5.6 Paradigmatic metaphors

In his studies of material metaphors, which, I contend, are a subclass of visual metaphors, Tilley thoroughly and convincingly shows that artifacts are a site of various kinds of significance, carrying values in a way possible only for crafted objects. While temporary metaphors, such as a cloud with a face, may be made by transfigurative perception, planned and culturally loaded metaphorical objects, such as Morris's *Cloud Table*, are substantial elements in every level of our being. Understanding this allows us to conclude that it is the visual metaphor whose ontological existence is surefire and the most substantial kind of metaphor, in that it serves as a model for all metaphors. Contrary to what is often argued in the literature, conceptual and linguistic metaphors are based on visual ones, rather than the other way around. From the point of view of material culture, Tilley says the following about the superiority of objects over language or concepts:

> Through the artefact, layered and often contradictory sets of meanings can be conveyed simultaneously. The artefact may be inherently ambiguous in its meaning contents precisely because it acts to convey information about a variety of symbolic domains through the same media, and because it may perform the cultural work of revealing fundamental tensions and contradictions in human social experience. In other words the artefact, through its silent "speech" and "written" presence, speaks what cannot be spoken, writes what cannot be written, and articulates that which remains conceptually separated in social practice.[72]

The primary status of material (visual) things, as well as our own physicality, over conceptual schemes, is also explained by Bruner under the establishment of cognitive psychology. Having studied the organization of knowledge and its representation, Bruner claims in his *Culture of Education* that material things guide our doings and our identities. Thinking is dependent on physical actions and doing is prior to mental representation. He uses the term "rebus" for the load that culture supplies for cognitive growth: "Rebus in its classical sense derives from the Latin 'res', and it denotes how things rather than words can control what we do. Our learned ancestors surely understood the expression *non verbis sed rebus*, explaining in things not words, understanding by doing something other than just talking." Being a member of a culture necessitates our taking part in the activities that the things around us demand, which in their turn constitute our being and humanhood, so Bruner claims: "tending the garden, paying the bills, repairing the downspout. Frequently, indeed, we know how to do those things long before we can explain conceptually what we are doing or normatively why we should be doing them."[73]

We are visual beings, and metaphors are basic for us. Indeed the conceptualist theory of metaphor, inaugurated in the 1980s, stressed both the foundational status of metaphors and their omnipresence. But, contrary to the conceptualist's main line of thought, these traits are due to our visual, not our conceptual, nature. Western rationalist thought, from Plato to Danto, from Kant to John Rawls, likes to characterize the human being as a conceptualizer, reaching picks through conceptual schemes. But the visual turn proves yet again that the empiricist ideas captured our essence much better. Nothing carries a deeper and more constitutive effect on us than the visual sphere. And it is in the visually based compositions that we reach our highs and lows—in everyday life, ethics, science, art and design, environment, information, and communication—and metaphors.

Without visual sources, imagistic infrastructures, aesthetic compositions, and their emergent properties, language and concepts *are just not enough to form metaphors*. Analyzing visual metaphor so far, I believe, allows us to take a theoretical route contrary to the conventional one to show that visual metaphor is the *paradigmatic kind* of metaphor. Opposing the prevalent application of the conceptual or linguistic structure to visual metaphor, I argue that linguistic and conceptual metaphors ought to be characterized through the visual mechanism, which is best captured in visual metaphors.

We have hitherto realized that studies show that perceptual features, in other words those features that are seen, have the primary role in the emergent part of metaphor—the part that makes it what it is. Accordingly, in comprehending metaphor people typically use imagery to produce emergent features.[74] Indurkhya's empirical studies of visuality help us to see how metaphors are dependent on visuality and perception, constructing a target by the visual properties of the source. In an educational article named "An Empirical Study on the Role of Perceptual Similarity in Visual Metaphors and Creativity," Indurkhya and Ojha present experiments concerning visual metaphors and their comprehension in which participants were presented with images of source and target in various levels of visual similarity. Their results led them to conclude that perceptual similarity highly affects, even determines, the emergence and creation of new features in metaphors, whether visual, linguistic, or conceptual. Moreover, they show that visual imagery plays a major role in the comprehension of every kind of metaphors:

Our experiments show that the participants had a preference toward perceptually similar images. Moreover, they took a longer time for conceptually similar images, but the addition of perceptual similarity reduces the response time. This suggests that *perceptual similarity may be facilitating the search for conceptual similarity as well as the creation of new conceptual relations*. Analysis of the first fixations revealed that whenever a perceptually similar image was available, most participants had their first fixation on that image."[75] (my italics)

For one of their experiments, they hypothesize "a pair of images with a high perceptual similarity index is more likely to be given a metaphorical interpretation." This led to the conclusion that metaphor comprehension is influenced, at least partially, by perceptual similarity at the level of color or shape. In other words, what they call a "high-level metaphorical process" was aided by low-level perceptual similarities. Other findings showed that "perceptual similarity correlates positively with emergent features that are neither part of the target nor of the source." Eye movement analysis for high-similarity images revealed that both the target and the source have similar attention patterns. This suggests a feature-based comparison. Indeed, visuality and metaphorical emergence are correlated if not internally linked. One more interesting and related finding was that when presented with dissimilar images, eye movements focused on the target image, whereas the source image received distributed attention. According to the researchers, "this suggests that features are searched in the source image that might apply to the object of focus in the target image. The features of the target are picked first, which in turn affects the features of the source that are selected."[76]

The metaphorical mechanism is predicated upon cross-categorical structures, non-conventional compositions, and visual combinations. Figurative language itself is dependent on the ability to see the figures in actuality, or to picture them in images as *new compositions*. Even conceptual metaphor is dependent on a structural perception of seeing or picturing one concept through a different one, which is enabled by the structural possibilities offered by visual media, "because it offers structural equivalents to all characteristics of objects, events, relations," in Arnheim's words.[77] Indurkhya's account of the perceptual and environmental origin of metaphors, following Arnheim's Gestalt approach, is helpful here as well. He argues that when facing "the sky is crying," the experience of rain is not required at that moment, "but words may evoke concrete percepts or episodes of rain, sorrow, etc. which in turn may activate a certain Gestalt organization that sees the sky as a sorrowful agent." The important point here, I think, is his emphasis on the inevitability of interaction with the external environment for the mutual evocation of percepts, words, and concepts. Indurkhya asserts that "all depends on the past experiences and interactions of the agent with its environment, so even when the agent is not experiencing the situation at that moment, the environment ends up playing a key role in how the described situation is re-experienced."[78]

I further claim that grasping novel compositions is, in a broad sense, a visual ability, even an aesthetic ability. This is the ability to perceive not only Pablo Picasso's *Baboon and Young* or Seletti's *Hot Dog Sofa* (Figure 2), but also to picture, as well as to create, warm and cold colors, Internet surfing, or a hobbyhorse made of a wooden stick, and to conceive—to see—the compositions "man is a wolf" and "love is a journey." Hence, it is the aesthetic aspect of intellectuality that is in charge of understanding metaphors. I follow here aestheticist, formalist, and mainly externalist claims that intellectual progress is a matter of aesthetic creativity, no less than it is a matter of conceptual reasoning—a matter of creating compositions.

The interplay between elements of composition, which determines the character of each of them, is best realized by visual (or sensuous) ones. An accurate formulation of the influence of context and juxtaposition of things next to each other is presented by Arnheim, concluding one of the deepest and most comprehensive studies of the nature of composition and the visual:

> the appearance of any item in the visual field was shown to depend on its place and function in the total structure and to be modified fundamentally by that influence. If a visual item is extricated from its context, it becomes a different object. Similarly complex situations arise in other areas of perception whenever "two and two" are put together. That is, when several items are seen as a unitary pattern.[79]

All elements gain characteristics or properties, sometimes the strongest that they possess, within their position in a structure and relations with other elements. Indeed, the structure of metaphor is formed in the final stage of composition. Those metaphorical properties that emerge from the very fusion of elements in their specific combination are most susceptible to this phenomenon. The metaphorical property of being a bun is gained by Seletti's *Hot Dog Sofa* (Figure 2) only through the metaphorical composition, and emerges only by it, because being a bun possessed by a sofa is critically different from being a bun possessed by a piece of bread. The former is cushion-soft, made of textile, big and seatable, and also full of humor and pop art reference. The latter is small and edible.

The nature of emergent properties indeed supports my anti-conceptualist case that external metaphors are not entailments of a pure conceptual scheme, but rather autonomous compositions possessing their own emergent properties. The emergent properties of metaphors cannot be captured by an internal conceptual structure. Because they emerge thanks to the power of composition, gained only through the external sphere, they have to be seen (or heard). Surely, no concept of sofa understood through the concept of bun can remotely capture the hotdog sofa metaphor. But also no concept of love understood through a journey can remotely capture the metaphors from which emerge paths and views that can only be possessed by relationships.

6

New Terminology for Metaphors: Visuality and Affordance

If we accept the visualist model of metaphor, a terminological shift from conceptual understanding to an understanding that reflects metaphor's being a medium by itself is required. We focused on the concept of "emergence," and it is time we introduced a related concept: "affordance." Affordance is logically related, if not equivalent, to the visualists' notion of the power of the object and its dynamic character, but brings us closer to the frantically visual era we face and its corresponding visual turn. "Affordance" I think also fits new theories of everyday aesthetics and philosophy of design. The term was coined by Gibson, with whom the visualists Gombrich, Arnheim, and Goodman conducted an ongoing discourse on perceptions and the nature of objects, and it is to be expected given that they all asserted in one manner or another that (in Gibson's words) "the observer and his environment are complementary. So are the set of observers and their common environment."[1] In this framework, Gibson addressed what the environment affords those who observe it and live in it. He first used the term "affordance" his *The Senses Considered as Perceptual Systems*, from 1966,[2] and extended the definition in his *The Ecological Approach to Visual Perception* from 1979. There he takes an enlightening *externalist* step, claiming that the theory may advance from the perception of the visuality of surfaces to the perception of what the surfaces afford, what he calls their affordances. Affordances are determined by the composition of the surfaces, and they are perceived visually:

> How do we go from surfaces to affordances? And if there is information in light for the perception of surfaces, is there information for the perception of what they afford? Perhaps the composition and layout of surfaces *constitute* what they afford. If so, to perceive them is to perceive what they afford. This is a radical hypothesis, for it implies that the "values" and "meanings" of things in the

environment can be directly perceived. Moreover, *it* would explain the sense in which values and meanings are external to the perceiver.[3] (original emphases)

Reintroducing ontology, rather than conceptual schema, as the sphere of metaphors, adjoined with grasping metaphors' own materials, perceptual dynamics, and abilities to invite their own categorization leads to defining metaphor in terms of its own space of possible relations with its audience. Furthermore, the question of metaphorical success, differentiating between reconstructions that are afforded by the target and those that do not stick, relates success directly to the affordance of the target. Gibson's attribution of affordance to the composition of the object or a piece of the environment, stressing its visuality, is plausible. It also easily linked to the omnipresence of metaphors, both the temporary and the stable, and their resultant connection to everyday aesthetics:

> If a terrestrial surface is nearly horizontal (instead of slanted), nearly flat (instead of convex or concave), and sufficiently extended (relative to the size of the animal) and if its substance is rigid (relative to the weight of the animal), then the surface *affords support*. It is a surface of support, and we call it a substratum, ground, or floor. It is stand-on-able, permitting an upright posture for quadrupeds and bipeds. It is therefore walk-on-able and run-over-able. It is not sink-into-able like a surface of water or a swamp, that is, not for heavy terrestrial animals.[4] (original emphasis)

Indeed, new theories of art and design have begun to adopt this term. An eye-opening iconographic 2021 study of the depiction of pointed amphorae in Athenian vase painting, by Yael Young, applies this term to explain the different uses of the amphora (as a piece of furniture, a toy, a sound box, etc.) that "stemming from its shape and material and the inherent potentialities for action, are perceived and exploited by the users."[5] A rich analysis of affordance is offered in the theory of everyday design objects which design theoretician Donald Norman formulated, first in 1988 and in a more elaborate version in 2013. Studying the interaction of use between a person and a product in his *The Design of Everyday Things*, Norman tries to answer the question of how we manage to interact with objects, even though we are surrounded by many of them: objects both artificial and natural, familiar and unique. In the framework of the externalist theoretical infrastructure of affordance, Norman attributes to affordance what he names "discoverability," the ability to figure out what an object does and how it works: "the perceived and actual properties of the thing, primarily those fundamental properties that determine just how the thing could possibly be used." The psychology of materials and things comprises the study of affordances of objects. A chair affords support, hence, it can be sat on, but can also be carried. Glass is for seeing through and breaking; wood's affordance is based on its solidity, opacity, support, and the possibility for it to be carved and written on; knobs afford turning; slots afford inserting certain things; balls afford throwing or bouncing. The affordance of scissors is easily discoverable thanks to its visible operating parts, and that moving the handle makes the blades move, while a digital watch does not afford visible relationships between the buttons and its possible actions.[6]

For a visualist definition of metaphor theory, the concept of "affordance" is a treasure trove, and I would like to further introduce the analysis of "affordance" to the field of metaphors and their visual nature. The perceptual space of interactions, founded on the appearance of a thing which the viewer or user is invited to explore, is the exact infrastructure of metaphor. Beyond the shape and material-bound uses of the thing itself, I believe affordance also accounts for what the object invites us to do with it in order to reconstruct something else. If we agree that an experience of the visuality of the source is the starting place for the comprehension of the metaphor, we must also agree that the phenomenon of discoverability of the space of uses of a thing stemming from its shapes and materials is basic to metaphor creation. Affordance applies to the three parts of metaphors: the use of the source to reconstruct the target, the space of possibilities of reconstruction afforded by the target, and the emergent properties of the composition amalgamating the source and the target. The pebble shape affords storing the charger of the powermat, the setting on the desk, and the holding of a cellphone (Figure 1). The shape of the sharpener affords holding pencils inside, as designed by Jamie and Mark Antoniades (Figure 3). The perceived shark properties afford to be reapplied to a specific kind of lawyers: the kind that attacks indiscriminately. While the eyes and mouth afford using them to personify so many things, so many things in turn afford seeing faces in them (though in this case they are the target of the metaphor).

Affordance, embodied in all of the three parts of metaphors, is presented in a beautiful account of metaphor in architecture in the formalist essay of Stanford Anderson, "The Fiction of Function." Here, he retroactively renounces the functionalist narrative of modernist architecture in favor of a formalist, one may say visualist, narrative. This account is a bit long, but worth reading in its entirety. Look, for instance, at what he says about the metaphorical structure of the pin-joints of the arches of Peter Behrens's *Turbine Factory* (1909; Figure 17) in light of self-suggestion (affordance) and a load of doorknobs:

Figure 17 Peter Behrens, *Turbine Factory*, Berlin, 1909. Photographer unknown.

Certain features of buildings may reveal internal functions sufficiently directly to be seen as more than metaphors for those functions: the length and repetitiveness of a factory elevation refers to similar characteristics of the processes it houses. Structural details may reveal their own function, but may also serve metaphorically: the great pin-joints of the arches of Peter Behrens's Turbine Factory in Berlin, beautifully machined and displayed on pedestals just above street level, insist on their own objectness while suggesting themselves as the engines of their own structural system and cognate to those engines of another mechanical system fabricated within. For that matter, it is virtually impossible to deprive building elements of metaphoric qualities associated with various functions: portals and doors loaded with the significance of arrival or departure; windows as the eyes of the building or as the frame through which a controlled view of the world is afforded.[7]

The substantial role of affordance in the world of things must include the field of metaphors, given that they are so ubiquitous. What is more, the notion of affordance is useful for shifting from a model of metaphor as an abstract conceptual scheme to the correct ontological, visual, particular model. A function may be abstractly well-planned prior to the execution of an artifact, but not many can predict the real-external space of particular uses. I am not referring here to a child using a car toy easily held as a percussion instrument. I am referring to well-designed objects such as Morris's modernist *Cloud Table* (Figure 16), which afforded a whole new a-hierarchical mode of sitting, revealing the titles of visitors as external from now on, contributing to the modernist zeitgeist. I refer also to reconstructing the Bankside Power Station on the Thames as the Tate Modern. The same goes with metaphors: the physical perceptual elements in a journey afford reconstructing relationships as journeys. A tree affords a reconstruction of knowledge thanks to its linear structure from its roots to the top, but it also affords the construction of the *White Tree* building (Figure 14) thanks to its branches (or, rather, its porches) and its height. A ship invites us to use it as a living space, as well as to build the *Ship Building* (Figure 8)—whereby that ship dialectically affords using a sailing vibe for a standing building.

We face here an intricate sort of realism. It is rightly noted by Nyíri, one of the inaugurators of the current visual turn in philosophy, that he aspires to reject relativism using his "commonsense realism." The limits of affordances, and the fact that this term refers to the direct perception of an object, fit here:

> verbal language emerges from the natural language of facial expressions and gestures, which are movement and image at the same time ... the strategy is specific in that it is based on the assumption that the human mind is a visual one—indeed, as I will stress, fundamentally a kinesthetic or motor one. The primary contact we make with reality is not verbally mediated; rather, it is direct, kinesthetic, perceptual, visual.[8]

Norman made sure to emphasize, in a prescriptive mode, that a design object whose uses are not directly discoverable, indeed requiring a manual to use, not only lacks affordances but also fails in its design. Writing about the structure of the visual world, following Arnheim's and Gombrich's attribution of primary status to the external visual sphere, Nyíri quotes Gibson in support of its externalist-visualist approach. Gibson termed it the "ecological theory of vision," as Nyíri informs us: "in his essay 'New Reasons for Realism' he explains that 'the structure of an array of ambient light from the earth' displays 'invariants … specific to the substances of which objects are composed, to the edges of objects, and to the layout of their surfaces,' adding some pages later: 'The doctrine of secondary qualities comes from a misunderstanding.'"[9]

The point of respecting objects' visual properties and the power of the surfaces, which I consider to be deeply related to affordance and metaphors, has been made time and again by the visualists. Arnheim emphasizes that an object's perceptual effect is not dependent on the observer's knowledge of its resource. "Rather, we must look for the visible properties of the percept that are responsible for the phenomenon."[10] Visual dynamics, for example, "is a property inherent in shapes, colors, and locomotion, not something added to the percept by the imagination of an observer who relies on his memories. The conditions creating dynamics have to be sought in the visual object itself."[11]

Acknowledging the power of the object's visuality does not exclude the idea of active perception, transfigurative look, the loaded eye (against the innocent eye), or Pygmalion power—all combine perceptual work with what the percept affords. Gombrich's characterization of colors in his "Visual Metaphors of Value in Art" explains their source of affordance. He differentiates between fixed or conventional visual code-symbols of value, religious ones, for example, and "visual qualities that lend themselves to symbolic use." Look how closely related this is to the idea of affordance (if not synonymous):

> A simple example of what I shall call a visual metaphor is the use of the colour red in certain cultural contexts. Red, being the colour of flames and blood, offers itself as a metaphor for anything that is strident or violent. It is no accident, therefore, that it was selected as the code sign for "stop" in our traffic code and as a label of revolutionary panics in politics. But though both these applications are grounded on simple biological facts, the colour red itself has no fixed "meaning."[12]

Gombrich's approach is as intricate or dialectic here as ever. The object has a lot to do with its space of perceptions and uses, but it is also saturated with cultural charge and the history of experience. I myself named the form charged with inextricable content, that which saturates the object, "deep form."[13] The fusion is that which creates the space of affordance—the possibilities which are afforded by the thing. This is exactly the structure of metaphor, the emergent properties of the newly reconstructed target (the third part of metaphor), which lends itself, but not without limitations, to the creative eye. Arnheim is right to note that in confronting structures we see roundness, smallness, remoteness, and swiftness. Similarly, in facing dynamic structures we see compactness, striving, twisting, expanding, and yielding.[14]

What is more, Arnheim offers a model of perceptual completion by the observer or user:

> a bridge is perceived as something to be walked over, a hammer as something to be gripped and swung. This extension is much more tangible than would be a mere association between an object and its use, or the mere understanding of what the object can serve to do. It is the direct perceptual completion of an object that looks incomplete as long as it is unemployed.[15]

Like Gombrich, Gibson, and Norman, Arnheim here employs a somewhat functionalist view. When an object is disarmed and stripped of its affordances, it looks weird. Arnheim reminds us that when functional objects are displayed in an art museum, regarded as shapes, "the absence of their visible function can change their appearance quite strangely. A pair of eyeglasses deprived of its connotation by such a display becomes spidery. Some modern artists have succeeded in alienating the familiar simply by presenting utensils of our daily lives as objects of contemplation."[16]

Thus, another part of affordance which is crucial for metaphors is the ability of the mind of the observer to complete the percept which presents only hints of its identity, but does invite a recognition trusting "our faculty to project and to supplement," as Gombrich labels it in his study of "conditions of illusion."[17] Both Gombrich and Arnheim refer to impressionism and Édouard Manet's paintings as a good example of this structure. Manet's stains are constructed as horses in *The Races at Longchamp* from 1866, according to Gombrich, because the observer is invited to recognize them as such. "The blob in the painting by Manet" affords its perception as horse, since Manet "has so cleverly contrived it that it evokes the image in us—provided of course, we collaborate."[18] He explains this invitation by relying on our readiness to take hints read contexts, and recall visual memory. Arnheim calls this invitation made by the perceived thing its "visual force." Following the psychologist Edward Titchener, he claims that partiality or incompleteness of a seen thing is not a disadvantage, but rather a positive quality. It helps us to distinguish between the physical nature of the object itself and the perceived one. This gap is embodied by an impressionist painting, such as Manet's, by comparison to those of the realists:

In spite of the considerable liberties which artists before the generation of Edouard Manet took in fact with the object they portrayed, the accepted convention held that a picture had to be intended as a faithful likeness. The comparison with Impressionist painting can also help us to understand the nature of Titchener's "visual hints" and "flashes." Instead of spelling out the detailed shape of a human figure or a tree the Impressionist offered an approximation, a few strokes, which were not intended to create the illusion of the fully duplicated figure or tree. Rather, in order to serve as the stimulus for the intended effect, the reduced pattern of strokes was to be perceived as such … The assembly of colored strokes on the canvas was responded to by the beholder with what can only be described as a pattern of visual forces.[19]

An analogous structure of trusting the viewer collaboration, projection, and working with the piece's affordances with an appropriate consideration of context exists in discourse according to Hopper's 2012 paper "Emergent Grammar." According to Hopper, spoken grammar relies on projection, namely "the ways in which speakers mold their utterances so that hearers can anticipate and thus prestructure a segment of discourse." As such, discourse analysis uses the concept of "projection" to characterize communicative situations. In other words, just like artists and designers expect the viewers or users to accept the invitation of the image or product to react perceptually by projecting a horse on a stain or sitting on a bench, the speaker expects a projection for the communication to take place. This is a parallel structure of affordance. According to Hopper: "Projection is what makes verbal communication an open and collaborative affair; as participants develop a sense of where the discourse is going, they can tacitly mold it, allow it to continue, harmonize with the speaker's goals, interrupt it with their own contribution, offer supportive tokens of various kinds, or predict when their turn will come."[20] Conversation, therefore, is a context for grammar's affordance, which has similar traits to the context of visual affordance.

6.1 Affordance in visual context

The significance of the context of appearance described above is marked by Yuriko Saito's concept of "circumstantial beauty," namely, considering beauty as "generated by a situation," which characterizes the Japanese structure of aesthetic appreciation, but appears in Western aesthetics as well. Saito refers, for example, to Archibald Alison's point that "the same sound of an eagle or an owl changes its character depending upon the time of the day (morning or night) and location (in captivity or in the wild)."²¹ This widens the extension of "affordance" to include and consider circumstances, which in turn bear on affordances as well. A well-known phenomenon of visual circumstances is the anisotropic character of visuality: a line looks longer in the vertical direction, but shorter in the horizontal. In the Müller-Lyer illusion, for instance, the two horizontal lines are of equal length but look different.²²

Social circumstances, too, affect the perceptual affordances—the uses and actions the object allows in its interactions with us—as shown by the design and material culture historian Judith Attfield. Her opposition to what she sees as the modernist rigid attribution of stable identity and agency to design objects is helpful in showing that the logical space of an object extends beyond its basic properties to the various gazes and uses it invites us to practice. Attfield criticizes "the central 'given' in design theory derived from modernism that still holds today. It assumes an agency on the part of the design process to be able to predict and control how the product will be put to use within certain parameters of space and place."²³ Therefore, Attfield proposes a more contextualist view of the material reality of our lives, seeing objects, especially the design objects, as "social things within a dynamic existence in the material world of everyday."²⁴

In her *Wild Things: The Material Culture of Everyday Life*, Attfield coins the wonderful term "things with attitude," those "that derive their meaning from their obvious visual presence"—for design objects. She thereby presents the extension of "design" as wide enough to include everyday objects within "the material culture of innovation-driven a vision of change as beneficial."²⁵ I am referring to Attfield's inclusive theory of design not only because design is a rich arena of material metaphors, indeed one that encompasses all that the creation of metaphor requires: a sense of categories and their transgression, familiarity, innovation, and most of all their visuality. I also refer to Attfield's theory of design and material culture as it opens yet another path toward the realization that cultural meaning is saturated in our material culture—our visual sphere—of things and their affordances. She claims that material culture ought to be theorized and studied as follows: "the metaphorical and physical limits of conceptual frameworks, definitions, hierarchical boundaries, and the cultural politics of locality, all aspects of order, need to be brought into play to contextualize the process that results in the physical manifestation of different cultural perspectives."²⁶ And this, in turn, sheds light on the nature of visual metaphors as *the* medium of metaphors.

A further, adventurous, proposition regarding metaphors may be offered here: the pebble-powermat, set on a desk or kitchen table (Figure 1), may open a chain of descendant metaphors, or at least may endow a metaphoricity to its environment. For example, the pebble-powermat may impart the property "being a bank of a stream" to that desk or table, or even lightly reconstruct it as such. *Hot Dog Sofa* (Figure 2) gives the living room an atmosphere of a fast-food court. Neil Morris's *Cloud Table* (Figure 16) reconstructs the living room with a new celestial lightness, and indeed was paradigmatic in the modernist progress toward redesigning the living room to be a casual, social-status-neutral, but nonetheless central part of the house. Maybe my aspirations here are too high. Indeed, a metaphorical influence does not often entail full, self-standing metaphors, but rather vibes, atmospheres, feelings, and conditional properties. However, it is evident that metaphors have an impact on their surroundings. A weeping willow tree may bear emotional elements which touch its close environment, and may thereby afford a wider impersonation of its surroundings. A shark lawyer affords fish or sea creatures or predators in an offensive arena. Attributing the shapes of hands, a neck, and a head to a corkscrew, for example (Figure 10), brings up a potential application of the human shape to kitchen accessories. Designing a picture to possess a sad composition not only allows pictures to potentially be sad, but allows for affordance of various kinds of emotions, for some pictures to generally be sadder or happier than other pictures. Labeling someone as the face of a business could mean that the others in the business are less representative.

My assertion here is related to Goodman's delineation of a mechanism of systematic label shifts generated by metaphorical application—only to some extent, but still significantly. The units of this mechanism, according to Goodman, are not merely specific labels, but complete sets of labels in conjunction with their hierarchies, commands, and values. These reorganize the realm of the target of metaphor. Goodman proposes that,

> metaphor typically involves a change not merely of range but also of realm. A label along with others constituting a schema is in effect detached from the home realm of that schema and applied for the sorting and organizing of an alien realm. Partly by thus carrying with it a re-orientation of the whole network of labels does a metaphor give clues for its own development and elaboration.[27]

For instance, by applying the "cold–warm" labels to people's characters, their whole apparatus is shifted from objects with temperature to the target realm of characters, and "takes over the new territory." Thus, according to Goodman, the relations between labels and pairs of labels migrate as well—the metaphor "heavy" for sounds migrates with the metaphor "heavier than" for another sound.

I do not think that metaphorical application is as organized by an apparatus of sets of labels as Goodman presents it to be. Additionally, I argue that *particular* metaphorical applications are as typical to the medium of metaphors as general applications. But Goodman's overall delineation of metaphorical nets is enlightening when it comes to the potential of ontological orders afforded by metaphors, as well as the affordance of a phenomenon reconstructed metaphorically. Hausman gives a relevant example of the antecedent ontological import of metaphor in science: "electrons are now entrenched as conditions on theory, although first recognized through creative reconstitution of scientific understanding of the way atoms function, which led to metaphors, which in turn became models of orbiting particles."[28]

No doubt properties of metaphorical things are embedded in the relationships with other properties, and are afforded as a result. Certainly relations between properties possessed by non-metaphorical things are often crucial. Metaphorical properties are always re-transfigured by each other. But the ontological-perceptual context sometimes plays a significant role in creating metaphorical identity, either of a thing or a metaphorical situation such as seeing a car staring at us—attributing "being eyes" to its lights, or from the opposite direction the seatability of the muffin chair (Figure 5). Indeed whether "being a muffin" is attributed to the chair depends on the shape of the top of the muffin. The muffin, in turn, exists thanks to the chair and its function. These, together, afford the third part of metaphor. And this third part could be presented as at least partially dependent on the context of darkness, in the case of the car, and of function, in the case of the muffin chair. Affordance goes all the way from the metaphorical thing to its surroundings. It invites a relationship with the surroundings. The lights glitter, create holes in the dark, and invite us to see them as metaphorical staring eyes. This is called "affordance." And affordance is about a visual space of an object, which the object invites us to grasp, but which is stretched beyond the object itself.

6.2 Constraints of metaphorical affordance

To grasp the affordance of a metaphor, one must grasp that metaphor's ontological constraints: the properties that the metaphorical structure may gain, or alternatively resist. Part of the affordance is the rigid core of the percept. Visualism indeed figures that the character of affordance is dialectically determined both by the structure's possibilities and limits. Arnheim reminds us that "percepts are stubborn enough to admit modifications only within the range of the ambiguities they contain ... Strongly subjective though the impulses are in such perceptual acts, they are still bound by a profound respect for what is given to the eyes."[29] Following these assertions, Goodman points to the limits of the context of classification delineated by the rightness of rendering and rigid conventions. Gombrich points to the minimal form to which a function may be projected in order to reconstruct the object accordingly.

An instructive demarcation of the possibilities as well as the constraints of metaphorical affordance is offered by Hausman in the context of his ontological theory of metaphorical referents, referents by his lights being the ontological derivatives of these possibilities and constraints. For Hausman there is a difference between the constraints of non-creative and creative media, and accordingly between an ordinary expression and those of metaphorical creations. Constraints of possibilities are established on a distinction between the near and far side of the referent: the near being "the properties that appear for interpretation," i.e., the object's intelligibility, "its interpretability or the relevance of its meanings as these are articulated by the metaphor"; the far side is the resistance of the object to irrelevant interpretation. This distinction is exemplified by "man is a wolf":

> The near, interpreted side of the referents of "man is a wolf" is the complex of meanings, including the idea of the hunting instinct, ferocity, tendencies to join packs, cleverness, rationality, etc., which interpretation discerns in light of the metaphor ... the far side is the condition of constraint that works against interpreting "man is a wolf" as referring to daintiness, which, if regarded as relevant, would enter as part of the near side of its referent.[30]

The metaphor of "the man is a shadow of a dream," according to Hausman's theory, "must have been formed as a way of leading us to an insight into the fragility and evanescence of being human."[31] Thereby, its referents resist attributions of materiality, stability, or invariance. Thus, the constraints are conditioned by the referent of metaphor: a dynamic center that accepts and rejects, discloses or reveals, different properties.

Hausman attributes a substantial significance to the far side, the restriction of affordance, of metaphor. Thus the uniqueness of the intelligibility that the referent affords as something new "and that is expressed by the relevant interpretations generated by creative metaphors." Non-creative objects, which have a general model of interpretation in the context of a well-established linguistic-cognitive system, thus lend themselves to a ready-made scheme of interpretation. By contrast the metaphorical referent, a created, new, referent, resists ready-made schemes. "Its intelligibility clashes with the established system of interpretation and forces an adjustment on it. Thus, 'the other side' of the referent, its insistence, functions with its constraints so as to help direct the course of interpretive thought in the future."[32]

6.3 Affordance and visual expressivity

Extending the idea of affordance to metaphors makes expressivity part of what an object affords. Metaphor is defined by Arnheim as being entrenched in perceptual hierarchies, visual patterns, and expressive properties. The expressive qualities that an object may invite us to perceive emerge through structures and directly perceived Gestalt perspectives. Arnheim dubs each such quality the "perceivable form of behavior" of the object, which is just another way of calling it an object's affordance. The formalist Roger Fry calls the expressivity that a composition affords its "visual elements of design," which are based on our physical existence.[33] Fry opposed mentalist ideas which attribute the emotions expressed in art or design to the creator, and instead asserted that expression is a structural property of composition. Similarly, Arnheim argues that dynamics are created by contrasts in color and gravity, just as organizations invite experiences of "weakness and strength, harmony and discord, struggle and conformance."[34] The interactions between contrasting elements in the composition and its center may evoke tension. We find a parallel proposal in Goodman's theory of artistic expression: expressivity is a property of the artwork, which is metaphorically exemplified and shown forth. That is to say, it is a metaphorical property of the work. The problem of the dualist view of expressivity (or the more extreme "inner model") which separates mind and matter, is brilliantly presented by Garry Hagberg in his *Art as Language*. Surveying the various versions of the question of how an object becomes expressive, Hagberg rightly classifies "the paradoxical source of philosophical mystery surrounding artistic expression,"[35] as an ontological or metaphysical problem. Hagberg is not a visualist, but he criticizes the internalist model of expressivity and the separation between the cause of expressivity and the physical external object. Thus, like the visualists he raises doubts regarding the attribution of "metaphysical priority to the artist" by dualist expression theories, which portray a two-part model of the artwork: a physical external artifact and meaning, which is a mental or conceptual entity. Doing so, the dualist theories overlook what he calls "the obvious metaphysical incompatibility of inward emotions and outward objects."[36]

The problem formulated by Hagberg finds its solution among the visualists by defining expressivity of inanimate things as dependent on their dynamics. This is done by Arnheim who rightly *attributes the source of expression to the perceived object itself*. In light of these formalist theories of expressivity, a theory of metaphors would benefit from stretching the Gestalt theory beyond the object up to its affordances. More accurately, Arnheim finds in the object both the source of its space of possibilities and the demarcation of this space. The model of the pathetic fallacy, which would have a mental content projected upon the object, is rejected thereof. Arnheim contends when projection is properly defined as external, "there remained the genuine phenomenon of expression inherent in the perceptual appearance of the object itself."[37] What is left is to explain how expressivity is in charge of some of the object's affordances. Dynamic compositions of objects "illustrate and recall the behavior of forces elsewhere and in general. By endowing the object or event with a perceivable form of behavior, these tensions give it character and recall the similar character of other objects or events. This is what is meant by saying that these dynamic aspects of the percept 'express' its character."[38] Thus, refuting the mentalist model of expression, time and again Arnheim returns to the assertion that expression dwells in the depths of structures, in forms and compositions and their material and non-material elements. For him, the structural properties both include sensuous data and used metaphorically to characterize an infinity of non-sensory phenomena: "low morale or the high cost of living, the spiraling of prices, the lucidity of argument, the compactness of resistance ... as soon as we open our eyes to the dynamic qualities conveyed by any such thing, inevitably we see them as carrying expressive meaning."[39]

I find W. J. T. Mitchell's idea of the metaphorical agency of pictures supportive of the supportive of the idea of expressivity as an affordance. The idea of the agency of pictures suggests that an image has a logical space (using Wittgenstein's terminology) of its own, rather than a conceptual scheme which is forced on it. Mitchell's project surely undertakes to analyze images in general, but see in particular how relevant his idea of the will of images is to the imagistic possibility of recomposing the appearance of a thing. In his 2005 *What Do Pictures Want?* Mitchell tries to shift the discussion from "what pictures mean," which suggests they are inert and passive, to what he sees as the "fundamental ontological question" about pictures' own desires, needs, drives, and requirements.[40] The notion of the living image is what he calls "an incorrigible, unavoidable metaphor."[41] Pictures and images do not contain living organisms, but we sure treat them as if they do.

Even if we do not go so far as to attribute agency or life to images, Mitchell's strong argument certainly suggests that expressivity is no less in the realm of visual things than animals and human beings. Look at Arnheim's insightful words about the sad willow, explaining that its expressivity comes prior to our attributions to it and our own feelings:

> If one thinks of expression as something reserved for human behavior, one can account for the expression perceived in nature only as the result of the "pathetic fallacy"—a notion apparently introduced by John Ruskin and intended to describe, say, the sadness of weeping willows as a figment of empathy, anthropomorphism, primitive animism. However, if expression is an inherent characteristic of perceptual patterns, its manifestations in the human figure are but a special case of a more general phenomenon. The comparison of an object's expression with a human state of mind is a secondary process. The willow is not "sad" because it looks like a sad person. Rather, because the shape, direction, and flexibility of the branches convey passive hanging, a comparison with the structurally similar state of mind and body that we call sadness imposes itself secondarily.[42]

It is only after we personify expression, after it is anthropomorphized, that the expressive thing allegedly becomes an entailment of abstract, rather than dynamic, mental content. *This is exactly what the current dominant conceptualist-cognitivist theories of metaphor miss.*

In retrospect, Kövecses the conceptualist shows how the conceptualist paradigm presents metaphor as motionless, possessing no dynamics, and thus overlooking its actual use. He recognized this as a major disadvantage. According to him, "conceptual metaphor theory started out as and remained for a long time, an essentially offline theory of metaphor. What this means is that conceptual metaphors were regarded as static connections (mappings) between two domains (such as LIFE IS A JOURNEY) in long-term memory." This applies to theories of complex metaphors as well, such as those of schematicity hierarchies, that consider different levels of metaphors and the concepts that form them. All these theories, Kövecses claims, did not "capture the dynamic processes that occur in the course of the actual use of metaphors."[43]

I think we have closed the circle here, with the implied admission of the need for a new, visualist, externalist theory of metaphor. Kövecses's brave and eye-opening recent critique of conceptualism, in light of the deep and comprehensive theories of metaphor and visuality which are offered by the visualist, is the right place to conclude with a concise visualist definition of metaphor.

CONCLUSION

A Definition of Metaphor

We started with a presentation of the visual perspective of metaphor, advanced to the linguistic turn of metaphor, and then to the conquest of the field by the conceptual theory of metaphor, which was critically addressed. Then the advent of the visualist theory of metaphor took place, delineating the ontological and visual sphere as the origin of metaphor, endowing it with its visual essence. This chapter is a very short one, aiming to present the visualist definition of metaphor I have been trying to formulate throughout our journey together.

My definition is visualist, ontological, and formalist. It is, therefore, anti-conceptualist, anti-internalist, and committed to externalism as the right philosophical infrastructure of the theory of metaphor and its definition. I will present it in a single list:

1. Metaphor is an aesthetic and creative medium, which is founded on visuality.
2. Metaphor originates in the external visual-ontological sphere.
3. Metaphor is an ontological structure or composition. In the visual-ontological sphere, metaphors operate by compositional means of cross-categorical allocations of properties, resulting in emergent properties of surfacing wholes. Again, the creative process of metaphor is not a mere attribution, but a construction.
4. Metaphor consists of three parts: (a) source; (b) target; (c) emergent properties. These emergent properties are enabled by the power of composition and are the amalgamation of properties from the source and target. The emergent properties of a metaphor are unique to it and can be possessed by it alone.
5. It is from the visual-ontological sphere that properties, structures, forms, and relations are borrowed—actually, reproduced—to reconstruct the target with emergent properties and introduce it to a new ontological group.

6. Contrary to the conceptualist definition, metaphors are not born in the mental sphere of thought or understanding the target-concept through the source-concept, nor are they primarily formed as conceptual-mental content. Nor are they abstract conceptual schemes with external entailments. Specific external metaphors gain their own emergent properties, which are not entailed by any alleged internal type-metaphor. What is considered external entailment by conceptualism are actually primary autonomous metaphors, which may be conceptualized later on.
7. Metaphors reconstruct groups, categories, and specific objects or phenomena as well as lay the foundation for all the various metaphorical practices, such as linguistic, conceptual, practical, material, or visual—along the line which goes from ordinary to artistic metaphors.
8. The use of the source to reconstruct the target creates a third element, an emergent, not predetermined composition, which is productive in itself and serves as a context of the newly modified emergent properties of the source and target. In addition to the reconstruction of the target, the metaphorical structure changes the source properties according to the context of the metaphorical composition, so they are new sub-properties.
9. Visual metaphors are paradigmatic among the various kinds of metaphor, and the foundation of all of them. In visual metaphors, the powerful nature of the composition, which allows the emergence of properties thanks to the context of composition and the mutual influence of the elements within, is embodied in the best way, serving as a model for every kind of metaphor.

Notes

Chapter 1 The Visual Dimension of Metaphors: Framework and Main Argument

1. E. H. Gombrich, *Art and Illusion: A Study in the Psychology of Pictorial Representation* (Princeton, NJ: Princeton University Press, 1969), 250.
2. Leon Battista Alberti, *Leon Battista Alberti: On Painting: A New Translation and Critical Edition*, trans. Rocco Sinisgalli (Cambridge: Cambridge University Press, 2011), 39.
3. Rudolf Arnheim, *Art and Visual Perception: A Psychology of the Creative Eye; the New Version*, expanded and rev. edn, 50th anniversary printing (Berkeley: University of California Press, 2009), 324.
4. Keller Easterling, *Extrastatecraft: The Power of Infrastructure Space* (London: Verso, 2014), 85 (n 15).
5. E. H. Gombrich, "Visual Metaphors of Value in Art," in *Symbols And Values: An Initial Study*, ed. Lyman Bryson, Louis Finkelstein, and R. M. MacIver (New York: Cooper Square, 1964), 266.
6. Gombrich, *Art and Illusion*, 84.
7. Gombrich, *Art and Illusion*, 76.
8. E. H. Gombrich, *Meditations on a Hobby Horse: And Other Essays on the Theory of Art*, 3rd edn. (London: Phaidon, 1978), 4.
9. Gombrich, "Psycho-Analysis and the History of Art," in *Meditations on a Hobby Horse*, 34.
10. Gombrich, *Art and Illusion*, 81.
11. Virgil C. Aldrich, "Visual Metaphor," *Journal of Aesthetic Education* 2, no. 1 (1968): 74, 75.
12. Gombrich, *Art and Illusion*, 88.
13. E. H. Gombrich, *The Sense of Order: A Study in the Psychology of Decorative Art* (Ithaca, NY: Cornell University Press, 1984), 3.
14. Rudolf Arnheim, *Visual Thinking* (Berkeley: University of California Press, 1969), 93.
15. Arnheim, *Visual Thinking*, 94.
16. Nelson Goodman, *Languages of Art*, 2nd edn. (Indianapolis, IN: Hackett, 1976), 51.
17. Goodman, *Languages of Art*, 69.
18. Arnheim, *Visual Thinking*, 174–5.

19 András Benedek, "A New Paradigm in Education: The Priority of the Image," in *Vision Fulfilled: The Victory of the Pictorial Turn*, ed. Kristóf Nyíri and András Benedek (Budapest: Hungarian Academy of Sciences and Budapest University of Technology and Economics, 2019), 12.
20 Arnheim, *Visual Thinking*, 232.
21 Arnheim, *Visual Thinking*, 13.
22 Arnheim, *Visual Thinking*, 233.
23 Kristóf Nyíri, "Towards a Theory of Common-Sense Realism," in *In the Beginning Was the Image: The Omnipresence of Pictures—Time, Truth, Tradition*, ed. András Benedek and Ágnes Veszelszki (Frankfurt am Main: Peter Lang, 2016), 17.
24 Kristóf Nyíri, in *Vision Fulfilled: The Victory of the Pictorial Turn*, ed. Nyíri and Benedek, 17.
25 Arnheim, *Visual Thinking*, 232.
26 Yuriko Saito, *Aesthetics of the Familiar: Everyday Life and World-Making* (Oxford: Oxford University Press, 2017), 1.
27 Judy Attfield, "Design as a Practice of Modernity: A Case for the Study of the Coffee Table in the Mid-century Domestic Interior," *Journal of Material Culture* 2, no. 3 (1997): 268.
28 Judy Attfield, *Wild Things: The Material Culture of Everyday Life* (Oxford: Berg, 2000), 97.
29 Saito, *Aesthetics of the Familiar*, 11.
30 Saito, *Aesthetics of the Familiar*, 2.
31 Saito, *Aesthetics of the Familiar*, 2–3.
32 Richard Rorty, *Contingency, Irony, and Solidarity* (Cambridge: Cambridge University Press, 1989), 16.
33 E. H. Gombrich, "On Physiognomic Perception," *Daedalus* 89, no. 1 (1960): 232.
34 Gombrich, "On Physiognomic Perception," 233.
35 Nelson Goodman and Catherine Z. Elgin, *Reconceptions in Philosophy and Other Arts and Sciences* (Indianapolis, IN: Hackett, 1988), 21.
36 Nelson Goodman, *Ways of Worldmaking* (Indianapolis, IN: Hackett, 1978), 105.
37 Goodman, *Ways of Worldmaking*, 65.
38 Gombrich, "On Physiognomic Perception," 232–3.
39 Gombrich, "On Physiognomic Perception," 232.
40 Congressional Record Volume 167, Number 7, Tuesday, 12 January 2021 [House], pp H133–H143.
41 Congressional Record Volume 167, Number 7, Tuesday, 12 January 2021 [House], pp H133–H143.
42 Gombrich, *Art and Illusion*, 89.
43 Rorty, *Contingency, Irony, and Solidarity*, 17.
44 Donald Davidson, *Inquiries into Truth and Interpretation*, 2nd edn. (Oxford: Clarendon Press, 2001), 247.

45 Rorty, *Contingency, Irony, and Solidarity*, 17.
46 Richard Rorty, *Objectivity, Relativism, and Truth: Philosophical Papers, Vol. 1* (Cambridge: Cambridge University Press, 1990), 163.
47 Rorty, *Contingency, Irony, and Solidarity*, 9–10.
48 Davidson, *Inquiries into Truth and Interpretation*, 252–3.
49 Gombrich, *Meditations on a Hobby Horse*, 6.
50 Gombrich, *Meditations on a Hobby Horse*, 8.
51 Gombrich, "On Physiognomic Perception," 232.
52 Gombrich, "On Physiognomic Perception," 232.
53 Ruskin, *Modern Painters*, III: 165.
54 Oscar Wilde, *The Complete Works* (New York: Harper & Row, 1989), 970. See more about Wilde's opposition to Ruskin in my Gal, *Aestheticism: Deep Formalism and the Emergence of Modernist Aesthetics* (Bern: Peter Lang, 2015), 18.
55 Ruskin, *Modern Painters*, III: 164.
56 Gombrich, "On Physiognomic Perception," 232–3.
57 Rudolf Arnheim, *Towards a Psychology of Art: Collected Essays* (London: Faber & Faber, 1966), 62.
58 Arnheim, *Towards a Psychology of Art*, 62.
59 Arnheim, *Towards a Psychology of Art*, 58.
60 Arnheim, *Towards a Psychology of Art*, 58.
61 Arnheim, *Towards a Psychology of Art*, 58.
62 Arnheim, *Towards a Psychology of Art*, 243.
63 Ian Verstegen, *Arnheim, Gestalt and Art: A Psychological Theory* (Vienna: Springer, 2005), 21.
64 Ian Verstegen, *Arnheim, Gestalt and Media: An Ontological Theory* (Cham: Springer, 2018), 32.
65 Arnheim, *Art and Visual Perception*, 454.
66 Arnheim, *Art and Visual Perception*, 455.
67 Leslie Cunliffe, "Gombrich on Art: A Social-Constructivist Interpretation of His Work and Its Relevance to Education," *Journal of Aesthetic Education* 32, no. 4 (1998): 71.
68 Arnheim, *Visual Thinking*, 14.
69 Arnheim, *Visual Thinking*, 14–15.
70 Arnheim, *Visual Thinking*, 15.
71 Bipin Indurkhya, "Interview," ed. Massimo Sangoi, *Humana.Mente Journal of Philosophical Studies* 23 (2012): 202.
72 Indurkhya, "Interview," 202.
73 Carl R. Hausman, "Criteria of Creativity," in *The Idea of Creativity*, ed. Michael Krausz, Denis Dutton, and Karen Bardsley (Leiden: Brill, 2009), 16.
74 Arnheim, *Visual Thinking*, 232.
75 Arnheim, *Visual Thinking*, 90.

76 Riccardo Fusaroli, and Simone Morgagni, "Conceptual Metaphor Theory: 30 Years After," *Cognitive Semiotics* 5, no. 1/2 (2013): 82.
77 Raymond W. Gibbs, Jr., "Conceptual Metaphor in Thought and Social Action," in *The Power of Metaphor: Examining Its Influence on Social Life*, ed. Mark J. Landau, Michael D. Robin, and Brian P Meier (Washington, DC: American Psychological Association, 2013), 21–2.
78 Arthur C. Danto, *The Transfiguration of the Commonplace: A Philosophy of Art* (Cambridge, MA: Harvard University Press, 1981), 176, 179, 189, emphases in original.
79 Arthur C. Danto, "Metaphor and Cognition," in *Knowledge and Language, Volume III: Metaphor and Knowledge*, ed. F. R. Ankersmit, and J. J. A. Mooij (Dordrecht: Springer Science+Business Media, 1993), 31.
80 T. J. Clark, *Farewell to an Idea: Episodes from a History of Modernism* (New Haven, CT: Yale University Press, 1999), 165.
81 See Goodman, *Ways of Worldmaking*, mainly, "When Is Art," 57–70, "The Fabrication of Facts," 91–108.
82 Indurkhya, "Interview," 200–1.
83 Aristotle, *The Rhetoric and the Poetics of Aristotle* (Scotts Valley, CA: CreateSpace Independent Publishing Platform, 2010), 126.

Chapter 2 Semantic Theories of Metaphor

1 Elisabeth Camp, "Metaphor and That Certain 'Je Ne Sais Quoi,'" *Philosophical Studies* 129, no. 1 (2006): 1.
2 Mary Hesse, "The Cognitive Claims of Metaphor," *Journal of Speculative Philosophy* 2, no. 1 (1988): 1, 3.
3 Richard Wollheim, "Metaphor and Painting," in *Knowledge and Language, Volume III: Metaphor and Knowledge*, ed. F. R. Ankersmit, and J. J. A. Mooij (Dordrecht: Springer Science+Business Media, 1993), 114.
4 Rudolf Arnheim, "A Plea for Visual Thinking," *Critical Inquiry* 6, no. 3 (1980): 489.
5 Arnheim, "A Plea for Visual Thinking," 489.
6 Wollheim, "Metaphor and Painting," 114.
7 Wollheim, "Metaphor and Painting," 116.
8 Wollheim, "Metaphor and Painting," 113.
9 Wollheim, "Metaphor and Painting," 122.
10 Danto, "Metaphor and Cognition," 22.
11 Danto, "Metaphor and Cognition," 23.
12 Danto, "Metaphor and Cognition," 23.
13 Danto, "Metaphor and Cognition," 26.

14 Danto, "Metaphor and Cognition," 26, 33.
15 I. A. Richards, *The Philosophy of Rhetoric* (London: Oxford University Press, 1965), 131.
16 Richards, *The Philosophy of Rhetoric*, 93, 43.
17 Max Black, "Metaphor," *Proceedings of the Aristotelian Society* 55, no. 1 (1955): 286.
18 Black, "Metaphor," 289.
19 Max Black, "More About Metaphor," *Dialectica* 31, no. 3/4 (1977): 441.
20 Black, "More About Metaphor," 442.
21 Black, "More About Metaphor," 443.
22 Black, "More About Metaphor," 454.
23 Monroe C. Beardsley, *Aesthetics: Problems in the Philosophy of Criticism* (Indianapolis, IN: Hackett, 1981), 142.
24 Monroe C. Beardsley, "The Metaphorical Twist," *Philosophy and Phenomenological Research* 22, no. 3 (1962): 294.
25 Beardsley, *Aesthetics: Problems in the Philosophy of Criticism*, 143.
26 Paul Ricoeur, *The Rule of Metaphor: The Creation of Meaning in Language* (London: Routledge, 2004), 115, 87.
27 Ricoeur, *The Rule of Metaphor*, 114.
28 Paul Ricoeur, *Interpretation Theory: Discourse and the Surplus of Meaning* (Fort Worth, TX: Texas Christian University Press, 1976), 45.
29 Beardsley, *Aesthetics: Problems in the Philosophy of Criticism*, 143.
30 Carl R. Hausman, "Language and Metaphysics: The Ontology of Metaphor," *Philosophy & Rhetoric* 24, no. 1 (1991): 40.
31 Hausman, "Language and Metaphysics," 40.
32 Marie-Dominique Gineste, Bipin Indurkhya, and Veronique Scart, "Emergence of Features in Metaphor Comprehension," *Metaphor and Symbol* 15, no. 3 (2000): 120.
33 Gineste, Indurkhya, and Scart, "Emergence of Features in Metaphor Comprehension," 118. One of the experiments he refers to was made by Camac and Glucksberg.
34 George Lakoff, "The Contemporary Theory of Metaphor," in *Metaphor and Thought*, 2nd edn, ed. Andrew Ortony (Cambridge: Cambridge University Press, 1993), 203.

Chapter 3 Cognitivist Theories of Metaphor: A Conceptual Turn

1 Bipin Indurkhya, "Rationality and Reasoning with Metaphors," *New Ideas in Psychology* 25, no. 1 (2007): 16.
2 Indurkhya, "Rationality and Reasoning with Metaphors," 19.
3 Donald A. Schon, *Displacement of Concepts* (Abingdon: Routledge, 2011), 74–9.
4 Schon, *Displacement of Concepts*, 192.

5   Bipin Indurkhya, "Emergent Representations, Interaction Theory and the Cognitive Force of Metaphor." *New Ideas in Psychology* 24, no. 2 (2006): 138.
6   Indurkhya, "Emergent Representations," 138.
7   Indurkhya, "Emergent Representations," 156–7.
8   Bipin Indurkhya and Amitash Ojha. "Interpreting Visual Metaphors: Asymmetry and Reversibility." *Poetics Today* 38, no. 1 (2017): 94.
9   Lakoff, "The Contemporary Theory of Metaphor," 203.
10 George Lakoff and Mark Johnson. *Metaphors We Live By*, paperback edn. (Chicago: University of Chicago Press, 2003), 57.
11 Beate Hampe, "Embodiment and Discourse: Dimensions and Dynamics of Contemporary Metaphor Theory," in *Metaphor: Embodied Cognition and Discourse*, ed. Beate Hampe (Cambridge: Cambridge University Press, 2017), 4–5.
12 On big meanings, see Menachem Mautner, *Human Flourishing, Liberal Theory, and the Arts: A Liberalism of Flourishing* (Abingdon: Routledge, 2018), Introduction and Chapter 6.
13 Roy Porat and Yeshayahu Shen, "Imposed Metaphoricity," *Metaphor and Symbol* 30, no. 2 (2015): 78.
14 Yeshayahu Shen, "Metaphors and Conceptual Structure," *Poetics Today* 25, no. 1 (1997): 5.
15 Christopher Peacocke, "The Perception of Music: Sources of Significance," *British Journal of Aesthetics* 49, no. 3 (2009): 260.
16 See, for example, Christopher Peacocke, "Does Perception Have a Nonconceptual Content?" *Journal of Philosophy* 98, no. 5 (2001): 239–64.
17 Peacocke, "The Perception of Music," 267.
18 Peacocke, "The Perception of Music," 262.
19 Peacocke, "The Perception of Music," 260.
20 Christopher Peacocke, "Music and Experiencing Metaphorically-As: Further Delineation," *British Journal of Aesthetics* 50, no. 2 (2010): 189.
21 Mark J. Landau, Michael D. Robinson, and Brian P. Meier, eds. *The Power of Metaphor: Examining Its Influence on Social Life* (Washington, DC: American Psychological Association, 2013), 7.
22 Landau, Robinson, and Meier, *The Power of Metaphor*, 7.
23 Hilary Putnam, "The Meaning of 'Meaning,'" in *Mind, Language and Reality: Philosophical Papers, Volume 2*, ed. Hilary Putnam (Cambridge: Cambridge University Press, 1975), 227. As is well known, focusing on the origin of meaning, Putnam's essay is canonical text inaugurated both natural kind externalism and a following semantic externalism in meaning theories.
24 Lakoff, "The Contemporary Theory of Metaphor," 204.
25 Lakoff, "The Contemporary Theory of Metaphor," 206.
26 Lakoff, "The Contemporary Theory of Metaphor," 207.

27 Lakoff, "The Contemporary Theory of Metaphor," 206.
28 Lakoff, "The Contemporary Theory of Metaphor," 207.
29 Lakoff, "The Contemporary Theory of Metaphor," 207.
30 Lakoff, "The Contemporary Theory of Metaphor," 207.
31 Landau, Robinson, and Meier, *The Power of Metaphor*, 19–20.
32 Éva Kovács, "Metaphors in English, German and Hungarian Business Discourse: A Contrastive Analysis," *Eger Journal of English Studies* 7 (2007): 111–28.
33 Éva Kovács, "Conceptual Metaphors in Popular Business Discourse," *Publicationes Universitatis Miskolcinensis: Sectio Philosophica* 11, no. 3 (2006): 71.
34 José Manuel Ureña Gómez-Moreno, "Non-Verbal and Multimodal Metaphors Bring Biology into the Picture," in *How Metaphors Guide, Teach and Popularize Science*, ed. Anke Beger and Thomas H. Smith (Amsterdam: John Benjamins, 2020), 181.
35 Gilles Fauconnier and Mark Turner, "Rethinking Metaphor," in *The Cambridge Handbook of Metaphor and Thought*, ed. Raymond W. Gibbs, Jr. (Cambridge: Cambridge University Press, 2008), 54.
36 Gilles Fauconnier and Mark Turner, *The Way We Think: Conceptual Blending and the Mind's Hidden Complexities* (New York: Basic Books, 2002), 299.
37 Fauconnier and Turner, *The Way We Think*, 300.
38 Fauconnier and Turner, "Rethinking Metaphor," 53.
39 Fauconnier and Turner, "Rethinking Metaphor," 53.
40 Zoltán Kövecses, "An Extended View of Conceptual Metaphor Theory," *Review of Cognitive Linguistics* 18, no. 1 (2020): 113.
41 Kövecses, "An Extended View of Conceptual Metaphor Theory," 123.
42 Kövecses, "An Extended View of Conceptual Metaphor Theory," 118.
43 Kövecses, "An Extended View of Conceptual Metaphor Theory," 119.
44 Kövecses, "An Extended View of Conceptual Metaphor Theory," 119.
45 Kövecses, "An Extended View of Conceptual Metaphor Theory," 117.
46 Paul Hopper, "Emergent Grammar," in *The Routledge Handbook of Discourse Analysis*, ed. James Paul Gee and Michael Handford (Abingdon: Routledge, 2012), 309.
47 Raymond W. Gibbs, Jr., *Metaphor Wars: Conceptual Metaphors in Human Life* (Cambridge: Cambridge University Press, 2017), 224.
48 Gibbs, *Metaphor Wars*, 223.
49 Gibbs, *Metaphor Wars*, 226–7.
50 Michalle Gal, "The Visuality of Metaphors: A Formalist Ontology of Metaphors," *Cognitive Linguistic Studies* 7, no. 1 (2020): 58–77.
51 Gibbs, "Conceptual Metaphor in Thought and Social Action," 22.
52 Lakoff, "The Contemporary Theory of Metaphor," 206–7.
53 Gibbs, "Conceptual Metaphor in Thought and Social Action," 17–18.
54 Gibbs, *Metaphor Wars*, 2.
55 Gibbs, "Conceptual Metaphor in Thought and Social Action," 18.

56 Gibbs, *Metaphor Wars*, 3.
57 Gibbs, "Conceptual Metaphor in Thought and Social Action," 24.
58 Gerard Steen, "The Paradox of Metaphor: Why We Need a Three-Dimensional Model of Metaphor," *Metaphor and Symbol* 23, no. 4 (2008): 214.
59 Steen, "The Paradox of Metaphor," 222.
60 Gerard Steen, "Deliberate Metaphor Theory: Basic Assumptions, Main Tenets, Urgent Issues," *Intercultural Pragmatics* 14, no. 1 (2017): 1–2.
61 Beate Hampe, ed., *Metaphor: Embodied Cognition and Discourse* (Cambridge: Cambridge University Press, 2017), 3.
62 Hampe, *Metaphor*, quoting Gibbs, 3.
63 Cornelia Müller, "Waking Metaphors: Embodied Cognition in Multimodal Discourse," in *Metaphor: Embodied Cognition and Discourse*, ed. Beate Hampe (Cambridge: Cambridge University Press, 2017). The term "communicativism" is actually not rare in cognitive literature. See, for example, Yuko Sakai's use of the term in *Communicativism and Cognitivism in Linguistics: From Plato Beyond Chomsky* (Scotts Valley, CA: CreateSpace Independent Publishing Platform, 2018), 978, 979, 570, 985; William H. Walcott's in Walcott, William H. *Knowledge, Competence and Communication: Chomsky, Freire, Searle, and Communicative Language* (Montreal: Black Rose Books, 2007).
64 Paul Hopper, "Emergent Grammar," *Annual Meeting of the Berkeley Linguistics Society* 13 (1987): 140.
65 Hopper, "Emergent Grammar" (1987), 141.
66 Hopper, "Emergent Grammar" (1987), 141.
67 Hopper "Emergent Grammar" (2012), 301.
68 George Lakoff, "The Invariance Hypothesis: Is Abstract Reason Based on Image-Schemas?" *Cognitive Linguistics* 1, no. 1 (1990): 40.
69 Lakoff, "The Invariance Hypothesis," 41.
70 Mark Johnson, *Embodied Mind, Meaning, and Reason: How Our Bodies Give Rise to Understanding* (Chicago: University of Chicago Press, 2017), 98.
71 Lakoff, "The Contemporary Theory of Metaphor," 208.
72 Susan Sontag, *On Photography* (New York: Rosetta Books, 2020), 2.
73 Andy Clark and David Chalmers, "The Extended Mind," *Analysis* 58, no. 1 (1998): 8.
74 Clark and Chalmers, "The Extended Mind," 10.
75 Johnson, Mark. "Embodied Understanding." *Frontiers in Psychology* 6 (2015): 2. Available online: https://doi.org/10.3389/fpsyg.2015.00875.
76 Johnson, *Embodied Mind, Meaning, and Reason*, 98.
77 Johnson, *Embodied Mind, Meaning, and Reason*, 99.
78 Christopher Tilley and Kate Cameron-Daum, *An Anthropology of Landscape* (London: UCL Press, 2017), 175.
79 Tilley and Cameron-Daum, *An Anthropology of Landscape*, 178.

Chapter 4 The Advent of the Visual Perspective of Metaphors

1. E. H. Gombrich, "The Visual Image," *Scientific American* 227, no. 3 (1972): 82.
2. Arnheim, "A Plea for Visual Thinking," 490.
3. Gombrich, "The Visual Image," 82.
4. Verstegen, *Arnheim, Gestalt and Art*, 22.
5. Aldrich, "Visual Metaphor," 73.
6. Aldrich, "Visual Metaphor," 74, 73.
7. Noël Carroll, "Visual Metaphors," in *Beyond Aesthetics* (Cambridge: Cambridge University Press, 2001), 347–68.
8. Aldrich, "Visual Metaphor," 76–7.
9. Aldrich, "Visual Metaphor," 74.
10. Gombrich, "Tradition and Expression in Western Still Life," *Meditations on a Hobby Horse*, 98.
11. Gombrich, "Visual Metaphors of Value in Art," 256.
12. Gombrich, "Visual Metaphors of Value in Art," 256.
13. Gombrich, "Visual Metaphors of Value in Art," 257.
14. Arnheim, *Art and Visual Perception*, 2.
15. Arnheim, *Art and Visual Perception*, 2–3.
16. Davidson, *Inquiries into Truth and Interpretation*, 262.
17. Rorty, *Contingency, Irony, and Solidarity*, 16.
18. Davidson, *Inquiries into Truth and Interpretation*, 263.
19. Gombrich, *Meditations on a Hobby Horse*, 3–4.
20. Arthur C. Danto, "The Artworld," *Journal of Philosophy* 61, no. 19 (1964): 571–84.
21. Arnheim, *Visual Thinking*, 29.
22. Hopper, "Emergent Grammar" (2012), 304.
23. Arnheim, *Visual Thinking*, 208.
24. Arnheim, *Visual Thinking*, 211.
25. René Descartes, *Principles of Philosophy*, trans. Valentine R. Miller and Reese P. Miller (Dordrecht: Springer, 1982), xxiv.
26. W. J. T. Mitchell, *Iconology: Image, Text, Ideology* (Chicago: University of Chicago Press, 1986), 20.
27. Mitchell, *Iconology*, 21.
28. Mark B. Turner and Gilled Fauconnier, "Conceptual Integration and Formal Expression," *Metaphor and Symbolic Activity* 10, no. 3 (1995): 183.

29 Fauconnier and Turner, *The Way We Think*, 3.
30 Fauconnier and Turner, *The Way We Think*, 43.
31 Gerald C. Cupchik, "A Critical Reflection on Arnheim's Gestalt Theory of Aesthetics," *Psychology of Aesthetics, Creativity, and the Arts* 1, no. 1 (2007): 16.
32 Arnheim, *Art and Visual Perception*, 5.
33 "Our mind, of course, works by differentiation rather than by generalization." Gombrich, *Meditations on a Hobby Horse*, 1–2.
34 Arnheim, *Art and Visual Perception*, 45.
35 Gombrich, "On Physiognomic Perception," 233.
36 Rudolf Arnheim, "Review of E. H. Gombrich, *Art and Illusion. A Study in the Psychology of Pictorial Representation*," *The Art Bulletin* 44, no. 1 (1962): 77.
37 David Blinder, "Review of E. H. Gombrich: *The Image and the Eye: Further Studies in the Psychology of Pictorial Representation*," *Journal of Aesthetics and Art Criticism* 42, no. 1 (1983): 85.
38 John Ruskin, *The Complete Works of John Ruskin: Modern Painters* (New York: T. Y. Crowell, 1905), 72.
39 Ruskin, *Complete Works*, 72.
40 Blinder, "Review of *The Image and the Eye*," 85.
41 Arnheim, "Review of *Art and Illusion*," 76.
42 Arnheim, "Review of *Art and Illusion*," 75.
43 Uta Grundmann and Rudolf Arnheim, "The Intelligence of Vision: An Interview with Rudolf Arnheim," *Cabinet Magazine* 2 (2001). Available online: https://www.cabinetmagazine.org/issues/2/grundmann_arnheim.php.
44 Grundmann and Arnheim, "The Intelligence of Vision."
45 Arnheim, *Art and Visual Perception*, 11.
46 Arnheim, *Art and Visual Perception*, 12.
47 Arnheim, *Art and Visual Perception*, 12.
48 Saito, *Aesthetics of the Familiar*, 53.
49 Saito, *Aesthetics of the Familiar*, 52.
50 Arnheim, "Review of E. H. Gombrich, *Art and Illusion*": 76.
51 Arthur C. Danto, "E. H. Gombrich," *Grand Street* 2, no. 2 (1983): 121.
52 Danto, "E. H. Gombrich," 120, quoting Gombrich, *The Sense of Order*, 232.
53 Arnheim, *Visual Thinking*, 87–8.
54 Arnheim, *Visual Thinking*, 88.
55 Arnheim, *Visual Thinking*, 89.
56 Goodman, *Languages of Art*, 69.
57 Gombrich, "The Visual Image," 84.
58 Danto, "E. H. Gombrich," 127.
59 Gombrich, "The Visual Image," 94.
60 Nelson Goodman, "Review of E. H. Gombrich: *Art and Illusion: A Study in the Psychology of Pictorial Representation*," *Journal of Philosophy* 57, no. 18 (1960): 596.

61 Arnheim, *Towards a Psychology of Art*, 154.
62 Arnheim, *Towards a Psychology of Art*, 154.
63 Arnheim, *Towards a Psychology of Art*, 155.
64 Arnheim, *Towards a Psychology of Art*, 152.
65 Goodman, "Review of *Art and Illusion*," 597.
66 Nelson Goodman, *Problems and Projects* (Indianapolis, IN: Bobbs-Merrill, 1972), 440.
67 Goodman, *Problems and Projects*, 440.

Chapter 5 Metaphors and Ontology

1   Gombrich, "Visual Metaphors and Values in Art," 272.
2   Gombrich, "Visual Metaphors and Values in Art," 272.
3   Arnheim, *Visual Thinking*, 62.
4   "To the Reader" by Denise Levertov, from THE JACOB'S LADDER, copyright (c)1961 by Denise Levertov. Reprinted by permission of New Directions Publishing Corp.
5   Arnheim, *Visual Thinking*, 62.
6   Arnheim, *Visual Thinking*, 62.
7   Verstegen, *Arnheim, Gestalt and Art*, 21.
7   Virgil Aldrich, "'Expresses' and 'Expressive,'" *Journal of Aesthetics and Art Criticism* 37, no. 2 (1978): 205.
9   Virgil C. Aldrich, "Form in the Visual Arts," *British Journal of Aesthetics* 11, no. 3 (1971): 219.
10 Aldrich, "Visual Metaphor," 77.
11 Aldrich, "Visual Metaphor," 86.
12 Aldrich, "Visual Metaphor," 78–9.
13 Arnheim, *Visual Thinking*, 68.
14 Aldrich, "Visual Metaphor," 79.
15 Aldrich, "Visual Metaphor," 86.
16 Hausman, "Language and Metaphysics," 25.
17 Carl R. Hausman, *Metaphor and Art: Interactionism and Reference in the Verbal and Nonverbal Arts* (Cambridge: Cambridge University Press, 1989), 103–4.
18 Hausman, *Metaphor and Art*, 107.
19 Hausman, "Language and Metaphysics," 25–6.
20 Gombrich, *Meditations on a Hobby Horse*, 2.
21 Hausman, *Metaphor and Art*, 107–8.
22 Hausman, *Metaphor and Art*, 121.
23 Arnheim, *Visual Thinking*, 90.
24 David R. Olson, "Education: The Bridge from Culture to Mind," in *Jerome Bruner: Language, Culture, Self*, ed. David Bakhurst and Stuart G. Shanker (London: Sage, 2001), 107.

25 Jerome Bruner, *Acts of Meaning: Four Lectures on Mind and Culture (The Jerusalem-Harvard Lectures)* (Cambridge, MA: Harvard University Press, 1990), 1.
26 Jerome Bruner, *The Culture of Education* (Cambridge, MA: Harvard University Press, 1996), 161.
27 Charles Forceville, "Developments in Multimodal Metaphor Studies: A Response to Górska, Coëgnarts, Porto & Romano, and Muelas-Gil," in *Current Approaches to Metaphor Analysis in Discourse*, ed. Ignasi Navarro i Ferrando (Berlin: De Gruyter, 2019), 367.
28 Charles J. Forceville and Eduardo Urios-Aparisi, *Multimodal Metaphor* (Berlin: Mouton de Gruyter, 2009), 23, 383.
29 Gibbs, "Conceptual Metaphor in Thought and Social Action," 19.
30 Arnheim, *Art and Visual Perception*, 454.
31 Arnheim, *Visual Thinking*, 13.
32 Arnheim, *Visual Thinking*, v.
33 Gibbs, *Metaphor Wars*, 225.
34 Gibbs, *Metaphor Wars*, 225.
35 Samuel Guttenplan, *Objects of Metaphors* (New York: Oxford University Press, 2005).
36 Arnheim, *Art and Visual Perception*, 453.
37 Bipin Indurkhya, "The Thesis That All Knowledge Is Metaphorical and Meanings of Metaphor," *Metaphor and Symbolic Activity* 9, no. 1 (1994): 67, 66.
38 Indurkhya, "Interview," 200.
39 Indurkhya, "Interview," 200.
40 Ryoko Uno, Eiko Matsuda, and Bipin Indurkhya, "Analyzing Visual Metaphor and Metonymy to Understand Creativity in Fashion," *Frontiers in Psychology* 9 (2019). Available online: https://doi.org/10.3389/fpsyg.2018.02527.
41 Indurkhya, "Rationality and Reasoning with Metaphors," 24.
42 Indurkhya, "Rationality and Reasoning with Metaphors," 27.
43 Bipin Indurkhya, *Metaphor and Cognition: An Interactionist Approach* (Dordrecht: Springer, 2011), 303.
44 Indurkhya, "Rationality and Reasoning with Metaphors," 29.
45 Indurkhya, "Rationality and Reasoning with Metaphors," 25.
46 Indurkhya, "Rationality and Reasoning with Metaphors," 28.
47 Johnson, *Embodied Mind, Meaning, and Reason*, 220.
48 Aldrich, "Visual Metaphor," 79.
49 Aldrich, "Visual Metaphor," 80.
50 Aldrich. "Visual Metaphor," 81.
51 Thierry de Duve, *Kant After Duchamp* (Cambridge, MA: MIT Press, 1998), 162; Katherine Kuh, *The Artist's Voice: Talks With Seventeen Modern Artists*, 1st Da Capo edn. (New York: Da Capo Press, 2000), 90.

52 Arthur C. Danto, *The Philosophical Disenfranchisement of Art*, revised edn. (New York: Columbia University Press, 2004), 34.
53 Aldrich, "Visual Metaphor," 82.
54 Ruskin, *Modern Painters*, III: 155, 158.
55 Arnheim, *Art and Visual Perception*, 454.
56 Arnheim, *Art and Visual Perception*, 454.
57 Rudolf Arnheim, *The Power of the Center: A Study of Composition in the Visual Arts* (Berkeley: University of California Press, 1982), 3–4.
58 Jane Forsey, *The Aesthetics of Design* (Oxford: Oxford University Press, 2013), 68.
59 See Jan Mukařovský, *Aesthetic Function, Norm and Value as Social Facts*, trans. Mark E. Suino (Ann Arbor, MI: Michigan Slavic Contributions, 1970).
60 Attfield, "Design as a Practice of Modernity," 270.
61 Attfield, "Design as a Practice of Modernity," 270.
62 Attfield, "Design as a Practice of Modernity," 272, 271.
63 Richard Shusterman, "Somaesthetics at the Limits," *Nordic Journal of Aesthetics* 19, no. 35 (2008): 18.
64 Yuriko Saito, *Everyday Aesthetics* (Oxford: Oxford University Press, 2007), 9.
65 Attfield, *Wild Things*, 132.
66 Christopher Tilley, "Metaphor, Materiality and Interpretation," in *The Material Culture Reader*, ed. Victor Buchli (Oxford: Berg, 2002), 28.
67 Tilley, "Metaphor, Materiality and Interpretation," 24.
68 Christopher Tilley, "Objectification," in *Handbook of Material Culture*, ed. Christopher Tilley, Webb Keane, Susanne Külcher, Michael Rowlands, and Patricia Spyer. Reprint (Los Angeles, CA: Sage, 2010), 62.
69 Tilley, "Objectification," 62.
70 Tilley, "Metaphor, Materiality and Interpretation," 28.
71 Tilley, "Metaphor, Materiality and Interpretation," 28.
72 Tilley, "Metaphor, Materiality and Interpretation," 28.
73 Bruner, *The Culture of Education*, 151.
74 Gineste, Indurkhya, and Scart, "Emergence of Features in Metaphor Comprehension," 118.
75 Bipin Indurkhya and Amitash Ojha, "An Empirical Study on the Role of Perceptual Similarity in Visual Metaphors and Creativity," *Metaphor and Symbol* 28, no. 4 (2013): 245.
76 Indurkhya and Ojha, "An Empirical Study," 40.
77 Arnheim, *Visual Thinking*, 232.
78 Indurkhya, "Emergent Representations," 155.
79 Arnheim, *Visual Thinking*, 54.

Chapter 6 New Terminology for Metaphors: Visuality and Affordance

1. James J. Gibson, *The Ecological Approach to Visual Perception*, classic edn. (New York: Psychology Press, 2014), 11.
2. James J. Gibson, *The Senses Considered as Perceptual Systems* (Boston, MA: Houghton Mifflin, 1966).
3. Gibson, *The Ecological Approach to Visual Perception*, 119.
4. Gibson, *The Ecological Approach to Visual Perception*, 120.
5. Yael Young, "The Representation of Pointed Amphorae in Athenian Vase Paintings: An Iconographic Study," *Art Style Magazine*, March 11, 2021, 159.
6. Donald A. Norman, *The Design of Everyday Things*, 1st Doubleday/Currency edn. (New York: Doubleday, 1990), 9–10; see also the new revised edition: Donald A. Norman, *The Design of Everyday Things*, revised and expanded edn. (London: Hachette UK, 2013).
7. Stanford Anderson, "The Fiction of Function," *Assemblage* 2 (1987): 22.
8. Nyíri, "Towards a Theory of Common-Sense Realism," 17.
9. Nyíri, "Towards a Theory of Common-Sense Realism," 23.
10. Arnheim, *Art and Visual Perception*, 419.
11. Arnheim, *Art and Visual Perception*, 416.
12. Gombrich, "Visual Metaphors of Value in Art," 257.
13. Gal, *Aestheticism*, "Opening: Deep Form"; and Ch. 4.1. "What Gives Form its Depth."
14. Arnheim, *Art and Visual Perception*, 444–5.
15. Arnheim, *Visual Thinking*, 90.
16. Arnheim, *Visual Thinking*, 90.
17. Gombrich, *Art and Illusion*, 171.
18. Gombrich, *Meditations on a Hobby Horse*, 10.
19. Arnheim, *Visual Thinking*, 107–8.
20. Hopper, "Emergent Grammar" (2012), 307–8.
21. Saito, *Aesthetics of the Familiar*, 47.
22. Arnheim, *Art and Visual Perception*, 419–20.
23. Attfield, *Wild Things*, 77.
24. Attfield, *Wild Things*, 32.
25. Attfield, *Wild Things*, 32.
26. Attfield, *Wild Things*, 78.
27. Goodman, *Languages of Art*, 72.
28. Hausman, "Language and Metaphysics," 35.
29. Arnheim, *Visual Thinking*, 91.
30. Hausman, "Language and Metaphysics," 36.
31. Hausman, "Language and Metaphysics," 32.

32 Hausman, "Language and Metaphysics," 36.
33 Roger Fry, *Vision and Design* (Mineola, NY: Dover Publications, 2011), 22.
34 Arnheim, *Art and Visual Perception*, 434.
35 G.L. Hagberg, *Art as Language: Wittgenstein, Meaning, and Aesthetic Theory* (Ithaca, NY: Cornell University Press, 1998), 121.
36 Hagberg, *Art as Language*, 120.
37 Arnheim, *Towards a Psychology of Art*, 53.
38 Arnheim, *Towards a Psychology of Art*, 53.
39 Arnheim, *Art and Visual Perception*, 445.
40 W. J. T. Mitchell, *What Do Pictures Want? The Lives and Loves of Images* (Chicago: University of Chicago Press, 2005), 11.
41 Mitchell, *What Do Pictures Want?*, 54.
42 Arnheim, *Art and Visual Perception*, 452–5.
43 Kövecses, "An Extended View of Conceptual Metaphor Theory," 122–3.

Bibliography

Alberti, Leon Battista. *Leon Battista Alberti: On Painting: A New Translation and Critical Edition*, translated by Rocco Sinisgalli. Cambridge: Cambridge University Press, 2011.
Aldrich, Virgil. " 'Expresses' and 'Expressive.' " *Journal of Aesthetics and Art Criticism* 37, no. 2 (1978): 203–17.
Aldrich, Virgil C. "Form in the Visual Arts." *British Journal of Aesthetics* 11, no. 3 (1971): 215–26.
Aldrich, Virgil C. "Visual Metaphor." *Journal of Aesthetic Education* 2, no. 1 (1968): 73–86.
Anderson, Stanford. "The Fiction of Function." *Assemblage* 2 (1987): 18–31.
Aristotle. *The Rhetoric and the Poetics of Aristotle*. Scotts Valley, CA: CreateSpace Independent Publishing Platform, 2010.
Arnheim, Rudolf. *Art and Visual Perception: A Psychology of the Creative Eye; the New Version*. Expanded and rev. edn, 50th anniversary printing. Berkeley: University of California Press, 2009.
Arnheim, Rudolf. "A Plea for Visual Thinking." *Critical Inquiry* 6, no. 3 (1980): 489–97.
Arnheim, Rudolf. *The Power of the Center: A Study of Composition in the Visual Arts*. Berkeley: University of California Press, 1982.
Arnheim, Rudolf. "Review of E. H. Gombrich, *Art and Illusion: A Study in the Psychology of Pictorial Representation*." *The Art Bulletin* 44, no. 1 (1962): 75–9.
Arnheim, Rudolf. *Towards a Psychology of Art: Collected Essays*. London: Faber & Faber, 1966.
Arnheim, Rudolf. *Visual Thinking*. Berkeley: University of California Press, 1969.
Attfield, Judy. "Design as a Practice of Modernity: A Case for the Study of the Coffee Table in the Mid-century Domestic Interior." *Journal of Material Culture* 2, no. 3 (1997): 267–89.
Attfield, Judy. *Wild Things: The Material Culture of Everyday Life*. Oxford: Berg, 2000.
Beardsley, Monroe C. *Aesthetics: Problems in the Philosophy of Criticism*. Indianapolis, IN: Hackett, 1981.
Beardsley, Monroe C. "The Metaphorical Twist." *Philosophy and Phenomenological Research* 22, no. 3 (1962): 293–307.
Black, Max. "Metaphor." *Proceedings of the Aristotelian Society* 55, no. 1 (1955): 273–94.
Black, Max. "More About Metaphor." *Dialectica* 31, no. 3/4 (1977): 431–57.
Blinder, David. "Review of E. H. Gombrich: *The Image and the Eye: Further Studies in the Psychology of Pictorial Representation*." *Journal of Aesthetics and Art Criticism* 42, no. 1 (1983): 85–9.

Bruner, Jerome. *Acts of Meaning: Four Lectures on Mind and Culture (The Jerusalem-Harvard Lectures)*. Cambridge, MA: Harvard University Press, 1990.

Bruner, Jerome. *The Culture of Education*. Cambridge, MA: Harvard University Press, 1996.

Camp, Elisabeth. "Metaphor and That Certain 'Je Ne Sais Quoi.'" *Philosophical Studies* 129, no. 1 (2006): 1–25.

Carroll, Noël. "Visual Metaphors." In *Beyond Aesthetics*, 347–68. Cambridge: Cambridge University Press, 2001.

Clark, Andy, and David Chalmers. "The Extended Mind." *Analysis* 58, no. 1 (1998): 7–19.

Clark, T. J. *Farewell to an Idea: Episodes from a History of Modernism*. New Haven, CT: Yale University Press, 1999.

Cunliffe, Leslie. "Gombrich on Art: A Social-Constructivist Interpretation of His Work and Its Relevance to Education." *Journal of Aesthetic Education* 32, no. 4 (1998): 61–77.

Cupchik, Gerald C. "A Critical Reflection on Arnheim's Gestalt Theory of Aesthetics." *Psychology of Aesthetics, Creativity, and the Arts* 1, no. 1 (2007): 16–24.

Danto, Arthur C. "E. H. Gombrich." *Grand Street* 2, no. 2 (1983): 120–32.

Danto, Arthur C. "The Artworld." *Journal of Philosophy* 61, no. 19 (1964): 571–84.

Danto, Arthur C. "Metaphor and Cognition." In *Knowledge and Language, Volume III: Metaphor and Knowledge*, edited by F. R. Ankersmit, and J. J. A. Mooij, 21–35. Dordrecht: Springer Science+Business Media, 1993.

Danto, Arthur C. *The Philosophical Disenfranchisement of Art*. Revised edn. New York: Columbia University Press, 2004.

Danto, Arthur C. *The Transfiguration of the Commonplace: A Philosophy of Art*. Cambridge, MA: Harvard University Press, 1981.

Davidson, Donald. *Inquiries into Truth and Interpretation*. 2nd edn. Oxford: Clarendon Press, 2001.

Descartes, René. *Principles of Philosophy*, translated, with explanatory notes, by Valentine R. Miller and Reese P. Miller. Dordrecht: Springer, 1982.

Duve, Thierry de. *Kant After Duchamp*. Cambridge, MA: MIT Press, 1998.

Easterling, Keller. *Extrastatecraft: The Power of Infrastructure Space*. London: Verso, 2014.

Fauconnier, Gilles, and Mark Turner. "Rethinking Metaphor." In *The Cambridge Handbook of Metaphor and Thought*, edited by Raymond W. Gibbs, Jr., 53–66. Cambridge: Cambridge University Press, 2008.

Fauconnier, Gilles, and Mark Turner. *The Way We Think: Conceptual Blending and the Mind's Hidden Complexities*. New York: Basic Books, 2002.

Forceville, Charles. "Developments in Multimodal Metaphor Studies: A Response to Górska, Coëgnarts, Porto & Romano, and Muelas-Gil." In *Current Approaches to Metaphor Analysis in Discourse*, edited by Ignasi Navarro i Ferrando, 367–78. Berlin: De Gruyter, 2019.

Forceville, Charles J., and Eduardo Urios-Aparisi. *Multimodal Metaphor*, Berlin: Mouton de Gruyter, 2009.

Forsey, Jane. *The Aesthetics of Design*. Oxford: Oxford University Press, 2013.

Fry, Roger. *Vision and Design*. Mineola, NY: Dover Publications, 2011.

Fusaroli, Riccardo, and Simone Morgagni. "Conceptual Metaphor Theory: 30 Years After." *Cognitive Semiotics* 5, no. 1/2 (2013): 1–290.

Gal, Michalle. *Aestheticism: Deep Formalism and the Emergence of Modernist Aesthetics*. Bern: Peter Lang, 2015.

Gal, Michalle. "The Visuality of Metaphors: A Formalist Ontology of Metaphors." *Cognitive Linguistic Studies* 7, no. 1 (2020): 58–77.

Gibbs, Raymond W., Jr. "Conceptual Metaphor in Thought and Social Action." In *The Power of Metaphor: Examining Its Influence on Social Life*, edited by Mark J. Landau, Michael D. Robinson, and Brian P. Meier, 17–40. Washington, DC: American Psychological Association, 2013.

Gibbs, Raymond W., Jr. *Metaphor Wars: Conceptual Metaphors in Human Life*. Cambridge: Cambridge University Press, 2017.

Gibson, James J. *The Ecological Approach to Visual Perception*. Classic edn. New York: Psychology Press, 2014.

Gibson, James J. *The Senses Considered as Perceptual Systems*. Boston, MA: Houghton Mifflin, 1966.

Gineste, Marie-Dominique, Bipin Indurkhya, and Veronique Scart. "Emergence of Features in Metaphor Comprehension." *Metaphor and Symbol* 15, no. 3 (2000): 117–35.

Glucksberg, Sam, and Boaz Keysar. "How Metaphors Work." In *Metaphor and Thought*, 2nd edn, edited by Andrew Ortony, 401–24. Cambridge: Cambridge University Press, 1993.

Glucksberg, Sam, and Boaz Keysar. "Understanding Metaphorical Comparisons: Beyond Similarity." *Psychological Review* 97, no. 1 (1990): 3–18.

Glucksberg, Sam, Patricia Gildea, and Howard B. Bookin. "On Understanding Nonliteral Speech: Can People Ignore Metaphors?" *Journal of Verbal Learning & Verbal Behavior* 21, no. 1 (1982): 85–98.

Gombrich, E. H. *Art and Illusion: A Study in the Psychology of Pictorial Representation*. Princeton, NJ: Princeton University Press, 1969.

Gombrich, E. H. *Meditations on a Hobby Horse: And Other Essays on the Theory of Art*. 3rd edn. London: Phaidon, 1978 [first published 1963].

Gombrich, E. H. "On Physiognomic Perception." *Daedalus* 89, no. 1 (1960): 228–41.

Gombrich, E. H. *The Sense of Order: A Study in the Psychology of Decorative Art*. Ithaca, NY: Cornell University Press, 1984.

Gombrich, E. H. "The Visual Image." *Scientific American* 227, no. 3 (1972): 82–97.

Gombrich, E. H. "Visual Metaphors of Value in Art." In *Symbols And Values: An Initial Study*, edited by Lyman Bryson, Louis Finkelstein, and R. M. MacIver, 255–81. New York: Cooper Square, 1964.

Goodman, Nelson. *Languages of Art*. 2nd edn. Indianapolis, IN: Hackett, 1976.

Goodman, Nelson. *Problems and Projects*. Indianapolis, IN: Bobbs-Merrill, 1972.

Goodman, Nelson. "Review of E. H. Gombrich: *Art and Illusion: A Study in the Psychology of Pictorial Representation*." *Journal of Philosophy* 57, no. 18 (1960): 595–9.

Goodman, Nelson. *Ways of Worldmaking*. Indianapolis, IN: Hackett, 1978.

Goodman, Nelson, and Catherine Z. Elgin. *Reconceptions in Philosophy and Other Arts and Sciences*. Indianapolis, IN: Hackett, 1988.

Grundmann, Uta, and Rudolf Arnheim. "The Intelligence of Vision: An Interview with Rudolf Arnheim." *Cabinet Magazine* 2 (2001). Available online: https://www.cabinetmagazine.org/issues/2/grundmann_arnheim.php.

Guttenplan, Samuel. *Objects of Metaphors*. New York: Oxford University Press, 2005.

Hagberg, G.L. *Art as Language: Wittgenstein, Meaning, and Aesthetic Theory*. Ithaca, NY: Cornell University Press, 1998.

Hampe, Beate. "Embodiment and Discourse: Dimensions and Dynamics of Contemporary Metaphor Theory." In *Metaphor: Embodied Cognition and Discourse*, edited by Beate Hampe, 3–24. Cambridge: Cambridge University Press, 2017.

Hampe, Beate (ed.) *Metaphor: Embodied Cognition and Discourse*. Cambridge: Cambridge University Press, 2017.

Hausman, Carl R. "Criteria of Creativity." In *The Idea of Creativity*, edited by Michael Krausz, Denis Dutton, and Karen Bardsley, 1–16. Leiden: Brill, 2009.

Hausman, Carl R. "Language and Metaphysics: The Ontology of Metaphor." *Philosophy & Rhetoric* 24, no. 1 (1991): 25–42.

Hausman, Carl R. *Metaphor and Art: Interactionism and Reference in the Verbal and Nonverbal Arts*. Cambridge: Cambridge University Press, 1989.

Hesse, Mary. "The Cognitive Claims of Metaphor." *Journal of Speculative Philosophy* 2, no. 1 (1988): 1–16.

Hopper, Paul. "Emergent Grammar." *Annual Meeting of the Berkeley Linguistics Society* 13 (1987): 139–57.

Hopper, Paul. "Emergent Grammar." In *The Routledge Handbook of Discourse Analysis*, edited by James Paul Gee and Michael Handford, 301–14. Abingdon: Routledge, 2012.

Indurkhya, Bipin. "Emergent Representations, Interaction Theory and the Cognitive Force of Metaphor." *New Ideas in Psychology* 24, no. 2 (2006): 133–62.

Indurkhya, Bipin. "Interview." Edited by Massimo Sangoi. *Humana.Mente Journal of Philosophical Studies* 23 (2012): 197–216.

Indurkhya, Bipin. *Metaphor and Cognition: An Interactionist Approach*. Dordrecht: Springer, 2011.

Indurkhya, Bipin. "Rationality and Reasoning with Metaphors." *New Ideas in Psychology* 25, no. 1 (2007): 16–36.

Indurkhya, Bipin. "The Thesis That All Knowledge Is Metaphorical and Meanings of Metaphor." *Metaphor and Symbolic Activity* 9, no. 1 (1994): 61–73.

Indurkhya, Bipin, and Amitash Ojha. "An Empirical Study on the Role of Perceptual Similarity in Visual Metaphors and Creativity." *Metaphor and Symbol* 28, no. 4 (2013): 233–53.

Indurkhya, Bipin, and Amitash Ojha. "Interpreting Visual Metaphors: Asymmetry and Reversibility." *Poetics Today* 38, no. 1 (2017): 93–121.

Johnson, Mark. *Embodied Mind, Meaning, and Reason: How Our Bodies Give Rise to Understanding*. Chicago: University of Chicago Press, 2017.

Johnson, Mark. "Embodied Understanding." *Frontiers in Psychology* 6 (2015): art 875. Available online: https://doi.org/10.3389/fpsyg.2015.00875.

Kovács, Éva. "Conceptual Metaphors in Popular Business Discourse." *Publicationes Universitatis Miskolcinensis: Sectio Philosophica* 11, no. 3 (2006): 69–80.

Kovács, Éva. "Metaphors in English, German and Hungarian Business Discourse: A Contrastive Analysis." *Eger Journal of English Studies* 7 (2007): 111–28.

Kövecses, Zoltán. "An Extended View of Conceptual Metaphor Theory." *Review of Cognitive Linguistics* 18, no. 1 (2020): 112–30.

Kuh, Katherine. *The Artist's Voice: Talks With Seventeen Modern Artists*. 1st Da Capo edn. New York: Da Capo Press, 2000.

Lakoff, George. "The Contemporary Theory of Metaphor." In *Metaphor and Thought*, 2nd edn, edited by Andrew Ortony, 202–51. Cambridge: Cambridge University Press, 1993.

Lakoff, George. "The Invariance Hypothesis: Is Abstract Reason Based on Image-Schemas?" *Cognitive Linguistics* 1, no. 1 (1990): 39–74.

Lakoff, George, and Mark Johnson. *Metaphors We Live By*. Paperback edn. Chicago: University of Chicago Press, 2003.

Landau, Mark J., Michael D. Robinson, and Brian P. Meier (eds.). *The Power of Metaphor: Examining Its Influence on Social Life*. Washington, DC: American Psychological Association, 2013.

Mautner, Menachem. *Human Flourishing, Liberal Theory, and the Arts: A Liberalism of Flourishing*. Abingdon: Routledge, 2018.

Mitchell, W. J. T. *Iconology: Image, Text, Ideology*. Chicago: University of Chicago Press, 1986.

Mitchell, W. J. T. *What Do Pictures Want? The Lives and Loves of Images*. Chicago: University of Chicago Press, 2005.

Mukařovský, Jan. *Aesthetic Function, Norm and Value as Social Facts*, translated by Mark E. Suino. Ann Arbor, MI: Michigan Slavic Contributions, 1970.

Müller, Cornelia. "Waking Metaphors: Embodied Cognition in Multimodal Discourse." In *Metaphor: Embodied Cognition and Discourse*, edited by Beate Hampe, 297–316. Cambridge: Cambridge University Press, 2017.

Norman, Donald A. *The Design of Everyday Things*. 1st Doubleday/Currency edn. New York: Doubleday, 1990.

Norman, Donald A. *The Design of Everyday Things*. Revised and expanded edn. London: Hachette UK, 2013.

Nyíri, Kristóf. "Towards a Theory of Common-Sense Realism." In *In the Beginning Was the Image: The Omnipresence of Pictures—Time, Truth, Tradition*, edited by András Benedek and Ágnes Veszelszki, 17–28. Frankfurt am Main: Peter Lang, 2016.

Nyíri, Kristóf, and András Benedek (eds.). *Vision Fulfilled: The Victory of the Pictorial Turn*. Budapest: Hungarian Academy of Sciences and Budapest University of Technology and Economics, 2019.

Olson, David R. "Education: The Bridge from Culture to Mind." In *Jerome Bruner: Language, Culture, Self*, edited by David Bakhurst and Stuart G. Shanker, 104–15. London: Sage, 2001.

Peacocke, Christopher. "Does Perception Have a Nonconceptual Content?" *Journal of Philosophy* 98, no. 5 (2001): 239–64.

Peacocke, Christopher. "Music and Experiencing Metaphorically-As: Further Delineation." *British Journal of Aesthetics* 50, no. 2 (2010): 189–91.

Peacocke, Christopher. "The Perception of Music: Sources of Significance." *British Journal of Aesthetics* 49, no. 3 (2009): 257–75.

Porat, Roy, and Yeshayahu Shen. "Imposed Metaphoricity." *Metaphor and Symbol* 30, no. 2 (2015): 77–94.

Putnam, Hilary. "The Meaning of 'Meaning.'" In *Mind, Language and Reality: Philosophical Papers, Volume 2*, edited by Hilary Putnam, 215–71. Cambridge: Cambridge University Press, 1975.

Richards, I. A. *The Philosophy of Rhetoric*. London: Oxford University Press, 1965.

Ricoeur, Paul. *Interpretation Theory: Discourse and the Surplus of Meaning*. Fort Worth, TX: Texas Christian University Press, 1976.

Ricoeur, Paul. *The Rule of Metaphor: The Creation of Meaning in Language*. London: Routledge, 2004.

Rorty, Richard. *Contingency, Irony, and Solidarity*. Cambridge: Cambridge University Press, 1989.

Rorty, Richard. *Objectivity, Relativism, and Truth: Philosophical Papers, Vol. 1*. Cambridge: Cambridge University Press, 1990.

Ruskin, John. *The Complete Works of John Ruskin: Modern Painters*. New York: T. Y. Crowell, 1905.

Saito, Yuriko. *Aesthetics of the Familiar: Everyday Life and World-Making*. Oxford: Oxford University Press, 2017.

Saito, Yuriko. *Everyday Aesthetics*. Oxford: Oxford University Press, 2007.

Sakai, Yuko, *Communicativism and Cognitivism in Linguistics: From Plato Beyond Chomsky*, Scotts Valley, CA: CreateSpace Independent Publishing Platform, 2018.

Schon, Donald A. *Displacement of Concepts*. Abingdon: Routledge, 2011.

Searle, John R. "Metaphor." In *Expression and Meaning: Studies in the Theory of Speech Acts*, 76–116. Cambridge: Cambridge University Press, 1979.

Shen, Yeshayahu. "Metaphors and Conceptual Structure." *Poetics Today* 25, no. 1 (1997): 1–16.

Shusterman, Richard. "Somaesthetics at the Limits." *Nordic Journal of Aesthetics* 19, no. 35 (2008): 7–24.

Sontag, Susan. *On Photography*. New York: Rosetta Books, 2020.

Steen, Gerard. "Deliberate Metaphor Theory: Basic Assumptions, Main Tenets, Urgent Issues." *Intercultural Pragmatics* 14, no. 1 (2017): 1–24.
Steen, Gerard. "The Paradox of Metaphor: Why We Need a Three-Dimensional Model of Metaphor." *Metaphor and Symbol* 23, no. 4 (2008): 213–41.
Stern, Joseph. *Metaphors in Context*. Cambridge, MA: MIT Press, 2000.
Tilley, Christopher. *Metaphor and Material Culture*. Oxford: Blackwell, 1999.
Tilley, Christopher. "Metaphor, Materiality and Interpretation." In *The Material Culture Reader*, edited by Victor Buchli, 23–56. Oxford: Berg, 2002.
Tilley, Christopher. "Objectification." In *Handbook of Material Culture*, edited by Christopher Tilley, Webb Keane, Susanne Külcher, Michael Rowlands, and Patricia Spyer, 60–73. Reprint. Los Angeles, CA: Sage, 2010.
Tilley, Christopher, and Kate Cameron-Daum. *An Anthropology of Landscape*. London: UCL Press, 2017.
Turner, Mark B., and Gilles Fauconnier. "Conceptual Integration and Formal Expression." *Metaphor and Symbolic Activity* 10, no. 3 (1995): 183–204.
Uno, Ryoko, Eiko Matsuda, and Bipin Indurkhya. "Analyzing Visual Metaphor and Metonymy to Understand Creativity in Fashion." *Frontiers in Psychology* 9 (2019). Available online: https://doi.org/10.3389/fpsyg.2018.02527.
Ureña Gómez-Moreno, José Manuel. "Non-Verbal and Multimodal Metaphors Bring Biology into the Picture." In *How Metaphors Guide, Teach and Popularize Science*, edited by Anke Beger and Thomas H. Smith, 175–208. Amsterdam: John Benjamins, 2020.
Verstegen, Ian. *Arnheim, Gestalt and Art: A Psychological Theory*. Vienna: Springer, 2005.
Verstegen, Ian. *Arnheim, Gestalt and Media: An Ontological Theory*. Cham: Springer, 2018.
Walcott, William H. *Knowledge, Competence and Communication: Chomsky, Freire, Searle, and Communicative Language*. Montreal: Black Rose Books, 2007.
Wilde, Oscar. *The Complete Works*. New York: Harper & Row, 1989.
Wollheim, Richard. *Art and Its Objects: With Six Supplementary Essays*. 2nd edn. Cambridge: Cambridge University Press, 2015.
Wollheim, Richard. "Metaphor and Painting." In *Knowledge and Language, Volume III: Metaphor and Knowledge*, ed. F. R. Ankersmit, and J. J. A. Mooij, 113–25. Dordrecht: Springer Science+Business Media, 1993.
Young, Yael. "The Representation of Pointed Amphorae in Athenian Vase Paintings: An Iconographic Study." *Art Style Magazine*, March 11, 2021, 159–79.

Index

Note: *italicised* page references indicate illustrations

active externalism 94
active perception 26, 35, 37–8, 59, 97, 114, 116, 117, 143–4, 162
   active agent 116
   physiognomic perception 23–4, *24*, 25, 26, 30–1, 32, 33, 34, 35, 37, 145
   projections 26, 35, 111, 113, 114
   transfigurative gaze 142, 143–4, 151, 162
affordance 4, 103, 108–9, 122, 136, 157–71
   completing the percept 163
   discoverability 158–9
   expressivity 23–4, 25, 27, 31, 32, 33, 35, 102, 116, 136, 169–71
   limits and constraints 161, 162–3, 167–9
   spoken grammar 164
   visual perception 14, 37, 40, 59, 108, 142
Alberti, Leon Battista 4
Aldrich, Virgil 10, 15, 32, 44, 58, 94, 99–100, 101, 134
   Beardsley, criticism of 127
   distinguishing visual from linguistic metaphors 101
   metaphor, definitions of 102, 127–30, 141–3
   on Picasso's eye 143
   triadic notion of metaphor 102, 127–30, 141–3
Alison, Archibald 164–5
Anderson, Stanford 159
anger, metaphors for 42, 76–7
animal metaphors 31, 52, 68–9, 101, 103, 145, 159
   Baboon and Young (Picasso) 28, 154
   Lion of Lucerne (Thorvaldsen) 103
   man is a wolf 47, 54, 131, 154, 168
   shark lawyer 69, 101, 159, 166
   Sweetheart Nutcracker (Hannon-Tan) 67–8, *68*, 83, 125–6

anthropology 65, 89, 96, 97, 150
anthropomorphism 171
antirealism 122
Antoniades, Jamie and Mark *see Sharpener Desk Tidy* (Antoniades)
architectural metaphors 5–9, 24, 79, 97, 102, 110, 118, 119, 137, 145
   Bankside Power Station (Herzog and de Meuron) 12–13, 118, 161
   Ship Building (Levi and Cohen) 8, *8*, 87, 97, 102, 110, 119, 161
   Turbine Factory (Behrens) 159–61, *160*
   White Tree building (Laisné and Rachdi) 106, *107*, 108–9, 115–16, 119, 125–6, 137, 161
Argument Is War metaphor 41, 42, 86, 110–11
Aristotle 45, 58
Arnheim, Rudolf 4, 10, 16, 32–5, 92, 99–101, 126–7, 129, 132–4, 154, 169–71
   active perception 37, 114
   affordances, account of 162, 163, 169, 170–1
   depth of thought and physical depth 20, 137
   everyday gaze 144–5
   external load of the seeing eye 111–14
   force of perceived things 114–15, 136
   Gestalt theory 32–3, 34, 108, 111, 153, 169, 170
   Gombrich's *Art and Illusion*, reviews 112, 113–14, 116–17, 121–2
   innocent eye model 14
   passive reception versus active perception 35, 37–8, 50
   perceptual classification 135, 136
   physiognomic perception 32, 34, 35, 145

primacy of the visual medium 18–19, 39, 51–2, 100–1, 103–4, 105–6, 134, 161–2
visual concepts 13, 40, 106, 114, 121–2
visual force 163–4
visual intelligence 40, 117–18
visual knowledge 13, 40, 117–18, 120, 122
visual storage 13, 14
visual thinking 18–19, 49–50, 94, 100, 106, 108, 114
art 29, 49, 111, 116–17, 134, 148–9, 152, 169
   as embodied meaning 43
   as language 42, 104, 105, 169
artistic metaphors 2, 4, 9, 23–5, 29, 42–4, 49, 103–5, 112–14, 143–4, 158, 162, 169, 174
   Aldrich on 127, 129–30, 142–3
   Arnheim on 103–4, 108, 112, 113–14, 121–2, 144, 163–4
   Baboon and Young (Picasso) 28, 154
   caricature 52
   cartoons 120
   Danto on 43–4, 103
   Dulle Griet (Brueghel the Elder) 27
   Jericho skull 10–11
   Lion of Lucerne (Thorvaldsen) 103
   mimetic model of art 112–13
   The Races at Longchamp (Manet) 163–4
   Wollheim on 48, 51–2, 103
   see also design; musical metaphors
Attfield, Judith 21, 146–7, 149, 165

Baboon and Young (Picasso) 28, 154
Bankside Power Station (Herzog and de Meuron) 12–13, 118, 161
Barnett, Richard 27
Beardsley, Monroe C. 47, 53, 55–6, 57–8, 110, 127
Behrens, Peter 159–61, *160*
Benedek, András 17–18, 19
Bianchi, Matteo *see Muffin Pouffe* (Bianchi)
Black, Max 47, 53, 54–5, 56, 63–4, 101, 130
blending 76–9, 97, 108–10
body cognition *see* embodiment
Boughton, Alice 43

boxing metaphors 84, 87
box, thinking outside of the 80–1
Braque, Georges 144
Brueghel the Elder, Pieter 27
Bruner, Jerome 132, 151–2
Burge, Taylor 94
Business Is War metaphor 75

Caliteiro Toothpick Holder (Salis) 5, 7
Cameron-Daum, Kate 96–7
Cameron, Lynne 86
Camp, Elisabeth 48
canonical/iconic forms 11–15, 30, 34, 144
capsize metaphor 78–9
car lights 9, 23, 28, 144, 148, 167
Carroll, Noel 101
cartoons 120
categories 3–11, 25, 26, 32, 38, 45, 66, 103–4, 111–12, 132–41, 158, 165, 173
   Attfield's treatment of categories in design 165
   Bruner's three stages of categorization 132
   conceptual accounts of metaphor 66, 80, 90
   familiar 26, 27, 30, 31, 145
   Gibb's notion of categorization 134–5
   modified in active perception 26
   reorganizing 15, 27, 31, 64, 121, 130
   visual categories 23, 103, 106, 114–15
Cezanne, Paul 2
Chalmers, David 94
chocolate bar-shaped notepad 5, *6*
Chomsky, Noam 90
Clark, Andy 94
Clark, Timothy James 44
Clifford, James 89
cloud metaphors 23, 31, 128, 141, 144, 145, 147–9, *147*, 151
Cloud Table (Morris) 147–8, *147*, 151, 161, 166
coffee tables 146–9
cognitivism 1, 38–46, 49, 67–70, 105–6, 132–6, 138–40, 152–3, 155, 173–4
   anti-conceptualism 155, 173
   blending, account of 76–9, 97, 108–10
   conceptualist turn 18, 19–20, 38–40, 44, 51–2, 61–98, 105

Danto's "metaphor and cognition" 43, 52
deliberate metaphor theory 85–8
embodied cognition 91–7, 105–6, 133, 140
emergent elements of metaphor, account of 1–2, 4, 76–7, 83, 91, 106, 110–11, 155
entailments of a conceptual scheme 4, 20, 22, 42, 65, 72–4, 83, 147, 148, 174
interaction theory of Bipin Indurkhya 37–8, 44–5, 59–60
see also conceptual metaphor theory
Cohen, Arieh *see Ship Building* (Levi and Cohen)
color and visual metaphors 103, 111, 127, 162
communicative approach to metaphor 88, 91
conceptualism *see* cognitivism
conceptual metaphors 34, 77–83, 88, 90, 91, 95–6, 106, 118, 119–20, 171
based on visual metaphors 132, 151, 152, 153
paradigmatic status of 4, 18, 61, 65, 71, 74–5, 87, 133
conceptual metaphor theory 1–2, 20, 28, 38–44, 53, 59–60, 61–97, 105–6, 132–42, 152, 171, 174
conceptual scheme *see* cognitivism
constructivism 15, 25, 37, 53, 55, 122–3, 142–3
aestheticist constructivism 31–2
artifactual reconstruction 143
constructivist realism 148
for familiarization 26–7, 30–1
of interaction theories 44, 59–60, 63–4
mental versus external constructions 1, 4, 26, 35, 80, 81, 105, 121–2, 174
metaphorical perception 25, 32, 44, 60, 129
social constructivism 35
see also active perception
context 11, 14, 44–5, 48, 54–7, 64, 103, 106, 136, 154, 164
affordance in visual context 164–7
anti-contextualism 48
and conventions 76–81

metaphorical composition 1–2, 3–4, 10, 47, 54–7, 126–7, 154, 174
properties of source 1–2, 3–4, 174
controversion theory 55–6
conventions 41–2, 65, 70–81
and context 76–81
convention-based possibilities in conceptualism 71, 74
as external 26, 65, 71, 73, 74, 76, 93
in social constructivism 35
Cork Cactus (Lerwill) 5, 7
corkscrew designs 23, *24*, 166

Danto, Arthur 43–4, 49, 50, 52–3, 57, 103, 105, 109, 117, 119–20, 143, 152
Darwin, Charles 138
Daumier, Honoré 52
Davidi, Gilad *see* pebble powermats (Padwa and Davidi)
Davidson, Donald 28–30, 47, 104, 105
de Duve, Thierry 143
deep form 162
de Meuron, Pierre 13
Descartes, René 50, 108, 125–6
design 3–5, 62–3, 146, 152, 158, 169
Caliteiro Toothpick Holder (Salis) 5, 7
Cloud Table (Morris) 147–8, *147*, 151, 161, 166
corkscrew designs 23, *24*, 166
desk cacti 5, 7, 11
Hot Dog Sofa (Job and Seletti) 5, *5*, 119, 154, 155, 166
The King and *The Queen* (Picasso) 87, *87*, 129
Muffin Pouffe (Bianchi) 5, 7, 95, 115, 119, 125, 167
pebble powermats (Padwa and Davidi) 3–4, *3*, 5, 11, 15, 16, 53, 64, 102, 119, 128, 159, 165–6
Sharpener Desk Tidy (Antoniades) 5, 6, 11, 13, 95, 159
Sweetheart Nutcracker (Hannon-Tan) 67–8, *68*, 83, 125–6
La Venus du Gaz (Picasso) 142–3, *142*
desk cacti 5, 7, 11
Dewey, John 19, 116
discoverability *see* affordance
disembodied mind 92, 93, 96
Domino, Fats 78

Duchamp, Marcel 143
dynamic character of precepts 114–15

Easterling, Keller 5–8
ecological theory of vision 162
embodied cognition *see* cognitivism; embodiment
embodiment 38, 43, 85–8, 91–7, 105, 128
emergence
  emergent grammar 79–80, 88–91, 106, 164
  emergent referents 58–9, 130–2, 168–9
  socially emergent cognition 88
emergent properties of metaphor 1–2, 9, 10, 16–17, 83, 106, 121, 126–30, 137, 152, 154–5, 162–3, 173–4
  and affordance 159
  Aldrich on 118, 127–30, 141–3
  Arnheim on 108, 118
  in art 127, 129, 142–3
  and blending 76, 108–10
  examples 3–4, 10, 16, 64, 67–8, 76–7, 79, 91, 101, 108–9, 115–16, 118–19, 125, 154
  Fauconnier and Turner on 76–7, 110
  as induced structures 115
  Indurkhya and Ojha on 59, 63, 152–3
  and interaction 53–7, 59–60
  metaphorical twists 55–7, 110, 127
  in music 125, 127
  and non-conceptualism 67–9
emoji 14, 95
emotions 4, 31, 34, 51, 69, 73, 96, 125, 145, 166, 169
entailments of a conceptual scheme 20, 22, 42, 65, 72–4
Ever Given (container ship) 35, *36*
everyday aesthetics 14, 20–2, 35, 84, 116, 144–50, 157, 158
everyday metaphors 9, 12, 23, 41, 44, 61, 144–50
extended mind *see* embodiment
eye movement analysis 153

face metaphors 23–8, *24*, 30–1, 35, 95, 121, 141, 144, 145, 148–9, 151, 159
  see also physiognomic perception
fashion 137–8
Fauconnier, Gilles 76–7, 78, 109–10

figurative language 20, 48, 102, 109, 153
Forceville, Charles 133
formalism 3, 23, 26, 43, 63, 89, 100, 159, 173
  anti-formalism 42, 49, 50
  formalist account of expressivity 169–70
  visual accounts of metaphor, relation to 4, 18, 26, 41, 95, 114
Forsey, Jane 146
Fry, Roger 169
functionalism 90, 120, 159, 163
Fusaroli, Riccardo 41

Gestalt theory 32–3, 34, 108, 111, 153, 169, 170
Giacometti, Alberto 118
Gibbs, Raymond 41–2, 64, 74–5, 80–2, 83–5, 86, 133, 134–5
Gibson, James J. 157, 162, 163
Glucksberg, Sam 66
Gombrich, Ernst 2, 8–11, 15–16, 25–7, 99–100, 102–3, 126, 146, 161–2, 168
  active perception 26, 37–8, 111
  Arnheim on 112, 113–14, 116–17, 121–2
  Danto on 117, 119–20
  Goodman on 25, 120, 122
  hobby horse, meditations on 105, 129, 131
  illusion 121, 163, 164
  innocent eye model, refutes 14, 25, 111–12, 117
  metaphor, definitions of 26–7, 103, 111
  musical metaphors 125
  physiognomic perception 23–5, 26, 27–8, 30–1, 33, 35, 37, 145
  pictorial representation 112, 119–20, 134
  Pygmalion power 9, 63, 97, 119, 121, 123, 162
  Ruskin's mimetic model of art, critiques 112–13
  "sense of order" 13
  visual thinking 97, 134
Gómez-Moreno, José Manuel Ureña 75–6
Goodman, Nelson 15–16, 25, 26, 40, 49, 109, 132, 157, 166–7, 168
  artistic expression, theory of 169

"figurative possession" 15
on Gombrich 25, 120, 122
Indurkhya follows 37–8, 139
innocent eye model, refutes 14, 25, 111
metaphor, definition of 118
"realist effect" 120
semantic theory of metaphor 47–8
"Seven Strictures on Similarity" 122–3
"ways of worldmaking" 44
Gray Tree (Mondrian) 15
Guetta, David 5
Guttenplan, Samuel 136

Hagberg, Garry 169–70
Hampe, Beate 65, 88
Hannon-Tam, Jim *see Sweetheart Nutcracker* (Hannon-Tan)
Hausman, Carl 32, 39, 57–9, 94, 127, 130, 138, 167, 168
Herzog, Jacques 13
Hesse, Merry 48
hobby horse 9, 105, 111, 129, 131, 154
Hopper, Paul J. 79–80, 88–90, 106, 164
Hot Dog Sofa (Job and Seletti) 5, *5*, 119, 154, 155, 166

iceberg analogy 138
iconic/canonical forms 11–15, 30, 34, 144
illusion 113, 121, 163, 164, 165
impressionism 112, 163–4
Indurkhya, Bipin 37–8, 44–5, 59–60, 61–4, 110, 136–9, 152–4
innocent eye model 14, 25, 111–12, 116, 117, 162
interaction theories 37–8, 44–5, 47, 54–6, 57, 59–60, 63–4, 130–1
internalism *see* cognitivism
iPhones 16

James, William 14
Jericho skull 10–11
Johnson, Mark 54, 61, 64–5, 66, 70, 75, 77, 80, 82, 92, 95–6, 105–6, 139, 140

Kant, Immanuel 152
The King and *The Queen* (Picasso) 87, *87*, 129
Kovács, Éva 75

Kövecses, Zoltan 54, 64, 76, 77–9, 171
Kuh, Katherine 143

Laisné, Nicolas 106
Lakoff, George 41, 61, 64, 71, 75, 76, 77, 80, 82, 90, 95, 105–6, 139
Love Is Journey metaphor 72–4, 93
metaphorical targets 54, 70
Landau, Mark J. 70
language as medium 56, 85, 106
Leibniz, Gottfried Wilhelm 50
lemon purse 11, *12*, 13
Lerwill, Nick 5, *7*
Levertov, Denise 126
Levi, Shimon *see Ship Building* (Levi and Cohen)
Life Is Journey metaphor 65–6, 69–70, 83–4, 171
light, metaphor of 4–5, 146
linguistic metaphors 1, 18, 43, 47–60, 68–9, 81–6, 103, 106, 126, 137–8
conceptualist critiques of 60, 81–2
emerging ontology 130–2
hackneyed 41
nonlinguistic 67, 80, 101
paradigmatic status 50–1, 64, 65
visual metaphors, based on 34, 132, 151, 152
see also poetic metaphors; semantic theories of metaphor
linguistic turn 18, 19–20, 22, 41, 44, 48–53, 59, 80, 99–101, 104–5, 134, 173
of aesthetics 42–3, 44, 49–53, 100, 103, 104
Lion of Lucerne (Thorvaldsen) 103
Lipps, Theodor 32–3
Louis Philippe, king 52
Love Is Journey metaphor 65, 70–1, 72–4, 93, 154, 155
Love Is Plant metaphor 70–1

Mac Cormac, Earl R. 137
Manet, Édouard 163–4
man is a wolf metaphor 47, 54, 131, 154, 168
Manor, Ehud 27
material culture 20–1, 96–7, 149, 150, 151, 165

material metaphors 53, 87, 96, 97, 133, 150, 151, 165
Matthews, Chris 84
Mautner, Menachem 66
Meier, Brian B. 70
Melanesian canoes 150
Mendini, Alessandro 23, *24*
mentalism 18, 25, 35, 42, 67, 69–70, 169
    see also cognitivism
Metamorphoses (Ovid) 9
metamorphosis 9, 10
metaphorical success 119, 120, 126, 128, 129, 136–7, 158
metaphorical twists 55–7, 101, 110, 127
mimetic model of art 112–13
Mitchell, William John Thomas 109, 134, 170–1
Mondrian, Piet 15
monotonous metaphors 61–2
Morgagni, Simone 41
Morris, Neil 147–8, *147*, 151, 161, 166
Muffin Pouffe (Bianchi) 5, *7*, 95, 115, 119, 125, 167
Mukařovský, Jan 146
Müller, Cornelia 86, 88
Müller-Lyer illusion 165
multimodal metaphors 75, 80, 88, 133
Musée d'Orsay 118
musical metaphors 69, 70, 125, 126, 127

network theory of meaning 48
non-conceptualism 67–9
non-monotonous metaphors 61, 62
nonverbal metaphors 58, 132
Norman, Donald 158, 161, 163
Nyíri, Kristóf 17, 19, 161–2

Obama, Barack 83–4, 87
Ojha, A. 152–3
ontological sphere, metaphors in the 1–11, 14, 18, 38–45, 97, 99–101, 119, 123, 125–55, 158, 173
    Aldrich on 141–2
    Arnheim on 10, 19, 34, 39, 114–15, 121, 134
    Black on 55
    Danto on 43–4, 57
    emerging ontology 130–2
    Gibbs on 80, 81, 84
    Gombrich on 9–10, 15, 16, 25, 26, 99, 100, 119, 120, 121
    Goodman on 15–16, 25, 40, 47–8, 167
    Hausman on 57, 58–9, 130–2, 138, 167, 168
    Hopper on 90
    Indurkhya on 37, 38, 44–5, 59, 61, 136–9
    Lakoff on 93
    neglect of 4, 38–9, 41, 43, 45, 53
    ontological productivity of metaphors 40, 55, 130
    Peacocke on 67
    readymades 141–4
    Saito on 19, 20
    social ontology 65, 71–2, 148
Ovid 9

Padwa, Alex *see* pebble powermats (Padwa and Davidi)
passing metaphors 23–8, 31
Pater, Walter 31–2
pathetic fallacy 31, 144, 170, 171
Peacocke, Christopher 67, 69–70
pebble powermats (Padwa and Davidi) 3–4, *3*, 5, 11, 15, 16, 53, 64, 102, 119, 128, 159, 165–6
Pelosi, Nancy 27
personification 26, 144, 145, 159, 171
phenomenology 91, 92, 140–1
Philipon, Charles 52
photography 2, 94
physiognomic perception 23–4, *24*, 25, 26, 30–1, 32, 33, 34, 35, 37, 145
    see also face metaphors
Picasso, Pablo 105
    Baboon and Young 28, 154
    The King and *The Queen* 87, *87*, 129
    La Venus du Gaz 142–3, *142*
pictorial representation 112, 119–20, 134
Plato 152
poetic metaphors 12, 18, 22, 23, 27, 31–2, 48, 65, 85, 126, 144–5
Popper, Karl 14, 120
Porat, Roy 66
prehension 102, 128, 142, 143
preperception 13–14
Price, Cedric 5–8
Putnam, Hilary 71, 94, 137

Pygmalion power 9, 63, 97, 119, 121, 123, 162
Pygmalion practice 10, 27

Rachdi, Manal 106
Rawls, John 152
readymades 141–4, *142*
realism 113, 117, 148, 162, 163–4
    about metaphors 119–23
    antirealism 122
    "commonsense realism" 161
    constructivist realism 37, 148
    ecological theory of vision 162
    realistic effect of metaphors 119–23
    truth to nature 31–2, 112
rebus 151
Reddy, Michael 71, 72
Relationship is Journey metaphor 72–4, 82–3, 86, 125–6, 144, 161
Richards, Ivor Armstrong 47, 53–4, 56
Ricoeur, Paul 56–7
Robinson, Michael D. 70
Romanticism 29, 31
Romeo and Juliet (Shakespeare) 58, 86
Rorty, Richard 22, 28–30, 40, 45, 47, 94, 104
Ruskin, John 31, 32, 112–13, 144, 171

Saito, Yuriko 20, 21–2, 116, 149, 164–5
Salis, Enrico 5, 7
Schon, Donald 62
Scott, Giles Gilbert 12–13
Searle, John 47
Seletti, Stefano *see Hot Dog Sofa* (Job and Seletti)
semantic theories of metaphor 25, 28, 37, 38, 43–4, 45, 46, 47–60, 101, 106
    see also linguistic metaphors
Shakespeare, William 58, 86
shark lawyer metaphor 69, 101, 159, 166
Sharpener Desk Tidy (Antoniades) 5, 6, 11, 13, 95, 159
Shen, Yeshayahu 66
Ship Building (Levi and Cohen) 8, *8*, 87, 97, 102, 110, 119, 161
Shusterman, Richard 148
Sia (singer) 5
similarities 28, 45, 59, 122–3, 128, 129, 138
    perceptual similarity 33, 152–3
"Seven Strictures on Similarity" 122
similarity-based metaphors 61–2, 78, 79, 122–3, 138
similes 66, 122, 128, 129, 141
snowmen 9–10
social constructivism 35
social ontology 65, 71, 148
somaesthetics 148
Sontag, Susan 94
Space is Time metaphor 76
Steen, Gerard 41–2, 86
Stern, Joseph 48
Suez Canal 35, *36*
Sweetheart Nutcracker (Hannon-Tan) 67–8, *68*, 83, 125–6

Tate Modern 12–13, 118, 161
temporary metaphors 121, 151, 158
textiles 149
theories are buildings metaphor 118
Thorvaldsen, Bertel 103
Tilley, Christopher 96–7, 149–50, 151
Titchener, Edward 163–4
Titian 51
transfigurative gaze *see* active perception: transfigurative gaze
tree metaphors 75–6, 108, 113, 119, 138, 145, 166, 171
    Gray Tree (Mondrian) 15
    tree of knowledge 108–9, 125–6, 161
    White Tree building (Laisné and Rachdi) 106, *107*, 108–9, 115–16, 119, 125–6, 137, 161
triadic definition of metaphor 1–2, 16–17, 91, 101–2, 125, 126–30, 141–3, 162–3, 173–4
Trump, Donald 27
truth 15–16, 48, 52, 92, 112–13, 122, 126, 139
    truth to nature 31–2, 112
Turbine Factory (Behrens) 159–61, *160*
Turner, Joseph Mallord William 112
Turner, Mark 41, 76–7, 78, 109–10

La Venus du Gaz (Picasso) 142–3, *142*
verbal metaphors 2, 49, 52, 58, 63, 75, 85, 86, 101, 104, 109, 116, 132, 137–8
Verstegen, Ian 34, 100–1, 127
visible metaphors 101

visualism 39, 57, 102, 106, 132, 134, 136, 140–1, 145, 167
　anti-visualism 38, 49–53
　relation to formalism 4, 18, 26, 41, 95, 114
　visual expressivity 27, 102, 169–71
　visual knowledge 13, 40, 114–19, 120, 122
　Visual Learning Lab 17
　visual memory 40, 163
　visual perception 14, 37, 40, 59, 108, 142
　visual sphere 2, 17, 20, 22, 39, 49, 51–2, 94–5, 100, 104, 105, 144, 162, 165, 173
　visual storage 13, 14, 33
　visual thinking 18–19, 49–50, 94, 97, 100, 106, 108, 114, 134
　visual turn 17–23, 33, 35, 38–9, 84–5, 93, 99–100, 119, 140–1, 150, 152, 161
visual metaphors 1–46, 48–53, 57–8, 63–4, 69, 90–1, 106, 142, 148, 173–4
　advent of 99–123, 173
　and color 103, 111, 127, 162
　emergent property of 127–8
　paradigmatic nature of 1, 2, 16–17, 18, 34, 91, 97, 103, 106, 119–20, 132, 145, 150–5, 165, 174
　scientific arguments, constructing 75–6

Wegener, Alfred 138
White Tree building (Laisné and Rachdi) 106, *107*, 108–9, 115–16, 119, 125–6, 137, 161
wide cognition 105–6
Wilde, Oscar 32
Wittgenstein, Ludwig 48, 79–80, 109, 170
Wollheim, Richard 48, 49, 50–3, 57, 103, 105
worldmaking 44–5, 48

Young, Yael 158

www.ingramcontent.com/pod-product-compliance
Lightning Source LLC
Chambersburg PA
CBHW062227300426
44115CB00012BA/2241